MARRIAGE

Experience *the* BEST

DR. STEVE STEPHENS

VISION™ HOUSE PUBLISHING, INC.

1217 NE Burnside Road
Portland, OR 97030

Marriage: Experiencing the Best
© 1995 by Steve Stephens

Published by Vision House Publishing, Inc.
1217 NE Burnside, Suite 403
Gresham, Oregon 97030

Printed in the United States of America

International Standard Book Number: 1-885305-12-5

95 96 97 98 99 00 01 02 03 04 — 10 9 8 7 6 5 4 3 2 1

To the best wife in the world,
Tami Sue Stephens.

Anything that is really important
must be kept on the cutting edge
and constantly fought for.
—H. Ross Perot

CONTENTS

ACKNOWLEDGMENTS

Tami, for putting up with me and listening to me read portions of this book over and over. But most of all, for loving me. You are fantastic.

My family of origin, especially my grandmother, parents, and five siblings and their partners. I love you all and enjoy every minute we spend together.

Allison and Jim Allison, for typing, talking, and encouraging me.

Monday night growth group, for over fifteen years of great discussions and even greater friendships.

New Vision Sunday school class, for praying for me and tolerating my teaching week after week.

Roger Kirchner, for his computer skills and invaluable feedback.

Pastors and youth pastors, who over the years have grounded me in my faith. In particular: Don Reid, Cliff Reynolds, Jerry Larson, James Jost, Stu Weber, Steve Wenning, Loren Fischer.

Those who read my manuscript and provided suggestions: Al Jansen, Wes Friesen, Bob Vandiver, Loren Fischer, Mike DeBoer.

The great team at Vision House Publishing, especially John Van Diest, David Van Diest, Doug Halverson, Kevin Cummings and Susan Abrahamson.

Marilyn McAuley, for expert editing.

Linda Graham, a great secretary who keeps my business life organized.

I thank you all.

INTRODUCTION

His face was beaming and his dark eyes twinkled. The handsome young man sat in my office and told me how he had recently met the woman of his dreams. "Life is fantastic," he said, "and God is so good."

The couple was married a month later and it was a year before I saw the young man again. This time he told me how wonderful marriage was with its moments of warmth, understanding, excitement, and fulfillment. I nodded my head in agreement and said, "But there are other moments that are not so wonderful."

He laughed and said, "Not for us. We're in love and it just gets better every day."

Several years later he sat in my office a third time. He looked tired and there was no twinkle in his eyes. "How can something that was so good cause so much pain?" he asked. A tear ran down his cheek as he told me his marriage was driving him crazy.

"The love is gone. I don't know what happened to it, but all I feel now is anger, hurt, confusion, and emptiness—a deep, overwhelming sense of emptiness. It's all over, I can't take it any longer."

I acknowledged his feelings and went on to say, "Life is like that. It can be wonderful and it can also drive you crazy, but don't give up. It doesn't have to be over. If you were in love once, you can recapture that love. The key to a good marriage is treasuring the wonderful times and working through the crazy times. Realize that if you push and pray you can make your marriage great again."

The young man left my office, returned to his wife, and

worked hard to rebuild his marriage. Ten years later the relationship is still not perfect; but both he and his wife are happy and thankful he didn't give up.

We live in an age of convenience. If our partner isn't working out, we look for a better model. Someone easier to maintain, more compatible, less demanding, and generally nicer. However, what most marriage counselors will tell you is that those who remarry tend to choose new partners with very similar problems as the old partners they just spent thousands of dollars to divorce. Our mate is a mirror reflecting back to us our own faults—our selfishness, impatience, insecurity, or unforgiveness. Changing mirrors doesn't change the view.

I'm not saying our spouses don't have areas they need to improve—maybe even major areas. However, we must start with ourselves and determine that we are going to be the best husbands or the best wives we can possibly be.

Pointing a finger rarely does anything but make a partner defensive. Then they point back saying, "What right do you have to complain when you do this and that." So husband and wife stand face to face, nose to nose, waiting for the other to make the first move to improve the marriage. Meanwhile, the relationship dies from stubborn neglect.

It's a sad state of affairs when we take better care of our cars and houses than we do our marriages. We change the oil, fill the tank, check the tires, and periodically tune up our cars. We change light bulbs, wash windows, paint walls, unplug toilets, and re-roof our houses, but what do we do to maintain our marriage? The truth is, more damage is done than repairs are made.

How important is your marriage? Is it more important to you than your car or your house? Are you willing to put in the time and energy and whatever else it takes to prove to your partner how valuable the relationship truly is to you?

Stop saying your marriage is important. Words are cheap. Rather, prove it! Prove it to your spouse by the effort you put forth.

The bottom line is: Do you have the tenacity to make your marriage great?

1

FACING THE ENEMY

Mondays were hardest. Two cups of coffee and a hot shower barely brought Jim to life. When he arrived at the office he faced a stack of phone messages and all the weekend mail. By 8:00 A.M. the day was already hectic with staff meetings, impatient clients, budget evaluations, and deadlines. So much for working for a Fortune 500 company. Days such as this made Jim question the worth of his high-powered corporate position. Only his six-figure salary kept him from quitting.

Driving home that evening, Jim felt exhausted. He couldn't wait to see his lovely wife, have a drink, and put his feet up for a little relaxation.

Jim and Lori had been married six years. Lori, a professional artist, worked out of a studio in their home. They had talked about having children, but both were too involved in their careers. Besides, they wanted to work out a few wrinkles in their relationship first.

Jim maneuvered his new BMW into the garage. The absence of Lori's car did not bother him. She often parked at the side of the garage. He slipped through the back door into the kitchen. The lights were off and everything was quiet. "Lori, I'm home."

Silence.

Jim walked through the kitchen to the living room. "This is weird," he said to himself. Lori always had dinner cooking when he came home from work. He loved her kiss at the back door and her "How was your day?" greeting. It was the one constant pleasure in his daily life and he missed it tonight.

Jim climbed the stairs and called again, "Lori, Lori, where are you?"

He opened the door to each room, turning on the lights, and looking for something...anything...that might tell him why she was gone. "Lori...Lori. Lori!"

She must be in the master bedroom. If not, at least she would have left a note. His heart pounded hard as he turned the doorknob.

Empty.

There was the note, propped on the pillow of the neatly made bed. He grabbed it and raced through the words.

Dear Jim,

I'm sorry, but I can't take it anymore. I saw a lawyer this morning and am filing for divorce. I will call you later in the week. Don't try to contact me. It's over and there is absolutely nothing you can do about it now. It's too late.

Lori

His hands shook as he read those last three words, IT'S TOO LATE. Tears blurred his eyes. His stomach felt sick. IT'S TOO LATE. His mind raced as his body collapsed on the bed. IT'S TOO LATE. Then something inside broke.

Sitting on the edge of the bed with his head in his hands, Jim cried. "What happened? How did something so good end up this way?" he sobbed.

It's an all too familiar story. Hundreds of couples break up each day. These couples start out with so much love and so many dreams. Just as Jim, they are asking, "What happened?"

Sometimes the husband leaves, sometimes the wife, and sometimes they both go at the same time. Some endings are loud and angry. Others happen with a quiet resignation. With certain couples the breakup is a surprise, whereas others have expected it for years. There are divorces that are public events with family and friends actively involved. Others slip by with people hardly even noticing. Sometimes a partner moves in with a lover, sometimes they live alone swearing never to love again.

Paul Simon was right. There probably are "fifty ways to leave your lover," but usually it comes down to at least one of nine reasons. Anyone interested in a lasting relationship needs to know why relationships end. Marriages are under attack and many fail because couples are not properly prepared. They do not know their enemy. Those who do don't take it seriously.

In 1940, twenty-three-year-old John F. Kennedy wrote a book entitled *While England Slept*. It was his thesis that England had not taken the threat of Nazi Germany seriously. England was not facing its enemy. As a result of its naiveté most of Europe fell to Hitler. If it had not been for America's involvement in the war and Hitler's strategic error of attacking Russia, England would have fallen.

Many marriages sleep beneath the shadow of the enemy. They know divorced friends or relatives but they sincerely believe it will never happen to them. Therefore, they never face their enemy. The shadow grows darker as they work and play. So much could be done, but they continue unaware. Some catch glimpses of the shadow but ignore it, thinking that in time it will go away. The only way to defeat the enemy is to know the enemy. Ignoring it and hoping for the best will not save the marriage.

The only way to defeat the enemy is to know the enemy. Ignoring it and hoping for the best will not save the marriage.

When couples come to me for premarital counseling I ask them, "What is most likely to sabotage your relationship?" I encourage them to study those forces bent on destroying their new love.

I believe that every marriage can triumph over these negative forces as long as both partners are serious about the battle. The following nine factors are challenging obstacles to overcome. They are the enemies that cast a deadly shadow over every marriage. So beware!

1. SELFISHNESS

We are all basically selfish. Some actually believe that selfishness is the root of all sin. In a relationship, we want the other to move around us and, likewise, they want us to move around them. We are the sun and our spouse is the planet. Historically, males have held this as a cultural and religious mandate. This was simply man's role. Many women today, in an attempt to make up for past injustices, are claiming selfishness as their modus operandi.

Marriage has been reduced to a selfish battle for power and control. A couple perceives each other as opponents fighting for the goal of "doing it my way," or "I'm right, you're wrong." In this egotistical contest, we forget that we are both on the same team. If our spouse loses, so do we.

We are in a three-legged race, trying to beat our partner to the finish line. In our attempts, we pull our partner off balance and tumble to the ground preventing each from reaching the goal.

Marriage involves leaving our selfishness behind. It involves cooperation, where we work together with neither taking control, but both submitting to the other.[1]

So many of our conflicts are petty. Most of us would be embarrassed to admit what our last conflict involved. It is usually the insignificant things such as, when did the party *really* start, or why did you fix broccoli. In the heat of the moment though, they seem terribly significant and we have to win.

Over and over again I hear in my office, "I will not let him control me" and "I can't let her push me around." We stand our stubborn ground over petty issues that seem so full of symbolic significance, but often the basic issue is merely whose selfishness is greater. We play the game of chicken, driving stubbornly toward each other, forcing our spouse to swerve. In this manner we prove our rightness and superiority. We are the sun, they are the planet, and don't forget it.

Unfortunately, the other does not always swerve and the crash is sometimes fatal.

Peggy and Carl had been married a year when they entered my office. They weren't talking. I saw them separately, asking Peggy first:

"What do you want out of this marriage?"

"A divorce. I've had enough of Carl's selfishness."

"What is it that Carl has done?"

"He refused to get me an ice cream cone. It was so hot and our drive was so long. All I wanted was an ice cream cone."

We talked of other things, then she left and Carl came in to talk. I asked him the same questions.

"What do you want out of this marriage?"

"I can't stand it anymore. I think the relationship is over. She is so demanding. This whole thing is over that stupid ice cream cone. We were late and she wanted to stop for ice cream. She pushed. I said no. She went hysterical. There was no way I was going to get her a cone. We were late."

Both stubbornly dug in their heels. Three months later this young couple filed for divorce. Sad, but true. The ice cream cone did not destroy the marriage—their stubborn selfishness did.

2. LAZINESS

Marriage is hard work. Many of us grew up with the Hollywood fantasy that once married you automatically live happily ever after. Wonderful relationships should just happen, shouldn't they? If relating is too much work, it's not worth it. Tony Campolo writes, "Love becomes nonexistent and marriages collapse primarily because most people do not work hard enough to create love and build marital relationships."[2] We fail to realize that things of value cost us time and energy. Marriages are demanding and draining. Good marriages do not come easily.

In fourth grade I decided to play the clarinet. I'm not sure why I chose that instrument, but I did. I imagined that soon I would play marvelous melodies and someday march in parades. I was shocked when I picked up the clarinet the first time and attempted to make music. I couldn't squeak out a single note. I blew harder, but my instrument remained silent. In frustration, I tinkered with the long, thin toy, putting my fingers over holes and pressing levers. Once in a while a noise jumped from the clarinet, but I wasn't sure how.

In time I learned how to blow past the reed properly and soon I could regularly produce five or six notes. Still, it was work. My music teacher recommended I practice a half-hour every day. On Tuesdays, a small group of potential musicians met in the library for instruction and to demonstrate their progress. When it was my turn I would wet my reed and blow. I would hit some notes, but more often an awful squeak forced its way from the clarinet. The patient instructor encouraged me to try again. I would, but the awful squeak returned. Then the instructor would ask in a knowing voice, "How has your practice been going?"

"Well, I've been awfully busy. I probably haven't practiced as much as I should have, but this week I'll try harder."

The truth is, I rarely practiced. I somehow thought I should simply be able to play without any effort. After about four months I quit my lessons. It was too much work. I was lazy.

A good marriage takes a lot of practice by both partners. I am frequently asked about situations where only one person is willing to work at their marriage. These situations are very difficult and the rule of thumb is that a successful marriage takes the full cooperation of both the husband and the wife.

3. DISAPPOINTMENT

We are all suckers for a good love story. Popular culture exploits this with a celebration of romantic love. Movies, television, novels, and music all feed the illusion that all you need is love. We grow up brainwashed with the myth of idealized love. Before children reach adolescence they start looking for their one and only, the perfect ten. Every girl dreams of her Prince Charming and every boy wants his Sleeping Beauty.

> *Yet she who marvels at how strong and silent he is, later complains that he lacks vulnerability and rarely talks. He who brags how beautiful she looks and loves her carefree manner, is frustrated later about how long it takes her to put on makeup and how she never gets anything done.*

We long for love so badly that when a likely candidate comes along we leap into our fantasy. Suddenly all the warts disappear and the image of our perfect mate is projected onto this person. In a way we lose touch with reality, for we fail to see this person as they really are. Maybe that is why we say we are "crazy" about someone or we are "madly" in love.

When we date we try to act out our fantasy. We attempt to orchestrate the evening so everything is perfect. Each partner strives to maintain the illusion. We try to look our best and act our best. We create a romantic atmosphere and pray that all goes smoothly. Each is the center of the other's attention with little or no responsibility except to have fun. Life seems wonderful when it consists of romantic dinners, concerts, movies, and ball games—especially when there is another person hanging on your every word.

In my late teens I had a number of terrible dating experiences. There was a young woman I wanted to impress by organizing a wonderful date. We drove to a special restaurant, but it was closed. After eating fast food, we planned to see a movie she selected. On the way to the theater I had a flat tire. I calmly changed it in a torrential downpour without the protection of rain gear. Then we got lost looking for the theater and by the time we found it, only front row seats were available. So there we sat, straining our necks. Somehow the illusion of romantic love was shattered that night.

When all goes as planned, the fantasy works. He thinks she is wonderful and she thinks he is fantastic. The couple sees each other and the world around them through eyes filled with love. Yet she who marvels at how strong and silent he is, later complains that he lacks vulnerability and rarely talks. He who brags how beautiful she looks and loves her carefree manner, is frustrated later about how long it takes her to put on makeup and how she never gets anything done. Unfortunately, the fantasy is superficial and never lasts. Every marriage goes through a disappointment cycle:

Fantasy Stage

"This is wonderful! My partner is everything I dreamed and more!"

Surprise Stage

"This isn't exactly what I expected; oh well, it's probably just a phase."

Questioning Stage

"What did I get myself into? Did I make a mistake?"

Disillusion Stage

"I can't believe I'm in this situation. Why was I so blind?"

Realistic Stage

"This relationship has some strong points and some weak points. It's not perfect, but neither am I."

Stabilized Stage

"This relationship is made of two struggling people and if we work together we can truly be happy and fulfilled."

Couples tend to pull apart when they get stuck in the questioning or the disillusion stage. They fail to see that this is part of the process. A young couple came to me with this problem. They had been married for only three months and were both depressed. He had expected her to always look beautiful and have a positive attitude. She was to fix gourmet meals, keep the apartment immaculate, socialize at a moment's notice, and work forty hours a week. There was no way she could meet his expectations and he felt deceived. "She did it before we were married, why can't she do it now?"

This is what I call *dating deception.* Courting is based on displaying our finest attributes; being more polite, generous, romantic, sensitive, and patient than we really are. We are not consciously trying to lie, we simply want our date to think the best of us, so we act in whatever way we think will make them happy. Add to this that our date, wanting to see us positively, maximizes our positives and minimizes our negatives. Once married the dating deception starts to fall apart, for it can't survive the scrutiny of twenty-four-hour observation.

Courting is based on displaying our finest attributes; being more polite, generous, romantic, sensitive, and patient than we really are.

Another problem that triggers disappointment is *naive-deception.* This is when we are not realistic with ourselves and say, "I thought he would change," or "I didn't think it was that big a problem."

Alisha knew Dale periodically went to X-rated movies, but she was confident that once married it would stop. Then during their engagement Dale visited a massage parlor and though Alisha was very offended, she told herself, "Boys will be boys. He has to sow some wild oats before he settles down." However, after they were married Dale did not settle down. X-rated movies and massage parlors were only the obvious aspects of a much deeper problem. Alisha was so disappointed that she couldn't even look at Dale, and whenever he approached her sexually she recoiled in disgust.

Blatant deception is a third type. In a self-calculating way, we pretend to be somebody we aren't. Years ago I spoke to a wonderful woman in her mid-sixties who was battling disappointment in her second husband. She had been married to her first husband almost forty years when he died suddenly of a heart attack. She lived alone for the next five years, until she met a suave and sophisticated gentleman about her age. They got along marvelously, except for one seemingly irreconcilable problem. She was an evangelical Christian. He was a self-proclaimed atheist. One thing she felt very strongly about—she would marry only within her own faith. When she confronted him with her convictions, he smiled and said, "No problem, I'll visit your church this Sunday and see what it's all about."

Within a month he converted to Christianity by accepting God into his life. After being baptized he became a member of the church. Six months later this older couple was married in an elegant church wedding. That was the last time he stepped inside a church. When his new bride asked why he refused to worship with her, he replied, "I'm an atheist and I've always been an atheist. The only way to get you to marry me was to pretend I was religious. I played my part, but now the pretense is over."

Every time two people interact they make either a deposit or a withdrawal from the other's love bank.

The bride was shocked at this blatant deception, but after working through her disappointment, she found that she truly loved this man. They discussed their situation and chose to renew their vows without the deception. Fifteen years later they are still happily married in spite of their rocky start and spiritual disagreement.

4. HURT AND UNHAPPINESS

We are all pulled toward those who make us feel good. We enjoy positive people who show appreciation and give praise. They boost our self-esteem, and their happiness is contagious. We know that we can relax and be ourselves because we feel safe with no need to be on guard, or trying to prove we are okay. With certain people we know we matter and are loved. We like people who like us and we enjoy spending time with them. Dr. Larry Halter, in his book *The Traits of a Happy Couple* writes: "Individuals enter and stay in a marriage as long as the relationship positives are greater than the relationship negatives."[3]

Dr. Willard Harley, a psychologist and author from Minnesota, has developed a concept called the *love bank*.[4] He suggests that every time two people interact they make either a deposit or a withdrawal from the other's love bank. A positive interaction makes a deposit, while a negative interaction makes a withdrawal. A couple is pulled together when there are many large deposits and few withdrawals.

When Michelle first met Todd she sensed he liked her. He was talkative and complimented her a number of times on her appearance. Michelle's love bank received a large deposit.

The next day Todd called her and asked her to go sailing. She quickly accepted and after a twenty-minute conversation, several more points were added to the account.

It was a beautiful day as Todd's boat skimmed across the waves. Michelle sat on the deck soaking up the sunshine. The two picnicked on a private beach and later watched a stunning sunset. Additional points were added to the account.

Over the next few weeks and months, Michelle's love bank continued its rapid growth and so did Todd's. A year and a half later, when Michelle and Todd announced their engagement, they both had sizable love-bank accounts. Their time together was both positive and enjoyable. They looked forward to seeing each other and both became experts at building up one another. When withdrawals did take place they were both quick to counter with a deposit to try to make up for the loss.

Nevertheless, whenever two people live together for very long, feelings are going to get hurt. We offend each other, step on toes, and even hit below the belt. At times we forget what is important, we have an immature or bad attitude, and we say things we wish later we hadn't. We all make withdrawals from our partner's love bank. Some of the withdrawals are intentional, others aren't. We are not always aware of our insensitivity.

I am more likely to be insensitive to Tami and make a withdrawal from her love bank when I am hungry or tired. Such times I tend to get grumpy and impatient. If Tami hears a certain tone in my voice, she asks if I am hungry. What she is really saying is, "Don't be mean." I usually get the message.

People may be insensitive when they have been hurt or are angry. They think to themselves, *If you hurt me, I'm going to hurt you back.* This sort of revenge rarely solves anything and usually escalates to anger. When some people are angry, the internal pressure blows and they say or do things they later regret—things they can't take back and their spouse doesn't easily forget. In the process more withdrawals are made from the love bank.

Each of us is unique. Some people are more sensitive to hurt than others. Hurts cut them deep and the pain lingers longer. For others, the hurt rolls off their backs and is quickly forgotten. I belong to a third group that is a little more confusing. We appear tough and thick-skinned, but we are actually tender.

Allowing hurts and negative interactions to pile up is dangerous. Most of us can handle one or two, maybe three hurts, but over the years they build and if not dealt with, the result is unhappiness. Each hurt is like a single brick, and as the bricks stack up they become a wall that destroys communication and togetherness.

5. HECTICNESS

For many of us life is a hundred-yard dash. We feel as if we sprint from one activity to the next. There never seems to be enough time to meet, or to finish half-completed projects. We easily fall into the March Hare syndrome—constantly checking our watch, fearing we'll be late for a very important date.

In my experience there are four types of hurried people.

The Overachiever. These people try to prove themselves. They are basically insecure and believe that if they are accomplishing something, they are okay. Overachievers always have to stay busy because their activity has become their identity and validates their existence. Their self-worth is based on doing rather than being. If there is nothing to do, they are lost.

The Perfectionist. These people must do everything just right. It's catastrophic if things are not in their proper place. Life fits into two categories—the right way and the wrong way. They believe they must always do it right no matter what the cost. For doing something wrong means being a worthless failure that will cause terrible things to happen. Since it is impossible to be perfect, these people are always rushing about trying to accomplish what will never be.

The Victim. They resent the hectic pace that has swallowed them. They feel pulled along by the current of those around them. They resent the demands and expectations placed on them, but they have a hard time saying no. Therefore, they get carried along in a direction they would not choose.

The Runner. These people are afraid to slow down because they would have to deal with their emotions and those of the people around them. They hide from emotions and depth. They skim along the surface of life, always too busy to plunge beneath the superficial. As long as they are running, they are one step ahead of being caught and having to deal with the difficulties of life.

These four types of hurried people rush through their day; when they finally do slow down, they are too worn out to be much good to anyone. They share tired talk and tired sex with their spouses who resent getting the leftovers and feel as though they are at the bottom of the priority list. Work, sports, children, hobbies, television, friends, cars, church, and a hundred other items seem to rank higher than the marriage. The message is, "You aren't important anymore," or "You don't matter," or simply "I don't love you."

6. NEGATIVITY

Most individuals are not attracted to negative people. They make others uptight and steal the joy out of life. Criticism, sarcasm, complaining, nagging, and put-downs push us away. We do everything we can to avoid them. This sort of negativity sours a marriage. A spouse becomes discouraged and thinks, *If everything I do is wrong, then why try?* They give up because they feel incapable of pleasing their mate.

Now there is always the other side of the story. A negative person is usually not happy either. They have been hurt or disappointed and are often frustrated with themselves, a particular person, or life in general. The more they focus on their frustration the more negative they get, and this negativity spills over onto everybody they meet. Since a spouse is often the closest person to them, they get the brunt of it, whether or not they are a part of the problem.

Often the negative person is trapped in their own negativity. In a wonderful and practical book called *Feeling Good,* Dr. David Burns suggests that people become negative as a result of cognitive distortions.[5] Four of these are as follows:

Over Generalization. One sees an isolated negative as a never-ending pattern of defeat.

Mental Filter. One picks out a single negative detail and dwells on it exclusively until one's entire vision becomes darkened.

Disqualifying the Positive. One rejects positive experiences by insisting they don't count for some reason or other.

Magnification and Minimization. One exaggerates the importance of negative things, and shrinks the importance of the positive.

Generally, negativity sucks the life out of a marriage and makes it very difficult for intimacy to grow.

7. FEAR

I am amazed at how many marriages suffer from fear. Women are more likely to admit they are afraid of their husbands. Yet I believe men are just as afraid, they merely hide it better. Women's fears are more specific and well-defined, whereas men's fears tend to be more general and vague. Listed are several of the most common fears I have observed:

Fear of Abandonment. This fear is usually born out of either emotional or physical abandonment by our parents. When we are children, such things as death, divorce, neglect, long separations, or alcohol and drug abuse create intense pain. Most parents do the best they can, but these situations create an insecurity that frequently shows itself in either self-protective distance or smothering possessiveness.

Those who choose distance believe if they get too close they will be hurt. Therefore, they avoid intimacy using any possible excuse. What they do not realize is that this lack of bonding and attachment creates a separateness that may tear the marriage apart. This guarantees the very hurt that the person is trying so hard to avoid.

Those who choose possessiveness believe if they have control, their mate will not leave them. Cathy's first husband abandoned her and she determined it would never happen again. So when she married Jack she kept a careful eye on him. She tracked his every move and interrogated him thoroughly whenever he was a few minutes late. Frustrated, Jack sat in my office saying, "I can't stand it any longer. Cathy is driving me crazy. She smothers me. If she doesn't back off, I'm going to have to leave." After exploring Cathy's insecurities and Jack reassuring her of his trustworthiness, Cathy was able to relax and deal with her fears in a more constructive way.

Fear of Anger. Many people grow up in families where anger was either not tolerated or it meant violence. Strong expressions of emotion, especially anger, make these people extremely uncomfortable. To them everything must be calm and rational—no raised voices, no intensity. When sparks start to fly they either panic (assuming something terrible is about to happen), retreat (trying to distance themselves as far as possible from the disturbance), or pacify (agreeing no matter what they think in order to quickly gain peace). The fear of anger creates all sorts of problems; worst of all it shuts down communication.

Richard was primarily a retreater, but at times he panicked and pacified. He grew up in a home where anger was not allowed. His wife, Sarah, came from an extroverted family who believed in "getting things off your chest." So when she confronted Richard with not watching their three-year-old daughter carefully enough, he panicked and retreated to his bedroom saying, "I'm sorry, I have this terrible headache and I can't talk about it now."

The next time Sarah confronted him on the same issue, he couldn't escape. He said whatever was necessary in order to restore peace. He never explained that he was watching the child and felt she should be given more freedom. He saw Sarah as being a restrictive and controlling mother. He agreed to be more careful to Sarah's face, but inside he had no intention of changing his style.

Richard's fear blocked a much needed area of communication and planted seeds for many more conflicts in the future.

Fear of Punishment. "If I don't do it right," or "If I bring up that unmentionable subject," or "If I don't see it their way, they will punish me." It might be the silent treatment or a verbal barrage. It might be a threat or actual physical abuse. It might involve guilt, shame, or embarrassment. No matter how it is applied, it is manipulation. This means of control might work on the surface, but the manipulated person builds a resentment and this resentment hardens their heart. They comply out of fear as they dream of retaliation or escape.

Ann did everything her husband asked. If he wanted steak, he got steak. If he wanted sex, he got sex. Outward compliance belied her inner fear. Over the years her fear turned into anger and her heart hardened. One day Ann broke. She could no longer take it. She packed up her bags, left a note on the kitchen table, and went to see an attorney. The broken relationship left the husband in shock. "She was such a good wife. What went wrong?"

We all have a frightened child within us and when we are afraid of our spouse, the marriage suffers a tarnished love. Love and fear do not fit together; the one drives out the other.[6] When fear creeps into the relationship, love fades. Someone once said that a relationship is either growing or dying. When fear is present, it is definitely dying.

8. BOREDOM

Madison Avenue has spent billions of dollars to refine and market sexuality. It surrounds us. We buy the package with little idea of what is inside. The package becomes the person in our world of superficiality. What you see is what you get. Physical attractiveness is subjective. It changes from generation to generation and from culture to culture. Today, in America, the perfect female is very thin, big bosomed, and tan with a healthy complexion. The perfect male is tall, dark, and handsome with a rugged muscular look. That could all change fifty years from now.

When people speak of "falling in love" or infatuation, they are really speaking of sexual attraction. Hormones created the passion Romeo and Juliet experienced. We enjoy physically pleasing people. The danger is what social scientists call *closure*. If he is handsome, we assume he is also intelligent, good mannered, hard working, and honest. Likewise if she is lovely, we assume kindness, good humor, creativity, and a host of other positive attributes.

Scott met Shelly on a blind date. The moment they met they felt love. Two months later they were married. They looked like the perfect couple. He was handsome and she was simply beautiful. Before even getting to know each other they were whisked away by the passion of the moment. The problem is that this passion and excitement did not last. What followed seemed boring by comparison.

Most marriages fall into a rut somewhere between the seventh and fourteenth year. Consciously or unconsciously, we make a major decision at this point.

Decision One

"This relationship is dead. I need to look elsewhere to find some excitement."

Decision Two

"This relationship is boring, but it's not that bad. I'm going to relax in this rut and make it as comfortable as I can."

Decision Three

"This relationship has developed some bad habits I can't tolerate, but if we both work at it we can pull out of this rut and recapture some of the excitement we used to have."

Marriages fall into patterns. Excitement turns into stability and predictability. Responsibilities increase, especially as a couple is active in the child-rearing years. Our interactions easily become a dull exchange of empty facts and scheduling information. One morning you awake and wonder what happened to the spark, the pizazz, the fireworks. Of course it is impossible for a couple to maintain the intensity of courtship, but boredom sets in when things fizzle down to nothing.

Sensitivity to boredom is different in every person. Some can tolerate large amounts. They simply lay back, relax, and enjoy the peace and quiet. Others cannot tolerate any at all. They crave variety and activity. This sensitivity also fluctuates at different periods in our life. For example, many find that as they hit mid-life their desire for excitement increases.

Closeness is more than simply being with a person; it is also belonging and connecting with that person.

Roseann was a serious and sedate school teacher. She and her husband had raised four children and were now ready for retirement. They were content with their simple lifestyle and had fallen into a comfortable pattern. Then Roseann suddenly woke up to something within her. She was no longer content. She wanted more meaning and activity in her life. She signed up for classes at the local community college, volunteered at the hospital, and became a greeter at her church. All these changes were a shock to her husband of thirty-five years. Especially when she asked him, "Are you going to start living or just sit in your old rocker and die?"

9. THE CREEPING SEPARATENESS

Loneliness kills. It creates an emptiness and emotional isolation. An unhappy marriage is one of the loneliest situations if life. Closeness is more than simply being with a person; it is also belonging and connecting with that person.

We all need love and touch. Someone special with whom we can share our fears, secrets, and dreams. Someone to laugh with us and cry with us. A person to walk silently beside us, or reach out and hold us tightly. We all need reassurance and affirmation. We may often stand alone, but we do not want to be lonely.

Everyone needs companionship. Even natural introverts who find fulfillment in solitude have moments when they see a beautiful sunset, or hear a tender love song, and yearn to share it with someone special. Adam must have felt such a yearning many times before meeting Eve. Marriage provides a beautiful opportunity for companionship, but marriage does not guarantee an end to loneliness.

Several years ago, Sheldon Vanauken wrote *A Severe Mercy*, a tender book about his marriage to his wife, Davy. He relates an incident when he and Davy looked around and saw, "A world where love did not endure. The smile of inloveness seemed to promise for ever, but friends who had been in love last year were parting this year." They stopped and asked why. Then one day in early spring they found their answer. "The killer of love is creeping separateness." Together they vowed to battle this enemy. They realized that people tend to gradually drift apart, sometimes without even noticing it, and they were not going to let it happen to them.[7]

> *The key for the porcupines is to learn how to lay down the quills so they don't stick out and poke their partner.*

Over the years I have also observed creeping separateness. A couple marries and becomes one. At first there is good communication, togetherness, romance, and all the other essentials that make a successful marriage. Eventually, time erodes their sincere commitment. It starts slowly—he does his thing and she does hers. There is nothing wrong with that, it is probably healthy, but they do not communicate about their activities. Soon she has her friends and he has his and somehow these friends pull the couple in opposite directions. Different hobbies, different causes, different experiences—all without a means of connecting the two. In time, there is more separateness than togetherness. There is more that is not known than is known about one another. The two feel like strangers. Oh, they may eat dinner together, sleep in the same bed, even go to church together, but they feel distant and disconnected. They look at each other and wonder what has happened and when did it happen. Something has pulled them apart and they can't figure out what it was—it just happened.

LAYING DOWN THE QUILLS

It was a cold night. Snow fell and the wind blew. It was the sort of night that calls you to curl up in front of a crackling fire.

Deep in the forest there was a clearing where two porcupines shivered in the cold; one on the east edge and one on the west. As the snow grew deep and the wind took on a sharp bite, the porcupines slowly drew together. The closer to each other they moved, the more heat was conserved and the more protected they were from the wind.

However, there was a problem in getting too close—their quills poked each other. Pain shot through each body and they quickly parted. Escape from the stabbing quills felt so good, but soon the cold pressed in again, and the two found themselves slowly and cautiously moving together. It was comforting to be close until the quills pricked, and the pain once more seemed greater than the cold.

As the night progressed, the two porcupines pulled together—then apart, over and over throughout the night.[8]

Many marriages are this way. Certain forces bring us together and we hope that is the end of the story. Boy meets girl, they fall in love, they marry, and live happily ever after. Unfortunately, life rarely goes so smoothly. Nobody is perfect and no relationship is made in heaven. Putting together two imperfect beings will create difficulties. As soon as we come together, something happens and we pull apart.

The key for the porcupines is to learn how to lay down the quills so they don't stick out and poke their partner. This is also true of marriage. The porcupine next to us is not our enemy, but our friend and ally, confidant and encourager, and a whole lot more. In the next nine chapters we will learn how to lay down the quills and make a marriage as healthy and fulfilling as possible. Remember, a good marriage does not come easily. It is much more than reading another self-help book. It takes self-evaluation, a willingness to change, a lot of hard work, and much prayer, but in the end it will be worth it.

Discussion Questions

1. When has your marriage been closest to divorce?

   How did you save the relationship?

2. Describe when you are the most selfish to your mate.

   Describe when you are the least selfish.

3. How does laziness slip into your marriage?

4. Which stage is your marriage currently in?

   Fantasy   Surprise   Questioning
   Disillusion   Realistic   Stabilized

5. Does your partner's love bank currently have a positive or negative balance?

   When was the last time you made a deposit to their account?

   When was the last time you made a withdrawal?

6. How do you treat each other when life is hectic?

7. On a scale from 1 to 10 (1 = all the time, 10 = not at all) how negative are you?

   In what ways do you express negativity?

8. Is there anything your partner could say or do that would frighten you? Explain.

9. What is the worst rut your marriage ever experienced?

10. List three examples of the creeping separateness in your marriage:

    a)
    b)
    c)

11. Of the following nine enemies to marriage, which one is the biggest threat to your relationship? Why?

    a) Selfishness   f) Negativity
    b) Laziness   g) Fear
    c) Disappointment   h) Boredom
    d) Hurt/Unhappiness   i) Creeping
    e) Hecticness   Separateness

12. Circle where are you today in the cycle of the porcupines.

    a) Shivering alone in the cold.
    b) Bleeding from the sharp quills.
    c) Watching your partner bleed?
    d) Trying to learn how to lay down the quills.

Notes

1. Ephesians 5:21.
2. Anthony Campolo, *Seven Deadly Sins* (Wheaton, Ill.: Victor, 1987), 14.
3. Larry L. Halter, *Traits of a Happy Marriage* (Dallas: Word, 1989), 48.
4. Willard F. Harley, Jr., *His Needs, Her Needs: Building an Affair-proof Marriage* (Old Tappan, N.J.: Revel, 1986), 15-24.
5. David Burns, *Feeling Good: The New Mood Therapy* (New York: Avon, 1980), 32-43.
6. 1 John 4:18.
7. Sheldon Vanauken, *A Severe Mercy* (New York: Harper, 1977), 36-37.
8. This story is attributed to Arthur Schopnhauer (1788-1860).

2

COMMITMENT

It began with a little itch on his right leg. No big deal. A little scratch and the itch went away.

Several days later the itch returned and scratching only made it worse. He visited the doctor and the itch vanished after applying the prescribed medication. Before long, Mun Ki developed strange sensations in both legs. He cooked up an old home remedy and his legs felt much better.

A week later a sore irritated the big toe on his right foot. It grew and spread to the toes on both feet. He became pale and shivered in the warm weather. By now he knew the cause of his misery. He tried all sorts of treatments and medicines, but nothing slowed down the disease. Finally, Mun Ki was forced to admit there was no cure for leprosy.

Three months after the first symptom appeared, Mun Ki sat with his wife and four children eating the evening meal. When the family finished eating, Nyuk Tsin, his wife, sent the children away. She knelt before her husband and said, "I shall be your *kokua*."[1]

This scene happens almost halfway through James Michener's epic novel *Hawaii*. In 1870 people diagnosed with leprosy were immediately banished to a leper colony on the island of Molokai. The government's strategy was: out of sight, out of mind. The officials did allow one provision for comfort—a healthy individual, fully aware of their actions, could volunteer to accompany a victim to the leper colony. These people were called *kokuas*, the "helpers." The *kokuas* lived with and nursed the leper until one of them died. Then if the *kokua* had not contracted the disease, they were free to return to civilization.

To be a *kokua* took more than love and courage, it took true commitment. As each *kokua* boarded the ship that would take them to a voluntary exile, the police marshal asked carefully, "Are you sure you know what you are doing?"

Engaged couples need to consider that same question. Passion and excitement capture couples and they rarely slow down long enough to think about the ramifications of a genuine commitment. They stand before friends and relatives promising to be faithful through better or worse, richer or poorer, sickness or health, for the rest of their lives. The promise is solemn and those giving it are sincere. Commitments are easily given but it is difficult to live up to them.

> *When most of us were first married, we were grossly unprepared.*

When most of us were first married, we were grossly unprepared. There was so much we didn't know, and what is frightening is that we never realized how unprepared we actually were. Few of us even realized what those sacred words entailed. A wedding vow is no small thing. It is the initiation of a new relationship—husband and wife. It is a commitment that is both total and timeless. Yet at the heart of that commitment there is also an assumption of trustworthiness; for if a commitment is not trustworthy, then by definition it is neither total nor timeless. Without trust the vow is false and ultimately meaningless. So it is here that we must begin.

WHAT IS A TRUSTWORTHY COMMITMENT?

Trust is the bedrock on which to build the foundation of a marriage. A foundation must rest on something solid. A builder who does not dig deep and plant firm footings risks disaster. I once heard of a contractor who built a complex of expensive condominiums in an exclusive river front development. The view was breathtaking, the architectural design received applause, and the choice of materials was top of the line. There was only one small problem. They built on unstable ground. Each year the complex slips an inch toward the river. That is not a fast rate, but in time these beautiful condominiums will collapse. Apparently the footing had been deep, but not deep enough to touch bedrock.

Eric Ericson, a well-known psychologist, writes that the first developmental task of children is "trust versus mistrust." Children learn early whether or not they can trust those around them. If they can, this sense of trust goes with them the rest their lives. Yet if they can't, mistrust becomes their lifestyle.

All children yearn to trust. It's the basis of all future growth. Trusting is the ability to feel safe and secure. Without trust a person is unable to relax and reach beyond themselves. Life becomes a risk.

Here are a few of the situations that can steal away trust in childhood:

- Death of a parent.
- Divorce of parents.
- Physical or sexual abuse.
- Neglect by parents.
- Intense long-term conflict of parents.
- Inconsistent discipline.
- Lack of expressed love and warmth by parents.
- Major trauma (e.g. death of a sibling, natural disasters, severe accidents, fire, hospitalizations).

These items block the development of security and can impact a person for the rest of his or her life. A damaged childhood trust makes it more difficult to trust as an adult. However, this trait can be re-established if both partners are patient and trustworthy.

In courtship the establishment of trust is critical and in marriage the continuation of that trust is equally critical. We build trustworthy commitments with honesty, dependability, and faithfulness. Let's look at each.

HONESTY

Integrity is the core of any intimate relationship. To either state or imply that something is true, when in reality it is not, destroys trust. If we discover our spouse lies in one area, we tend to question them in all areas. We no longer believe what they tell us. Our trust is gone. We can't trust one who is dishonest.

DEPENDABILITY

When someone is dependable we can relax. We don't need to worry or be afraid. In a dependable marriage, we can count on our spouse—we know they will be there when we need them. We base this dependability on a number of assumptions:

- Our spouse cares about us.
- Our spouse is concerned with our best interests.
- Our spouse won't maliciously hurt us.
- Our spouse is responsible.

If we question any of these four assumptions, we tend to pull back and be cautious. When a partner is undependable, we quickly learn that trust leads to disappointment.

FAITHFULNESS

In marriages, faithfulness is a symbol of commitment. It is a statement that our heart belongs to our spouse. This loyalty takes precedence over all other allegiances—parents, relatives, co-workers, and friends of each gender. Faithfulness insists that we allow no one to compete with this special place of affection. Our partner is truly our one and only. Emotional or physical affairs are unthinkable when we have a faithful heart.

> *In marriages, faithfulness is a symbol of commitment. It is a statement that our heart belongs to our spouse.*

Marital trust is built over time. As our honesty, dependability, and faithfulness remain strong, our spouse sees us as trustworthy. However, there are four trust breakers that are so severe they destroy trust. These are not mere setbacks; they take one back to the beginning. Trust is more than damaged, it is annihilated. It no longer exists. They shatter either honesty, dependability, or faithfulness, and sometimes all three.

The following four trust breakers are critically important. To minimize them is to minimize a faulty foundation.

1. **Abandonment**
(Emotional/Physical)
2. **Abuse**
(Emotional/Physical/Sexual/Verbal)

3. Addictions
  (Alcohol/Drugs/Sexual)
4. Adultery
  (Emotional/Physical)

However, trust can be rebuilt if both partners are willing. It is not easy and it takes time. Wounds can heal, but trust breakers leave deep scars and threaten the future of a relationship. Anyone in a relationship where the above is currently happening should seek professional help immediately. Don't say, "It's no big deal," or "If I can hold on, it will get better." These four trust breakers are big deals and without help, situations tend to get worse.

When a couple comes to my office with a specific problem I often ask, "How long have you been aware of this difficulty?" It is not unusual for people to say, "Ten or twenty years."

"Why did it take you so long to seek help?"

"We just thought it would go away."

Problems don't just go away, they tend to get worse. They might start as a little seed, but given time they grow and grow and grow. Yet if we confront the problem early, there is hope.

Cindy was tired of Scott's late nights. She knew he had trouble with alcohol and that most of the nights he was at the local bar. When he stumbled in at 3:00 A.M., he apologized and promised he would never do it again. Cindy finally had enough of his empty promises. She confronted him with two choices: either he go into a month-long alcohol rehabilitation program or she was leaving.

"Do you really mean it?"

"Absolutely!"

"Okay, where do you want me to go?"

"St. Vincent's drug and alcohol unit has a bed waiting for you. I arranged it this morning."

"Let's go. If I'm going to do it I might as well get it over with."

Two years later, Scott is still sober with no relapse. Cindy says he is a new man and the marriage is better than ever. She has even learned to trust him all over again. With trust re-established, there can be a sincere commitment.

If there is no trust in the beginning, the original commitment is on a false foundation. If the trust is present at the beginning but broken later, the initial commitment is drained of meaning.

The marriage may have the appearance of commitment but its spirit is severely wounded. Unless this trust is recaptured, the commitment is merely a social and financial illusion.

WHAT IS A TOTAL COMMITMENT?

Tonya and Sid were the perfect couple—young, attractive, intelligent, and deeply committed to God. They had been married less than two years when a drunk driver hit their car broadside. Sid walked away without a scratch. Tonya was unconscious with severe head injuries. She was rushed to the hospital and was in surgery for six hours. When she came to, the right side of her body was paralyzed and she could hardly speak. Sid propped pillows behind her head and placed a straw between her cracked lips so she could drink.

Three weeks later Tonya was released from the hospital. The doctors said the paralysis was permanent and she would be confined to a wheelchair. She couldn't walk or feed herself; her speech was slow and slurred; she couldn't even go to the bathroom without assistance.

As Sid sat in my office he looked exhausted and my heart went out to him.

"I love Tonya," he said, "but this isn't what I expected out of marriage. One minute we were happy and carefree, the next she's an invalid. This isn't fair! She's not the same person I married."

During the next few weeks Tonya's situation worsened. Terrible headaches kept her bedridden. Her right arm and leg atrophied into awkward and unusable positions. Discouragement and pain pulled Tonya deeper into herself as friends and relatives stopped visiting. It was just too hard to see Tonya in this state.

When I saw her, her face twitched as she slowly tried to articulate her thoughts. She told me she couldn't read anymore and it was hard to concentrate on what she heard.

"The only way I make it through my day is to repeat to myself different Bible verses I memorized as a child. Over and over I repeat them and pray that God will take me home." Then she gave me a strange look and her voice softened. "I told Sid to leave me, but he won't. Do you know what he said?"

I shook my head.

"He said he loved me and he'd never leave."

Her eyes filled with tears as she looked beyond me to something only she could see. "Isn't he crazy?" A tear fell down her cheek.

I grabbed a tissue and gently wiped the tear away. "No, he's not crazy. He's committed—totally committed."

Most of us aren't called to give as much as Sid.

Total commitment is the willingness to share everything—especially ourselves. Each of us are to give all of ourselves to all of our spouse. Life is no longer a solo journey, but a joint endeavor. Two giving themselves freely and equally of everything they can, fulfills the spirit of total commitment.

In this type of commitment we share our time, our possessions, and most significantly, our personhood. We give all we can—with no holding back. We reach deep into our soul to share emotions, beliefs, needs, traits, history, and dreams.

Total commitment is so broad that it is hard to focus in on the specifics, but our strengths and our sexuality are two specific areas we need to share with our spouse. Though these are just two of many critical areas to commit to each other, they do provide a place to begin.

STRENGTHS

We are hesitant to discuss our strengths because we think it is arrogant or presumptive. However, since they are God given and we have nothing to do with it, we should not engage in such thinking. Rather, we need to acknowledge and understand our strengths so we can use them to enhance life with our spouse.

Usually, each of us excel in one or two of these areas and we are slightly retarded in one or two. In other words, we all have both strengths and weaknesses and both are part of the marital commitment. We need to know each other's strengths in order to encourage and build one another up in those areas. We also need to know each other's weaknesses so we can be understanding and compensate for them.

To be committed means to give who we are and part of who we are involves the following ten areas of intellectual strength:[2]

Verbal Intelligence. This is the ability to put one's thoughts into words. Writers, poets, and public speakers can express themselves in language, finding the right word for the right situation. My six-year-old daughter has good verbal intelligence. One evening I came home from work and said, "Brittany, you sure look beautiful."

"Daddy, I do not."

Taken back by her response, I asked, "What do you mean?"

"Look at my nose. It's runny and runny noses are not beautiful." There wasn't anything else I could think to say.

Mathematical Intelligence. People with this ability love numbers. They do not need calculators to add, subtract, multiply, or even divide. Calculations come naturally to them. They snicker at those of us who have math phobias or who struggle in this area.

People laugh when they hear how I deal with my checkbook. I have two strategies that simplify my accounting. First, I round everything up to the next dollar. Second, I have a special line item every month. It's called *Bank Adjustment.* When I get my statement from the bank, I compare what they say I have with what my ledger says and adjust it to what the bank says. I figure they must know what they are doing. One month the bank said I had four hundred dollars more than I had calculated, so I added it to my total. Tami and I celebrated. Then the next month the bank indicated they had made an error and took back the four hundred. We ate macaroni and cheese for the next thirty days.

Visual Intelligence. This ability involves seeing size, shapes, angles, distance, and perspective. It also involves seeing the interaction between objects. Some with good visual intelligence can even discern subtle hues of color and shadow. Artists, architects, and carpenters have visual intelligence.

My father has visual intelligence. He can look at a wall and say, "That's about seventeen-and-a-half feet long." I pull out my tape measure and he is right; seventeen-and-a-half feet.

This ability makes me very nervous when he parallel parks. We drive along and he says, "There's a spot!" I insist that we will never fit. He laughs and says, "There's at least a foot." I hold my breath as the car squeezes into the space, almost scratching the cars in front and back. Most people would never attempt this feat, but my father not only tries it, he does it without even slowing down. "Don't worry," he says, "there's plenty of room."

When the car finally stops and I can breath again, I check the front and back bumper. Dad was right. There was a foot to spare—six in the front and six in the back.

Musical Intelligence. I envy those with the ability to sing and play instruments. Some read music and others can play by ear. My parents insisted that I take four years of piano lessons in hopes that I might develop some musical ability, but it didn't work. Meanwhile, my brother Dale, who never had any piano lessons, can sit at the piano and reproduce almost anything he has ever heard. He has musical intelligence.

Music is a wonderful ability which God did not grant me. Now I love to sing—in the shower, driving in the car, or playing with my children. I'm always singing. I don't always remember the words or have the tune correct so I make up something.

Our children quickly picked up my love for music. Unfortunately, they rarely have the words or tunes correct either. We sing our own versions of popular songs. My wife just sits and shakes her head when Brittany sings, "Row, row, row the car," or "Mary had a little dog."

Mechanical Intelligence. This is the ability to use one's hands to fix things. Mechanics, plumbers, electricians, and repairmen usually have this ability. Traditionally it's a man's field, but if something breaks down in our home, I rarely know what to do. My grandmother once told me you only need one tool to fix things—a hammer. If something doesn't work, you just start tapping it until it does.

My wife has better mechanical intelligence than I do. If the garbage disposal breaks, I will run to the garage for the hammer while she tears it apart and before I know it, it's fixed.

Another part of mechanical intelligence is putting things together. Tami and I will purchase a simple little toy for the children, and when we open the box there are hundreds of pieces and a fifty-step guide to assembly. I'm a fairly intelligent human being, but these instructions rarely make sense to me. Within fifteen minutes I'm so frustrated I have to take a short time out. Then along comes Tami, she reads the instructions and quickly puts the whole thing together. I'm sure glad I have a wife with mechanical intelligence.

Logical Intelligence. Problem solving, trouble shooting, and thinking in a sequential manner is all a part of this ability.

Corporate executives, business administrators, and anybody involved with management have logical intelligence. These people think clearly from point A to point B to point C. All is in order and well structured. *Organization* is their middle name. They keep the world running smoothly, but they also drive those of us who are less logical a little crazy. Have you ever gotten into an argument with someone who is totally logical? It's just not fair. Anyway, who said arguments had anything to do with logic? Besides, being logical doesn't always make that person right.

Physical Intelligence. Dancers, athletes, and actors all have this ability. They are aware of their body. They can control and coordinate it with strength, grace, and expression.

My three children, at least at this point in their lives, do not have physical intelligence. They trip, run into walls, lose their balance, fall off chairs, bump their heads, and skin their knees.

My wife, on the other hand, was a gymnast and has great coordination. Several years ago our community had a strong wind storm and we lost some of the shingles on the roof. The next day I asked my wife to hold the ladder while I climbed up and replaced them. Once on top of the roof I had a hard time getting to the right spot. The shingles were slippery and the pitch was steep. I carefully crawled on my hands and knees up the roof— two feet forward, then I would slip back two feet. After about fifteen minutes of absolutely no progress, Tami called up and suggested she give it a try. I gladly traded her places thinking, *Does she really think she can do any better?* Well, she did. Tami stood up, got her balance, confidently walked up the steep pitch, and replaced the shingles.

Personal Intelligence. The person with this ability is in touch with their feelings, needs, and motives. In an attempt to better understand themselves they study psychology. Their world is inward and at times introspective as they ponder who they are and why they are that way. A psychotherapist once wrote about having a memory that "was accompanied by a good deal of emotion."[3] It involved building little houses and castles with stones. To fully understand why he had this strong feeling, he went to the beach every afternoon for a number of months and built little houses in the sand. In this way he hoped to recapture the events of his childhood that produced this emotion and, therefore, know himself a little better. This displayed personal intelligence.

Sharing our strengths along with our weaknesses is an important part of marriage.

My daughter, Brittany, may have it as well. When she had just turned two, my wife left her with me for the afternoon. We were playing and having a wonderful time when suddenly Brittany disappeared. I looked all over for her and finally found her in her closet, curled up with her blanket, her favorite doll, and a pacifier. In surprise I asked, "Brittany, what are you doing in your closet?" She pulled out her pacifier and said, "Daddy, I was getting a little stressed and I needed a break."

Social Intelligence. This is the ability to bring people together and help them feel relaxed. They can make a group laugh or organize them into action. People naturally gravitate to those blessed with social intelligence. This person might be an up-front type leader, but they might just as likely be a behind-the-scenes type person.

Everybody likes Sam. The party doesn't start until he arrives. He is a natural mingler. If Sam is around, people have a good time. Sam is also the type of person you can call if there is a problem. He always seems to know the right thing to say. When you talk, Sam gives you all his attention and you sense he really cares. He even sends me a birthday card every year. Sam definitely knows how to deal with people.

Spiritual Intelligence. Some people have a special sense of good and evil. They have an awareness of God and the intangible forces of the universe. Those with spiritual intelligence have an extra measure of faith and can see beyond what is visible. This ability is possible for more than saints and mystics. It is also possible for everyday people such as you and me.

George was a successful physician working at a prestigious hospital who felt called by God to be a medical missionary. He knew God would take care of him and he felt that if God said go, he should go.

———◆———

Sex is neither sacred nor profane. It is simply a part of life.

———◆———

Once in a while, when I meet a particular person or am in a certain situation, a shiver goes up my back and I get a definite sense of evil. I can't rationally explain this, but I believe it's a part of spiritual intelligence.

Sharing our strengths along with our weaknesses is an important part of marriage. It's the commitment of both our best and worst qualities that makes our vows so meaningful. It is easy to commit to the positive aspects of people—those admirable characteristics that everybody loves and respects. However, a commitment of the total person also involves those negative aspects we wish did not exist. Just ask Tonya and Sid.

Talk to each other about your strengths and weaknesses. Commit yourself to help build up your partner's strong areas by encouraging them to be everything God made them to be. Also, commit to protect and help compensate for your partner's weak areas—promising never to ridicule or use these areas against them.

SEXUALITY

Sexual intercourse is the consummation of the marriage commitment. It's the symbol of marital completeness. If there is no intercourse, a marriage may be annulled. The ceremony does not count if the commitment isn't total.

No marriage can exist totally isolated from the issue of human sexuality. Partners may be either embarrassed or obsessed by the subject, but it can't be ignored. To some it is a god and to others it is a demon. All of us are sexual beings; it is a part of who we are. Sex is neither sacred nor profane. It is simply a part of life.[4] Unfortunately, many couples see intercourse as merely a sexual act. They miss the power and significance of sexuality to a healthy marriage.

Sexual intercourse has four levels of meaning: reproduction, pleasure, communication, and unity.

Reproduction. Some couples see reproduction as an unwanted side-effect of sexual intercourse. People use pills, birth control devices, wishful thinking, and abortions to avoid child birth. Tami and I tried for over two years to have a child. Three emotional miscarriages left us both very aware of the miracle of birth. Reproduction is miraculous. That a male and female can come together sexually and produce a child is beyond words.

Tami's fourth pregnancy went full term. At 4:30 A.M. she woke me and said, "I think I'm ready." We jumped into the car and sped to the hospital. On the way, I turned to Tami and said, "Life will never be the same after today." I was right.

When Brittany's head crested I was curious and amazed. When she slid out and her pink chin quivered with her first cry, I was so ecstatic that tears streamed down my cheeks. There is nothing as awe-inspiring as watching the birth of a child.

Two years later, I was at the same hospital. Once more I was experiencing that wonderful ecstasy as I watched the delivery of our second child, Dylan. I had a son! My joy was suddenly clouded with alarm as I looked at a very blue baby. I looked at the physician and saw his troubled face. Then I realized Dylan had not cried. He was just lying there. Panic gripped me. My thoughts screamed, *What's wrong? Do something! Get him air!* The physician pushed on the baby's chest and Dylan let out a cry. The most wonderful cry I have ever heard.

Children are a blessing. Sexual intercourse is a joyous part of creating this blessing. It is a means of continuing the human race and guaranteeing that the stream of life will flow from generation to generation.

Saint Augustine, with many of the early church fathers, believed that reproduction was the only justification for sexual intercourse. However, a complete reading of the Holy Bible shows that God is interested in more than just the creation of babies. He is also concerned with the fulfillment of adults. Jesus said, "I am come that they might have life, and that they might have it more abundantly."[5]

Pleasure. Sexual intercourse is one of the most intense physical pleasures of life and it is important that its sheer delight be a part of marriage. When a husband and wife come together there is a celebration of human sexuality. However, this pleasure is not merely the biological release of energy and anxiety. It is also the result of two emotional factors:

1. Giving. This is where each partner seeks mutual pleasure, rather than just individual gratification. It is where the process of sharing satisfaction becomes as significant as the point of personal orgasm. The real fulfillment is wrapped up in the total joyous giving of one's self to another and the total joyous giving of another to oneself.

2. Reaffirming. Pleasure is gained from the reaffirmation of the original pledge of mutual love. Therefore, the act of sexual intercourse takes on an element of psychological satisfaction where our personhood is enhanced, romance is rekindled, and security is reinforced.

Every individual has desires and drives for sexual pleasure. The physical ecstasy, when truly shared, creates an emotional intimacy. The world outside the couple stops. Two individuals—body, soul, and spirit—are totally focused on each other. That is intense pleasure, plus a lot more that words can't even express.

Communication. The Hebrew word to describe intercourse is *Yada* meaning "to know" and it is a euphemism for the sex act.[6] This same word also describes intellectual and spiritual knowledge. In English, the word intercourse means "communication" and in a sense that is quite appropriate, for sexual intercourse is a special means of communication. Let's see how it provides a unique and intimate modality for mutual expression, exposure, and exploration.

1. Expression. Someone once asked Mozart, "What are you trying to express by your music?" The famous artist replied, "If I could express it in words, I wouldn't need music."

The marriage act is the means by which two people, committed to each other, can express the whole meaning and quality of their relationship. Sex extends the means through which a couple can communicate love and mutual concern. It enhances the meaning of marriage by becoming an expression of solidarity, intimacy, acceptance, affection, romance, and tenderness. It provides a language for the husband and wife not matched by words or any other act.

2. **Exposure.** Sexual intercourse involves the opening up of ourselves to our partner. The nakedness alone is symbolic that nothing is hidden and that one is at a point of extreme personal vulnerability. For sexual intercourse to be most meaningful, it requires the unhindered sharing of our innermost thoughts, feelings, and very being. This surrender of our private identity to another is both frightening and satisfying; for in the sexual relationship we willingly expose ourselves to the risk of rejection. To reveal oneself to another and to be trusted with that person's intimate self-revealing provides a new and deepened personal awareness that can both strengthen and complete one's identity. One's self-disclosure leads to the other's self-disclosure making this process truly reciprocal and, unless blocked, unending.

3. **Exploration.** Human sexuality provides knowledge of our mate. It is through the process of exploring the mystery of another person that we discover the mystery of ourselves. This desire for intimate involvement with another person inevitably leads to mutual growth. It draws a man and a woman toward each other in their search for understanding.

Communication is a necessity and communication through intercourse is one of the most meaningful experiences in marriage. The process of expression, exposure, and exploration within the context of sexuality allows and sustains a process of growth that should only get better as the anniversaries come and go.

Unity. Sexual intercourse brings together two total individuals and makes them one. The book of Genesis says, "Therefore shall a man leave his father and his mother, and shall cleave unto his wife; and they shall be one flesh."[7] To cleave to one's mate takes in every aspect of the relationship between husband and wife. It

49

is through giving and receiving that two distinct personalities are considered one single unit. This solidarity involves the creation of a physical, social, mental, and spiritual unity.

1. Physical Unity. This is the most obvious manifestation of the one-flesh relationship. The intimate body contact, the tender sexual embrace, and the private meeting of male and female make the marriage act an intensely physical encounter. However, sexual intercourse is more than an encounter between two bodies. It is the reaching out of the spirit through the body, for nowhere does flesh and spirit touch so intimately. The body is essentially an epiphany of personhood and when it is given, so are all the secrets that it contains. Every instance of sexual intercourse is significant in itself; for the physical is inseparable from the totality of the oneness.

2. Social Unity. This is essential because it creates the promise of companionship. Loneliness is an awful thing. We all desire to share our hopes and fears, our joys and frustrations with one who understands. We want to belong and be taken from our isolation. Belonging has power and the one-flesh relationship is the most profound form of belonging. It is a companionship that requires and provides radical self-giving, unique self-exposure, and unrestrained self-commitment.

3. Mental Unity. It is impossible to consider the act of sexual intercourse apart from the mind, for the primary sex organ is the brain. The one-flesh relationship is an intimate blending that involves a unity of personality. Sexual intercourse is an expression of the individual. It is more than the meeting of two bodies, it is the meeting of two persons. Physical sexuality is the vehicle for the expression of psychological sexuality, yet the vehicle and the expression are so intertwined in the marriage act as to be virtually inseparable.

In sexual intercourse the most intimate aspects of two personalities touch and in this is created a union of two intellects, two emotions, and two wills. Isolate or exclude any one of these three from the physical union and the act runs the risk of being incomplete, meaningless, self-centered, or exploitive.

The intellect is needed to establish the proper attitude, the emotions to create the proper atmosphere, and the will to initiate the proper action. When an integration of this type takes place, a trust and surrender develop which cannot otherwise occur.

4. Spiritual Unity. We are all spiritual and sexual individuals. These two important aspects of our existence are closely related; both are private, unavoidable, and easily distorted. Sexual intercourse is symbolic of a commitment that has a specific spiritual dimension.

The marriage act is the sealing of a spiritual covenant with God and with our partner. It is an oath to God concerning our relationship to another. Therefore, the marriage covenant is a promise that only death can break. Sexual intercourse is a reaffirmation of the sincerity of that promise, but even more, for it is a statement about the couple. It states the existence of a permanent and exclusive commitment between two people. The faithfulness to this covenant involves the decision to stand together through and in spite of periods of conflict, struggle, boredom, and monotony. However, a total life commitment involves more than mere fidelity. Sexual intercourse is most satisfying when it occurs within the security of a total and timeless partnership that is interested in the personal growth of each member.

When two people join to become one in the process of sexual intercourse, a comprehensive unity takes place. To maintain our sexual integrity, we must recognize the facts and implications of a union of this nature. Physical, social, mental, and spiritual dimensions give intercourse a unique significance. However, one must be alert to the danger of so ethereal a view of sexual unity that it does not correspond with the reality of human experience.

The giving of ourselves sexually is symbolic of giving of our personhood. To focus on the levels of reproduction or pleasure without considering the deeper significance of communication or unity is to miss the substance of commitment. All four levels are meaningful and important. Yet there is a sequence of intimacy from least to greatest: reproduction, pleasure, communication, and unity. The greater the intimacy the more total is the commitment.

There are many aspects to a total commitment. Strengths and sexuality are merely two of these. Each spouse gives all they are to their mate. This mutual submission is done in a spirit of harmony, sensitivity, friendship, compassion, and humility.

WHAT IS A TIMELESS COMMITMENT?

The wedding vows read, "Till death do us part." That's a terribly long time. How can anyone seriously enter into such a permanent obligation? That's impossible! Far too idealistic. After all, people change, situations change.

- What if you fall out of love?
- What if you don't even like your partner anymore?
- What if somebody more compatible comes along?

Several years ago I went to a seminar on marriage at an international psychological convention. During one of the workshops the question arose: "At what point should one divorce?" The scholarly presenter suggested, "When your needs are no longer met." Someone else added, "When you are unhappy or uncomfortable."

It is easy to give up and forget that "love returns in waves...you just have to wait it out."
Alan Alda

The discussion continued with the emphasis that life is too short to waste your time in a relationship that does not bring you pleasure, self-actualization, and ultimate fulfillment.

I was sitting in my chair getting more and more restless and trying hard to bite my tongue. Finally, I could hold back no longer and I blurted out, "But what about commitment?"

The room went silent, then people started chuckling. The presenter stepped forward and explained to me, as a father would to a slightly retarded son, "Commitment is an old-fashioned word.

Marriage is a social contract and if it no longer meets the needs of the parties involved it must be either renegotiated or nullified."

I shook my head and said in my most intellectual voice, "That's the wimpy way out," but nobody was listening.

Relationships go up and down while love comes and goes. Someone once asked Alan Alda, the famous television and movie star, how he managed to have such a long and successful mar-

Our love is more than a feeling, it is a choice.

riage. His answer was that most relationships begin with a "vibrant" love, but soon fade into "utter discontent." It is easy to give up and forget that "love returns in waves...you just have to wait it out."[8] Alan Alda was right; love is like the tides of the ocean. Sometimes they come in and the passion is high. You feel the love and the relationship is wonderful. Then there are times when the tide is out—sometimes way out. The relationship is dry and lifeless. The love is gone. You look out at the sea and wonder if the tide will ever return. But if you're patient and stay at the beach, the waves will again crash on the shore. The excitement and romance will return. You will even feel the love again.

The intent of the marriage commitment is permanence. Yet we live in a culture that sees everything as disposable. If the tide is out at your beach, just go to another. We are impatient and the grass is always greener on the other side of the fence. Robert Fulghum, in his book *It Was On Fire When I Lay Down On It* counters with, "The grass is greenest where it is watered."[9] Unfortunately we don't water our own grass. It is much easier to pick up our things and move. If the relationship does not work out, divorce and try another. Frequently a terminated marriage says more about who we are, than about what was wrong in the relationship.

People trade in marriages the way they trade in cars. A couple in their late twenties came to me for pre-marital counseling. When I confronted her with some potential difficulties in the relationship, she agreed.

"Dr. Stephens, I don't think this marriage has much of a chance to last more than a year."

"Then why are you getting married?"

"He's such a nice guy and I think I should give it a try. If it doesn't work, it just doesn't work."

I was shocked.

Marriage commitments are serious. Two people pledge their integrity to each other. They promise to enjoy the good times and work through the bad. They vow that they will allow nothing to tear apart their union. The future may be unknown, but their honor, determination, and hard work will carry them through.

Tami and I have committed to never use the word *divorce*. Just saying the word opens the option. Threatening it cheapens our integrity. Therefore, we strike the word from our vocabulary. We are both committed to work through any problem and grow deeper in our relationship year by year. This does not guarantee we will always feel wonderful about each other. What it does mean is that our love is more than a feeling, it is a choice.

There is also the realization that it takes two to create marital difficulties. If there is a problem, I ask what is it I have done to either contribute to, or cause the situation. We will work out the problem together.

However, merely staying together does not guarantee a healthy relationship. Many couples proudly announce their commitment for life while they have endured many years of emotional divorce. Years ago I heard a speaker ask the audience what their relationship was like with their spouse, then asked them to determine if they were:

- roommates,
- checkmates,
- cellmates,
- stalemates,
- helpmates.

The first four options may have a timeless commitment, but it seems as if they are following the letter of the law and ignoring its spirit. The last option, being helpmates, is the heart of a timeless commitment. Two partners helping each other to be their best.

A timeless marriage with timeless growth and intimacy as its aim is a goal that any marriage can achieve if both parties are willing to fight for it.

Earlier in this chapter I said that commitment is based on trust and when trust is broken, the commitment is shattered. Adultery, abandonment, abuse, and addiction destroy the heart of a marriage. The relationship might stay together, but the intimacy is dead. You must circle *cellmates* in the previous paragraph to describe the interaction. A legal divorce is only a technicality.

Yet if the offending party is truly repentant and if the offended can recapture a spark of trust, then it is possible to renew the timeless commitment. This is a difficult thing to do, but when possible, it is well worth reviving the healthy aspects of a relationship.

The dream of growing old together is a wonderful dream. I love to hear of couples celebrating fifty years together—couples who have been true helpmates. At times I have asked them how they do it. The usual answer is, "We have had good times and bad times, but through it all we have been committed to each other."

That is the type of trustworthy, total, and timeless commitment that provides security. It fosters a nurturing environment where two can mature and grow. Anything less is not really a commitment. We live in a world of false vows and counterfeit promises, where people play at marriage. They don't want to be tied down or vulnerable. Half-hearted commitments make marriage a mockery. They doom the partners to superficiality and loneliness.

RENEWING THE COMMITMENT

Commitment is the foundation to any marriage. When it fails, the marriage crumbles. Building a firm marriage gives it the possibility of withstanding anything.

Doug and Diane had made a total and timeless commitment. One evening when Diane was out of town visiting relatives, Doug picked up a prostitute. The next morning he was appalled at what he had done—it was so stupid and terribly wrong. He knew he had to tell Diane, but he was afraid she would leave him.

Diane was shattered. "How could you do this?" she asked, her voice cracking. "I thought you loved me. I thought you were a Christian."

Doug hung his head and cried. "Is there any way you could forgive me?"

A few days later they walked into my office. Doug stuttered through their story as Diane stared at the floor. It was hard for her to look at him and yet she made it clear she didn't want a divorce. Doug was repentant and willing to do anything to reestablish trust. Diane was numb, but she wanted to forgive him and try to rebuild the relationship.

After nine months of intense counseling, these two stood before their minister. It was a sunny June afternoon. She wore her wedding dress and he a tuxedo. Friends and relatives applauded as they renewed their vows to honesty, dependability, and faithfulness. They knelt before God and committed themselves to him. Then they kissed a wild, passionate kiss while the guests cheered and whistled.

I wish the story ended there. A month later Doug applied for life insurance. Part of the routine health exam involved an AIDS test and Doug's results were HIV positive. He couldn't believe it—one night of illicit activity and his life was at risk.

Diane was angry and scared. The two held each other, crying and praying. The next day she went to a community health clinic for anonymous testing. Several days later she found her results were negative, but she should be retested in six months.

Diane moved out to think things through and decide what to do. A week later she returned home with a commitment to stay beside Doug through this terminal crisis. During the next five years her commitment was total.

She went back to the clinic six months later and got a clean bill of health. Together they told friends and relatives of the disease. She went to the doctor with him, encouraged him, and prayed for him. She packed up his personal items when he could no longer work. When he was too exhausted to walk, she pushed him in his wheelchair. She nursed him at home when he could no longer take care of himself.

As the years passed, Doug drastically lost weight, had horrible night sweats, grew large warts on his face, and struggled with his breathing. Before her very eyes, Diane watched Doug slowly die. She was constantly by his side.

Together they went to local churches and high schools, speaking about AIDS and abstinence. Together they committed each day to God and to each other. It wasn't easy and it wasn't romantic. During the last year, Doug was always sick and Diane was always exhausted. She was there by his side, holding his skinny hand and praying the night he died.

The last time I saw Doug and Diane together I asked her why she stayed with him. She smiled and said, "I told him, 'till death do we part,' and I meant it."

"But aren't there times you regret staying with Doug?"

"Not for a minute. During the past few years I've learned that love isn't leaving when things get rough. It's giving and growing through the hard times. I love Doug more now than when we were first married. The bad times taught me what real marriage is all about."

I said, "Most people couldn't do what you've done, but you've shown real commitment in action. Thanks."

Diane blushed and I whispered, "You're quite a lady."

Discussion Questions

1. Describe what you remember about your wedding and giving of your vows.

2. On a scale from 1 to 10 (1 = excellent, 10 = poor) how would you rate yourself in the following areas?

   a) Honesty
   b) Dependability
   c) Faithfulness

3. Which of the four A's (abandonment, abuse, addictions, and adultery) would be hardest for you to deal with?

   Which would be easiest?

   How would you deal with the hardest and easiest if they happened in your marriage?

4. In the story about Sid and Tonya, would you be able to do what Sid did? Why or why not?

5. Of the following ten strengths, circle the ones you are good in and underscore the ones where you are slightly retarded.

   Identify which ones apply to your spouse using a check for good and an X for slightly retarded.

Verbal	Personal
Musical	Visual
Physical	Logical
Mathematical	Social
Mechanical	Spiritual

6. Are you better at pointing out your partner's strengths or weaknesses? Explain why.

7. How giving and reaffirming are you in your sexual relationship? Explain.

8. In your sexual relationship, are you more comfortable with:

   a) expression,
   b) exposure,
   c) exploration?

9. Other than strengths and sexuality, what are three additional aspects of a total commitment?

   1.
   2.
   3.

10. Is a timeless commitment possible? Explain.

11. How long did your parents' marriage last?

How does this impact your view of a timeless commitment?

12. How would you describe your commitment to your mate?

Notes

1. James Michener, *Hawaii* (New York: Random, 1959), 470-486.

2. Howard Gardiner, *Frames of Mind: The Theory of Multiple Intelligences* (New York: Basic Books, Inc., 1983). These strengths are an expanded and modified version of intelligence as presented by Dr. Howard who lists six types of intelligence: linguistic, musical, logical/mathematical, spatial, bodily/kinesthetic, and personal.

3. C. G. Jung, *Memories, Dreams, Reflections* (New York: Vintage, 1989), 173ff.

4. Harry Hollis, *Thank God for Sex* (Nashville: Broadman Press, 1975), 11-12.

5. John 10:10, KJV.

6. Genesis 4:1.

7. Genesis 2:24, KJV.

8. Elizabeth Kaye, "Arlene and Alan Alda: A Love Story," *McCall's* (January 1976), 122.

9. Robert Fulghum, *It Was On Fire When I Lay Down On It* (New York: Villard Books), 162.

3

POSITIVE REGARD

He treated her with respect and kindness. He built her up and did not dwell on her mistakes. She knew that he not only loved her, he liked her. He took the time to know who she was and what made her that way. He watched her and listened to her. He saw beyond her physical self to her very soul. He knew her emotions and her needs. He encouraged her as she reached out to her goals and dreams.

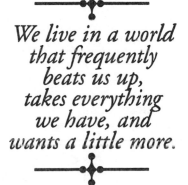

We live in a world that frequently beats us up, takes everything we have, and wants a little more.

If someone attacked her, he defended her. If someone doubted her, he believed in her. If someone rejected or ignored her, he let her know how much she mattered. It is called *positive regard,* and husbands and wives need this from each other.

We live in a world that frequently beats us up, takes everything we have, and wants a little more. By the end of the day we are exhausted, frustrated, and sometimes discouraged. We journey home hoping to regroup, but at times our marriage can be more exhausting than our work.

Positive regard is simply being kind and supportive to each other. It's letting our partner know he or she is important and special. Don Quixote, in that masterpiece by Cervantes, had positive regard for Aldonza Lorenzo. He called this simple farm girl the "fairest of the fair" and he went out to conquer kingdoms in her name. He told everyone he met that she was the most beautiful damsel in the world and he saw it as his mission to convince others to "believe, confess, affirm, swear, and defend that truth."

Positive regard is being nice to each other. It's enjoying each other's company. This is one of the factors that bring two people together—it's also needed to keep them together. People don't stay where they aren't wanted and without positive regard a person doesn't feel wanted.

Positive regard is a process with three aspects: knowing, accepting, and respecting. We must know our partner to accept him or her. We must accept our partner in order to respect our partner. Without respect there can be no genuine love. It is love that drives us to want to know more about our partner. Thus, we repeat the circle of positive regard, developing a deeper intimacy with each trip through its three aspects.

PART ONE

Do you know your mate? I mean really know who he or she is. We get to know each other during courtship and then too often we stop learning new things about one another. This is unfortunate because we are all constantly growing and changing. Often times the needs and feelings we had five years ago are different from those we have today.

We usually want to know more about those we love. To know know more, we have to study. A healthy marriage requires us to be good students desiring to learn more about our spouse. Many of us have developed poor study habits. There are three basic techniques that make one a good student of his or her spouse.

• **Watch** and notice their likes, dislikes, and numerous other characteristics.

• **Listen** to really hear their concerns and expectations.

• **Ask** simple questions, rather than assuming we know our partner's thoughts and feelings.

Knowing each other is a lifetime process. We are deceived if we ever think we fully know our spouse. Most of us barely know ourselves, so how can we claim to truly know someone else? Yet to maintain a healthy, growing marriage we must work at continually learning more about each other. For without knowing, our relationship is based on illusion, assumption, or apathy. All of which can destroy a marriage.

A good student approaches a subject with a plan. Since we all have a past, a present, and a future this provides a simple outline for our study.

THE PAST

We are a product of our past. Not just our personal past, but also our ancestral past. We cannot separate ourselves from our roots. History often shapes us in ways we are totally unaware. To know our spouse we must gain some sense of their history. We need to dig into the family histories with the same motive an archeologist digs for ancient ruins—to reveal the unknown.

Ancestral Past. In America we have a tendency to disconnect from our past because we live too much in the here and now. We often know little about our ancestors and ethnic heritage. This is unfortunate because our personal history can tell us a great deal about who we are.

During the first two or three sessions of therapy I frequently gather as much information as I can about a person's family tree. From this valuable information I can usually identify potential problems with which one might struggle.

The other day a gentleman had his first appointment, and after gathering a family history I said I was concerned with two areas: sexuality and anger. He looked at me astonished. "How in the world do you know that?"

"It's actually quite simple," I said, "your paternal grandmother and your father both have a history of promiscuity. Your maternal grandmother, your mother, and an uncle are hot-tempered. Therefore, these are two of your family's traits and the likelihood is that you will also struggle with them."

To know our spouse, we must know their heritage. Try to gather information about their grandparents, parents, uncles, and aunts. If we can go back further that would be helpful. Ask your mate questions. If they don't know maybe a parent or an aunt, or someone else in the family, can provide some history. Ask about:

- Ethnic heritage
- Family traits
- Migrations

- Religious background
- Occupations
- Education
- Traditions
- Traumas
- Temperament
- Major events, achievements, or turning points
- Addictive tendencies (alcohol, drugs, sex, gambling, food)
- Psychological struggles (depressions, anxieties, phobias, suicides, breakdowns, psychosis)
- Interesting family stories

Personal Past. One psychiatrist has said that the child is the father of the man. Over and over again I hear stories of childhood traumas that have impacted people for the rest of their lives.

- The little girl whose parents divorced when she was four, later had difficulty trusting any relationship.

- The boy whose best friend died when he was eight, later became a chaplain to help others deal with their grief.

- The ten-year-old girl who was seduced by her campfire leader into a lesbian interaction, later became very promiscuous in an attempt to prove her heterosexuality.

- The teenage boy who was publicly humiliated, later developed a social phobia and has panic attacks every time he leaves his house.

Many psychologists believe that our basic personality is imprinted by the time we are five, and our identity is crystallized prior to our twentieth birthday. Therefore, knowing about the early years of our partner is critical. Sit down together and discuss the following questions:

- What is your earliest childhood memory?

- What were the major accomplishments, events, and traumas in your life?

- Who in your family were you the closest to? Who were you the most distant from?

- How do you think the birth order in your family affected you?

- How did your mother and father parent you?

It is important that each partner be willing to share their personal past with the other. Take turns at both sharing and listening. Be aware, though, that some past events may be so humiliating it is frightening to share them.

I had seen Leslie and Leonard for six months of marriage counseling when Leslie called my office in tears. She told me that, after sixteen years of marriage, she still had a big secret from her past that she had never disclosed. The next day she sat in my office and shared how her father had sexually abused her between the ages of four and seventeen. Though she felt humiliated, she knew she had to tell her husband.

Leonard was in the waiting room when I asked him to join us. As Leslie shared her story, he wept in powerful sobs. When she finished, the room was silent. Then Leonard said, "Leslie, I was not only crying for you. I was crying for me because my mother sexually abused me, and I've never told a soul."

The two embraced. Their secrets were out and they felt they knew each other better than ever.

THE PRESENT

It takes time and effort to know our partners. After a study of how the past affects personality, our research moves to the present. There are many facets to a person's current psychological makeup. Two of these facets involve a person's needs and emotions.

Needs. We all have psychological needs. Some psychologists believe that these needs are the core of human personality. To ignore our partner's needs leaves us ignorant of the driving forces behind who they are. In the book *Love* Leo Buscaglia writes that "love recognizes needs."[1] Yet we must know what to look for in order to recognize the needs. Here are ten common psychological needs.[2]

1. **Achievement.** To achieve a goal. To overcome an obstacle or challenge.

2. **Affirmation.** To draw near and relate to others. To interact with individuals or groups.

3. **Autonomy.** To have physical and/or emotional space. To experience freedom. To resist restriction.

4. **Control.** To order and manage one's environment (including self, others, and things).

5. **Impact.** To be seen and heard. To get and hold the attention of others.

6. **Growth.** To explore and understand. To ask or answer questions. To gather information.

7. **Nurture.** To assist others in need. To help, support, console, protect, comfort, encourage, nurse, heal.

8. **Play.** To have fun. To relax and enjoy oneself.

9. **Security.** To feel safe and supported. To be protected from harm or humiliation. To be loved.

10. **Stimulation.** To seek and enjoy sensory input (tactile, auditory, visual, olfactory, gustatory). To have sexual interactions.

We are attracted to those who know our needs and can sensitively meet them. It's paramount that we know our mate's needs for if they aren't being met, our spouse may be tempted to seek other relationships where their needs will be met. This creates a potentially dangerous situation that could undermine the basic commitment of marriage.

Emotions. Emotions are the guts of who we are. Some people are expressive with their feelings, others repress them; but it would be foolish to deny their importance. To know our spouse we must peek into their heart and discover what emotions influence their thoughts and shape their behavior. There are hundreds of emotions and a thousand gradations of each. Following are thirty-three basic emotions that can start you on your journey to discovery. Begin with these three questions and then make up a few of your own.

To know our spouse we must peek into their heart and discover what emotions influence their thoughts and shape their behavior.

- Which of these emotions is most often felt by your spouse?

- When was the last time your spouse felt each of these emotions?

- What triggers each of the following emotions in your spouse?

Anger	Joy	Fear
Grief	Stress	Relief
Suppression	Guilt	Satisfaction
Disgust	Hurt	Loneliness
Sadness	Depression	Caution
Impatience	Humiliation	Nervousness
Regret	Confusion	Strength
Boredom	Peace	Jealousy
Hope	Courage	Exhaustion
Resentfulness	Bashfulness	Curiousity
Betrayal	Numbness	Determination

Knowing the needs and emotions of our spouse provides a great beginning to our study. There are also many other aspects of who we are in the here and now. There are roles we play, beliefs we hold, traits we manifest, choices we make, perceptions we defend, intuitions we experience, and behaviors we display. These facets, and many more, create a gem more precious than any diamond or emerald ever found on this small planet.

THE FUTURE

The future is a great unknown. To some it appears full of hope and excitement. To others it seems to hold only fear and despair. Goals and dreams are the flip sides of the same coin. They push us forward toward the positive. They define our character and direct the course of our marriage. If we do not know the goals and dreams of our partner, our marriage is bound to run aground.

Goals. Someone once wrote that most people aim at nothing and usually hit it. Goals are the targets of life. They are specific and measurable, even though they come in many shapes and sizes. The following are twelve target areas:

a) Educational
b) Financial
c) Occupational
d) Spiritual
e) Personal
f) Relational/Marital
g) Parental
h) Physical
i) Intellectual
j) Emotional
k) Political
l) Recreational

Each of these areas provides something at which to aim. That is the focus of any goal. Sit down together and talk through each of these twelve target areas. It's amazing what you might learn. If you don't know the goals of your mate, you might find you're both aiming in different directions.

Dreams. These are the fantasies and wishes of life. This is where our mind wanders when time and money, and all other obstacles, are erased. Yet dreams can come true. If we don't know our partner's dreams we miss a wonderful opportunity to make them happy.

When we were first married, Tami had a dream of building our own house. After a number of years that dream came true. Our dreams don't have to come true to bring happiness; sometimes just the process of dreaming and sharing our dreams with each other brings about joy.

Tami and I just finished a discussion of our dreams. She told me about seven of hers.

- Own a bed and breakfast
- Build an orphanage in the Caribbean
- Help educate needy children
- Be a ballet dancer
- Play the piano
- Travel to Australia
- Cruise the Greek Isles

Some of these dreams I knew about and they belong to both of us. Others are very personal to her. One of her dreams caught me totally by surprise. I didn't know Tami wanted to be a ballet dancer. Now that I do, I'm better able to help her dream become a goal and a reality.

Our spouse is our most valuable asset. They have an incredible impact on our life. Why is it we often know our job, our house, even our car better than we know our mate?

I know a woman who made a list of a hundred dreams on her twenty-first birthday. Some were big and some were small. Number 16: Visit the White House. Number 37: Water ski. Number 42: Hang glide. Number 56: Eat escargot. Number 59: See a play on Broadway. Number 80: Climb the Eiffel Tower. Number 98: Read *War and Peace*. Her goal was to accomplish two or three of her dreams each year.

Twenty years have flown by and this woman has now crossed off more than fifty dreams on her list. Her husband has been very supportive of her first fifty dreams and together they look forward to fulfilling the next fifty.

Knowing our spouse is the first step to positive regard. It sends a message that they are important and we are committed. We know the color of their eyes, their favorite food, and what they like to do in their spare time, but we don't really know *who* they are. Too often our knowledge of each other is superficial. We skim over the surface of life never taking the time to dig deep.

Knowing our spouse takes time and effort; it doesn't just happen. It takes watching with keen eyes, listening with attentive ears, and asking with an open mind. Our spouse is our most valuable asset. They have an incredible impact on our life. Why is it we often know our job, our house, even our car better than we know our mate? To have a healthy marriage we need to take care of it. To do that, we must be willing to know and be known by our partner.

PART TWO: ACCEPTING

The old saying "opposites attract" is often true. The difficulty is, once opposites marry they drive each other crazy.

Our opposites tend to fascinate us because they add variety to life and pull us from our comfortable rut of familiarity. Opposites stretch us beyond ourselves, forcing us to broaden our horizons. They add depth and provide opportunities for growth. It is from them that we learn our most difficult lessons. They expose us to thoughts, feelings, and experiences that are foreign to us. They balance our lopsidedness and make us more complete.

In many ways, Tami and I are opposites. When it comes to decorating our house, she likes pictures of flowers that are light and airy with a lot of pastels. Now flowers are nice, but I like dark pictures of landscapes or people. Early in our marriage we agreed not to buy a print unless we both liked it. For several years the walls of our house were empty.

Another area we differ on is music. Tami enjoys jazz and the big band sound. I enjoy folk music. To me, music needs lyrics and the more thought provoking the better. Tami listens to music for relaxation, not to think. Therefore, at our house there are two cassette tape cases: one for Tami and one for me. Yet over the years we have accumulated enough tapes for a third case. This consists of tapes Tami has played for me and I have played for her and somehow we have both come to appreciate. Through the years both of our musical tastes have broadened.

These differences are healthy but they are also frustrating. The biggest frustrations come when we start thinking of opposites in terms of right and wrong. What that usually means is "I'm right, you're wrong." Taste in decorating and music is seldom an issue of right versus wrong. It is simply a matter of what I like versus what Tami likes. Most of us agree with that principle. However, when it comes to personality traits we frequently become more judgmental.

In working with people, I have discovered that most couples have little understanding and no tolerance for differences. They want each other to think and act as they do. They are astonished that someone would actually approach life differently and think it was okay. So they begin a process of trying to convert their partner to the "right way" or the "best way." This is like trying to convince a Norwegian that Egyptian is the right language or a Japanese that Spanish is best. It is not an issue of right or best, just different. One popular author goes so far as to suggest, tongue in cheek, that men are from Mars and women are from Venus. As couples, we need to acknowledge our differences and accept them.

Here are ten areas of differences I frequently find in couples. Look through the list and try to find which differences apply to you and your mate:

EXTROVERTS VS. INTROVERTS

Extroverts love crowds—the more people, the merrier. They are expressive and frequently think out loud.

Introverts, on the other hand, would rather spend the evening in solitude or with a close friend than go to a party. Being more reserved they tend to think through all the options before talking.

Dennis always planned romantic evenings alone with Suzy. When she learned about such an evening, she would invite others to join them. After a few years Dennis came to believe Suzy didn't like him. He thought, *Why else would she not want to spend time alone with me?*

One day he confronted her with his concern. She burst out laughing, "Are you crazy? Of course I love you. I also love people. They energize me."

"But they wear me out," Dennis replied.

"Really?"

This led to a marvelous discussion for Dennis and Suzy to talk about their different needs. She needed to socialize and he needed peace and quiet.

There are times when I hate the telephone. It interrupts whatever I happen to be doing. If it's for me, I handle the caller's need and hang up as soon as possible. You guessed it—I'm an introvert.

Now Tami is not an introvert. If a phone call is for her, she lights up and visits enthusiastically with the caller. When she hangs up I ask, "What did you talk about?"

"Oh, nothing."

"But you were on the phone for thirty minutes."

"It sure didn't seem that long."

"Why did they call?"

"Just to talk."

I scratch my head and mumble, "How can you spend thirty minutes talking about nothing."

However, I'm glad I married an extrovert. She pulls me out of my solitary ways and encourages me to socialize.

LEAPERS VS. LOOKERS

Leapers take risks. When they see an opportunity they want to jump on it before it's too late. They appear to be fearless, or at least oblivious to potential danger.

Lookers are more cautious than leapers. They like to carefully check everything out before making a decision. They gather information, analyze, ponder, consider options, question, ruminate, evaluate consequences, pray, investigate, and then decide.

When I was a teenager, I would spend several weeks each summer visiting my grandparents in southern Oregon. On the hot, dry afternoons my uncle and I would hike up to Rough and Ready Creek and go swimming. Uncle Walt dove from the rocky bank into the cool, clear water. He was a leaper, but I was a looker. I took my time and carefully tested the temperature of the creek. Once my toes were used to the water, I moved up to my ankles, then to my knees, and then my waist. Inch by inch I slipped into the water, making sure each part of my anatomy acclimated totally before I moved in deeper.

Another common difference between these two approaches to life is that leapers like new and unique experiences, while lookers like the comfortable and familiar.

Lyman loves to travel. He dreams of visiting each of the fifty states and ultimately every continent, even Antarctica. He is an adventurer and explorer. Every vacation Lyman wants to go somewhere new. Sonya, his wife, would be happy visiting Cannon Beach each summer. She enjoys renting the same cozy cabin year after year and just relaxing.

Leapers help lookers stretch and grow. Lookers help leapers think and plan before they leap. We need each other.

OUTLINERS VS. DETAILERS

Outliners have a general focus and look at the big picture. They think in terms of direction and getting things done.

Detailers look at the nuts and bolts. Their concern is *how* to get things done.

Outliners are abstract thinkers who see the whole forest, while detailers are concrete thinkers who see the individual trees. Outliners develop outlines and detailers fill in the outlines with details. Both perspectives are important.

When Tami and I go on vacation our differences are evident. Several years ago we decided to drive from Portland, Oregon, to Disneyland. I developed a big picture for our trip. We would drive down I-5 to Los Angeles and spend one day in Disneyland and another at Knott's Berry Farm, then drive up the coast, spend a day in San Francisco, cross over to I-5, and drive home.

Tami looked at my agenda and asked, "How many hours are we going to drive the first day? What hotel are we going to stay at in Los Angeles? Would we just take casual clothes or should we take something nicer?"

"I don't know,"I replied. "Don't bother me with the details. We'll get there and we'll get back. That's what's most important."

The big picture was most important to me, but the details were important to her. She came alongside me and filled in all the holes in my agenda. I created an outline and she breathed life into it. Without the outline we would have no direction, but the outline would break down without the details.

SPENDERS VS. SAVERS

Many couples argue over money, especially if one is a spender and the other a saver. If spenders have money, they want to spend. Sometimes they use it on themselves, but they might also give it away to friends or worthy causes.

Savers save for some future rainy day. They do not like to spend unless it's very important.

I have a friend who is a generous spender. He loves to buy gifts for people and he will frequently empty his checkbook this way. His wife has the same habit so together they spend themselves into debt. Seven major credit cards are up to their limit. Yet birthdays, weddings, and other special occasions still come along; big sales entice; and good causes call for help. Each of these events present new opportunities to spend.

I once knew a couple who loved to save. They enjoyed the challenge of getting by on less and thus watching their savings grow. They worked hard and found extra ways to make money. They passed by the luxuries and maintained the simplest of lifestyles. In their fifty-some years of marriage they went on only two or three vacations, but they were able to save large sums of money. Unfortunately, they both passed away without enjoying the benefits of all their thrift.

It seems that more often than not, rather than two spenders or two savers in a marriage, there's a spender and a saver.

The spender views the saver as a parental tightwad always saying no. The spender wishes their partner would relax and have a little more fun.

The saver views the spender as irresponsible, impulsive, and extravagant. The saver fears their spouse will drive them to bankruptcy.

If these two can learn to work together as a team, they would soon discover that there is a time to spend and a time to save.

PLANNERS VS. FLEXERS

Planners love structure. They want everything organized and neatly packaged. They like schedules and deadlines. They want their life to be neat and tidy. Their philosophy is, "There is a place for everything and everything has its place."

Flexers bend with the flow of life. They see planners as being rigid and over-controlling. They tend to be more spontaneous and laid back. They take things as they come. Benders don't worry about schedules or deadlines. Loose ends don't bother them because things will work out. Planners frequently see this as lazy and irresponsible.

Sandy is a very structured person. With four children she feels she has to be. She takes her role as housewife seriously and her home runs like a well-oiled machine. That is, until her husband, Chuck, comes home from work.

Chuck is easy-going and he likes to do whatever strikes him at the moment. Frequently, all of Sandy's plans for the evening fly out the window when Chuck suggests, "Let's go to a movie," or "Let's visit grandma."

Sandy likes Chuck's great ideas, but they interfere with her schedule. She often goes to bed frustrated at Chuck's change of plans, and Chuck lays next to her confused, wondering why she didn't enjoy the evening.

Planners like everything well ordered. When a person walks into my office, one of the first things they notice is my bookshelf. The books, neatly set in rows, stand upright beside colleagues of similar height. Organized carefully by subject, there is a section for marriage and relationships, one for children and parenting, as well as other groupings for emotions, codependency, counseling techniques, and group dynamics.

Ron's office is next to mine and his bookshelf has a different personality. Some of his books are stacked horizontally, others are lined up vertically, and still others rest on top of the vertical rows. It looks helter-skelter and disorganized to me. A book on marriage stands beside a book on depression and lying on top of these two is a book on men's issues. When I sit in his office I want to straighten his books.

SCURRIERS VS. AMBLERS

Scurriers are always busy. They are on the move from dawn to dusk, racing from one point to the next. Speed and efficiency are the scurrier's watchwords—accomplish as much as you can as fast as you can. They are similar to the rabbit in *Alice in Wonderland* who is constantly checking his pocket watch and then rushing off to some very important appointment.

Amblers take their time. They stop and smell the roses. They don't let the rapid pace of our modern world push them. They set their own pace; they look and listen; they relax and play. They might not do as much, but they enjoy what they do.

I'm a scurrier. When I need to get from point A to point B, I look for the quickest, most direct route. I like the freeways—I can move fast without waiting for stop signs and red lights.

Tami is an ambler. Speed does not determine what route she takes. More than once I have asked, "Why did you go that way?" She smiles and says, "Why not?"

She's right. She smiles because she knows what I'm thinking—why didn't you go the fastest way?

The answer is simple. She didn't go the fastest way because she is different from me. Tami chooses her routes based on familiarity and beauty. One time she told me she drove a certain way because it was spring.

"What does that have to do with it?" I asked.

"In springtime there is a field along this road that has the most beautiful lilac bushes you've ever seen."

I need to slow down and look for lilac bushes more often. Tami's ambling helps me to relax and enjoy life more. She encourages me to take my time and savor the moment. It's a good balance; I slow down and she speeds up. In the process we have both come to appreciate and accept each other's different paces.

THINKERS VS. FEELERS

Thinkers focus on facts and principles. They base decisions on objective data and everything else is irrelevant. If they step on somebody's toes or hurt their feelings, then that's just the way life is. Truthfully, they probably didn't even notice the impact they had. Thinkers tend to be task oriented, while feelers tend to be relationship oriented.

Feelers focus on people and emotions. They base decisions on subjective information and show great concern about the impact on others.

Thinkers see feelers as overly concerned with pleasing others, whereas feelers often view thinkers as insensitive.

In our culture, seventy-five percent of men are thinkers and seventy-five percent of women are feelers. Now thinkers have feelings and feelers do think. It's just that they process situations with a different focus. Men are more likely to be analytical and cold. Women are usually more compassionate and warm.

Thinkers focus on their head as they seek truth. They want to make sure they get all the facts straight. Feelers focus on their heart as they seek peace and harmony. They want everybody to be happy.

John was logical. When Andrea didn't have her facts straight, he corrected her. He was so busy establishing who was right and who was wrong that he didn't realize he was destroying their relationship. It hurt Andrea deeply.

Whenever she tried to communicate her feelings to John, he would say, "What's that have to do with what we're talking about?"

"They're my feelings," Andrea tried to explain.

"But facts are facts regardless of what anybody feels about them," John said. "Feelings have nothing to do with this."

Both are right. The head can easily hurt the heart and the heart often appears irrational to the head. Like so many differences, balance is the key. Truth without sensitivity can be cruel even as sensitivity without truth can be misguided sentimentality. We need both truth and sensitivity.

DREAMERS VS. WORKERS

Dreamers are creative people who love to come up with ideas. They are optimistic and oriented toward the future.

Workers are practical. They like to take other people's ideas and make them happen. Workers tend to be pessimistic and focus on the present.

Dreamers frequently have their head in the clouds; whereas workers have their feet firmly planted on the ground. Dreamers can drive workers crazy. One worker said, "Why can't he be more realistic? He comes up with all these wild ideas that will never work." Another worker said, "She comes up with all these great projects, but she never follows through and puts them into action."

Workers discourage dreamers. Dreamers tell me, "Workers are stuck in a rut and have no vision. Workers are wet blankets who are always emphasizing the negative and telling me why something won't work."

I'm a dreamer. I love to come up with new ideas. More than

once I have driven down the freeway fine-tuning some concept only to discover I have missed my exit. Tami has come to recognize my faraway look and will ask, "What are you thinking about?" This brings me back to the here and now.

Then I tell her about my latest idea. Tami is a worker, but she has learned to humor and help me. She listens to my ideas then tells me what she thinks will work and what won't. It used to offend me when she wasn't excited about my dreams. She's usually not excited about certain ideas because they are impractical, and she's usually right. I have learned to trust her over the years.

We make a good team. I stretch her in creative ways she never imagined, and she reminds me of my limitations and responsibilities. She encourages me to dream; but like a kite, she keeps me connected to the ground. When the wind takes me too high, she pulls me back to reality. It's a wonderful arrangement as long as we appreciate the differences.

COLLECTORS VS. TOSSERS

Collectors gather things. They hate to throw anything away for they know they will need it as soon as it is gone. After all, lunch boxes from the fifties are now collector's items; paisley shirts from the seventies are popular again in the nineties.

Tossers get rid of things. They have a philosophy that if something isn't used within six months or a year, it probably never will be. They see the collector's treasures as clutter. Collectors love to go to garage sales and tossers love to have them.

Andy Warhol, famous artist and painter of the Campbell soup can, was also a famous collector. When he died, he left several warehouses full of his things. On the other hand, I have a client who is a not-so-famous tosser. She told me she moves into a different house every second year just to get rid of all the "junk" she has collected since her last move. When she moves, everything gets tossed except the necessities.

My grandfather was a collector. The land around his house was a museum of everything imaginable: trucks, concrete mixers, gold-mining pans, cans of nuts and bolts, chains, rusty bins, pieces of scrap metal, cans of mysterious substances, assorted car parts and old engines, wooden barrels, and much more. I always wondered why he didn't clean up the place. Then I watched him work on a project one day. He would stop and say how he needed something to finish it. Then he would walk out back to some pile of useless junk, bend over, and pick out exactly what he needed.

Several years ago I visited Iceland, the ancestral home of my grandfather's parents. While there I gained additional insight into my grandfather's life as a collector. In the isolated area of Myvatn, during the nineteenth century, supplies were often short. There were years when the Danish trade ships never crossed the North Atlantic. Families had to get by with what they had. To survive you had to be a collector—nothing could be wasted. My grandfather inherited this trait. However, I didn't inherit my grandfather's compulsion to collect. I'm a tosser.

JUGGLERS VS. HOLDERS

Jugglers are multi-channeled. They can balance many things simultaneously without missing a thing and enjoy the process. If they are forced to focus on only one item or project, they become bored.

Holders are single channeled. They deal with one thing at a time and when forced to cope with more, they become stressed and overwhelmed.

Debbie, a mother of three, balances a heavy load. Besides the maintenance of a large home, she has a part-time accounting job, writes articles for a national magazine, takes piano lessons, works at her church, and volunteers once a week at school. Her husband, Lance, marvels at the way she handles everything with such ease. He shakes his head in amazement for he is single channeled.

It's sad that often we honor people more in death than in life.

One week Debbie was out of town on business and Lance took over her schedule—at least he tried. After three days he thought he was going crazy.

Jugglers assume that their spouse can juggle as well as they can. Many a holder tries their hand at juggling only to find they can't do it. They think it's because they aren't as organized, or need more practice, or if they were stronger they could keep up and do more. Holders are not inferior to jugglers; they are just different. Holders need to finish one task before moving on to the next. They are more compartmentalized. Each thing gets one hundred percent of the focus during its allotted time.

Jugglers often appear distracted. Nothing seems to get all their attention at any given time because they are also processing two or three other things. It frustrates holders when jugglers don't pay more attention, but if they did they would probably drop something. Juggling is an art and it has its place just as holding is important and has its place.

These are just a few of the many differences that crop up between a husband and wife. Differences can be a wonderful strength to a marriage. They create a balance if each spouse is willing to work together as a team. If a couple stands back to back, they can use their differences to battle life. When they stand face to face, these differences turn inward and partners then battle each other. Accepting and appreciating our partner's differences sends a strong message of positive regard.

PART THREE: RESPECTING

In northern India, there stands one of the most beautiful and expensive buildings in the world. It is a monument of love and respect. It is also a tomb.

The death of Shah Jahan's wife in 1632 left him devastated. To honor her, he gathered twenty thousand workers who spent the next twenty-one years constructing this amazing temple. It's a domed, white marble building with four slender minarets set in an exquisite garden and surrounded by a red sandstone wall. He spared no expense, for his love of her was so great. Even the name of the temple reflected his respect for his beloved wife. He named it Taj Mahal, "crown of the palace."

Whenever I hear this story I wonder whether Shah Jahan communicated his respect for his wife during her life as well as he did after her death. It's sad that often we honor people more in death than in life. We go to a funeral to pay our respects. Why don't we pay our respects when our loved ones are with us? Maybe we are too busy or too shy, or maybe we just don't think about it. So we save our honor until it is too late—when they can't hear our kind words and acknowledge our respectful behavior.

Everybody deserves respect. That doesn't mean everything a person *does* deserves respect. We live in a world that doesn't give much respect. Throughout society we see a lack of respect between parents and children, employees and employers, the government and its citizens. Nobody seems to respect anybody.

Respect is a reflex of the heart toward someone we deeply treasure.

Yesterday, I watched a little gray-haired grandmother in a white Cadillac back out into traffic without looking. A van slammed on its brakes, barely missing the gray-haired woman. Now this was, without question, the grandmother's fault, but she rolled down her window and screamed obscenities at the other driver.

If respect exists no place else in the world, it should at least be present in our marriage. Respect begins with how we think about people. Our thoughts influence how we feel, and our feelings display themselves in words and actions. It's a simple sequence that begins with how we think.

THINKING

Respect is born within us, and then demonstrated outwardly through our actions and conversation. How we think about a person ultimately impacts everything else. Respect is thinking the best of our spouse and giving them the benefit of the doubt by not jumping to negative conclusions. Respect involves thinking positively; for as we think positive, we feel positive. What we focus on is what we feel.

If we think of our spouse as special, they become special. If we think poorly of them, that is what they become. Our thoughts shape our perspective. So say to yourself: "My spouse is my special treasure. He/she is not perfect, but neither am I, nor is any other human being." These are the sort of thoughts that help a marriage grow. Nurturing respectful thoughts about our spouse is critical to positive regard.

Comedian George Burns wrote an entire book on his thoughts about his wife. He entitled it *Gracie: A Love Story*, and George's attitude of respect toward Gracie permeates its pages. Summarizing their forty-year relationship he says, "Gracie was my partner in our act, my best friend, my wife and my lover, and the mother of our two children. We were a team both on and off stage.... Marrying Gracie was the best thing that ever happened to me."[3]

We all have strengths and weaknesses. Respect searches for strengths. It wants to know and accept. Have you ever met a person who at first seemed plain and ordinary, but over time began to look more attractive? What happened? You saw their soul. Respect looks for the beauty in an individual. It is not distracted by the superficial. No matter how ordinary the external, the inside holds something special. To recognize the inner value of our spouse is the first step in the giving of respect.

FEELING

Our feelings are a critical part of who we are. They give us depth and substantiate our thinking. They become the spring from which our words and actions flow. Yet they are often difficult to explain and describe. Respect is a reflex of the heart toward someone we deeply treasure. On an emotional level, we feel respect in at least three different but overlapping ways.

Appreciation. This involves feeling thankful for the partner we married—standing back and smiling at all the little things our partners do each day to make our lives easier. Yet we often grow callused and take them for granted. When we fail to appreciate what they do, we communicate a lack of respect for who they are.

I encourage you to stop for a moment and contemplate your spouse's positives. The way they deal with the children in stressful situations, or the way they stand by you when life is not going as you think it should. The way they put up with your odd idiosyncrasies, or sacrifice their preferences for yours. If we consider the wise words, loving embraces, patient waiting, generous gifts, welcome smiles, and so much more—we should be thankful.

Consideration. Respect feels empathy. It puts ourselves in their shoes. Respect causes us to feel joy when our mate is happy, and sorrow when they experience loss or disappointment. Because we value them, we walk beside them with sensitivity. When we give our full attention it shows we respect them. We listen with our ears and our heart, taking what we hear seriously without having to agree or understand. When we ignore or neglect our spouse, we communicate that they are not valuable to us.

Inspiration. Respect creates an excitement and enthusiasm toward our spouse. We can't wait to see them. We want to be with them. We admire who they are and feel a certain awe when we are in their presence. This awe might not involve a breath-catching gasp or a case of nervous shivers, but it does bring inspiration. It is a feeling that we are in the presence of someone special or unique. Inspiration says an emotional "Wow!" It wants to shout our partner's praise, gaze at their face, or hear their voice. It stirs up a passion that wants to create, achieve, impress, and give. This inspiration is the spark that motivates us to build our marriage into the best it can possibly be.

SPEAKING

Respect communicates. One couple told me that they always practice the Thumper principle. Do you remember Thumper in Walt Disney's movie *Bambi?* He was Bambi's rabbit friend. Thumper said, "If you can't say somethin' nice, don't say nothin' at all."

What a great principle! Respect speaks nicely and politely. It uses words and a tone of voice that translates into courtesy. Unfortunately, most couples have a difficult time practicing the Thumper principle.

Robert Fulghum writes about the logging practice in the Solomon Islands. He explains, "If a tree is too large to be felled with an ax, the natives cut it down by yelling at it." Yes, you read it right! Woodsmen creep up on the selected tree and scream at the top of their lungs. "They continue this for thirty days. The tree dies and falls over. The theory is that the hollering kills the spirit of the tree."[4]

In our civilized culture, people call their loved ones names, yell, scream obscenities, degrade, humiliate, and ridicule. The effect is the same as it is on the trees in the Solomon Islands—it kills the spirit.

We get angry and words slip out of our mouth. We say things we regret. Once the words are out, they can never be erased. Our spouse may forgive us, but they never forget. Each word creates a little wound. The wounds may heal, but the scars remain.

- You're driving me crazy.
- You idiot!
- All you ever do is complain.
- Jerk.
- Why don't you ever listen?
- Were you born in a barn?
- You're impossible.
- When will you ever learn?
- Why in the world did I ever marry you?
- I've had enough of this.

We program people by what we say. If we speak to our spouse with disrespect, they will feel disrespected and our love begins to die. The above messages depreciate and humiliate our partner. They communicate very clearly that we don't respect them and we hold them in low esteem.

ACTING

How do we behave respectfully toward our spouse? One way is to show them courtesy and politeness in every interaction. In his book *Stop! You're Driving Me Crazy* George Bach gives four rights. These rights are actually ways to demonstrate respect.

- **The right to feel.** Respecting our partner's emotions in a non-judgmental, compassionate way.

- **The right to know.** Providing our partner with honest and accurate information about things that impact them.

- **The right to be heard.** Listening to our partner with our full attention and taking what they say seriously.

- **The right to space.** Realizing that at times our partner needs physical and/or emotional space; respecting their privacy and allowing them their space.[5]

It is not always easy to give respect, but when we provide these four rights we show a serious intent to act in a respectful way—even when it is inconvenient and uncomfortable.

Another way to demonstrate respect is to show love. There are many types of love and each wears a different face. Three types that act with respect are as follows:

Sacrificial Love. In January 1936 Edward VIII ascended the throne of the British Empire. As the year progressed, he fell in love. The press quickly picked up the story and spread the news. However, a situation that would normally provide an opportunity for celebration turned into a crisis. There were three problems with King Edward's romantic interest. She was a commoner, an American, and divorced.

Especially because of the divorce, the British government strongly opposed accepting Mrs. Wallace Simpson as their queen. On the evening of December 11, 1936, King Edward VIII

Respect is the most important piece to the marriage puzzle. Without respect nothing else will fit together properly.

announced on the radio, "I have found it impossible...to discharge my duties as king, as I would wish to do, without the help and support of the woman I love." At that point the King of England sacrificed his throne for his love. Six months later he married her.

Friendship Love. In 1918 DeWitt Wallace developed a new idea for a magazine. It would consist of a collection of condensed articles and he would call it *The Reader's Digest*. He put together a proposed sample and sent it to publishers throughout the country. Nobody seemed interested. DeWitt was terribly discouraged.

About the same time he met Lila Bell Acheson, the daughter of a Presbyterian minister. Before long the two fell in love. Lila encouraged him to keep trying his wonderful idea for a magazine. Boosted by her faith in him, DeWitt started mailing circular letters to potential subscribers.

In October 1921 Lila married DeWitt. On returning from their honeymoon, they found a bundle of letters from interested subscribers. Together they worked on Volume 1, Number 1, which appeared in February 1922. DeWitt Wallace included Lila Bell Acheson as his co-founder, co-editor, and co-owner. Over the years their little magazine grew. Now printed in seventeen languages, *Reader's Digest* sells over twenty-eight million copies a month and the company grosses approximately $500 million a year.

DeWitt and Lila were friends. They encouraged, supported, and believed in each other. They worked side by side to make their dream come true, and in the process they respected each other. DeWitt once said, "I think Lila made the *Digest* possible." I can imagine that Lila would probably say the same about DeWitt.

Protective Love. The public had no idea how serious the situation was. In September of 1919 President Woodrow Wilson collapsed with a nervous breakdown. A week later, he suffered a cerebral hemorrhage that paralyzed his left side and almost killed him. Incapable of performing his presidential duties, his wife stepped in and coordinated his executive responsibilities, allowing the political scene in Washington to go on as normal. She protected him from the press and his advisors, and kept him informed on major domestic and international events as she nursed him back to health. If you wanted to get to the president, you had to go through Mrs. Wilson. For the next six months, until his term ended, Mrs. Wilson kept everything on an even keel. It was not until years later that the public realized how ill the president had been and that it was Mrs. Wilson who had run the presidency; thus, protecting him from the physical, mental, and emotional strain that such an office requires.

With three types of love we have just seen a king, a minister's daughter, and a president's wife show respect for their spouses. One sacrificed his throne; one battled beside her husband; and one protected her partner from the pressures of a political office that might have killed him. All three acted with respect, and demonstrated that love without action holds little meaning.

Some marriage counselors say that respect is the most important piece to the marriage puzzle. Without respect nothing else will fit together properly.

Respect begins with our thoughts; our feelings eventually follow. As respectful thoughts and feelings grow, they make themselves known through our talk and walk. If they are not evident, the opposite is communicated by default. There is no middle ground. We either respect our partner or we don't. Respect proclaims that who they are and what they say is important to us. If they are important, we will take the time and effort to build a healthy marriage. We will then read the following chapters on Communication, Making Peace, Forgiveness, Giving and Receiving, Togetherness, Romance, and Ministry with interest. Not because they are easy or natural, but out of respect. The very fact that you have read this far in a book on marriage, tells me where your heart is.

"SAD, SAD, SAD"

Positive regard starts with knowing our spouse, expands into accepting what we know, and ends up with respecting them. Without positive regard a couple has nothing. There might be a commitment but it has no heart. The partners might stay together because of their sense of loyalty or duty; yet the commitment is hollow and possibly even destructive. To live together without knowing each other represents loneliness and alienation. To spend day after day together without acceptance leads to conflict and rejection. To be married without respect opens the door to abuse and humiliation. A marriage without positive regard is a marriage in name only. In reality it is an emotional desert where love and caring shrivel in the heat.

In the late sixties Elizabeth Taylor and Richard Burton starred in the movie *Who's Afraid of Virginia Woolf.* It is the story of a marriage that has no positive regard. It is a relationship of incessant bickering, yelling, name calling, sarcasm, and put downs. George and Martha order each other around and argue about the color of their son's eyes. It's a pathetic marriage. Even George shakes his head and says, "George and Martha, sad, sad, sad...." This couple does not know, accept, or respect each other. George explains it by saying, "One day it snaps and you don't give a damn." So they fight, emotionally beating each other up in the process. George asks, "Total war?" Martha replies with glee, "Total!" Near the end of two hours of conflict, George sums it up, "There is no moment anymore when we could come together."

Without positive regard a relationship is nothing but "sad, sad, sad."

Discussion Questions

1. What event in your partner's past had the most impact on who he/she is today?

2. On the following list, circle your mate's top three needs.

   Achievement   Affiliation
   Control   Nurture
   Growth   Autonomy
   Stimulation   Play
   Security

3. Name three dreams that are important to your spouse.

   a)
   b)
   c)

4. On a scale from 1 to 10 (1 = very accepting, 10 = rejecting) how tolerant are you to differences between the two of you?

   How do you express your:

   Tolerance?
   Intolerance?

5. In the following list of differences, which best fits each of you? (Circle the wife's, underline the husbands.)

   a) Extrovert   or   Introvert
   b) Leaper   or   Looker
   c) Outliner   or   Detailer
   d) Spender   or   Saver
   e) Planner   or   Flexer
   f) Scurrier   or   Ambler

g) Thinker	or	Feeler
h) Dreamer	or	Worker
i) Collector	or	Tosser
j) Juggler	or	Holder

6. How do you show your spouse:

   a) Appreciation
   b) Consideration
   c) Inspiration

7. When was the last time you may have damaged the spirit of your mate by acting as a logger from the Solomon Islands? Describe the scene.

8. Do you agree with Dr. Bach's four rights (the right to feel, to know, to be heard, and to have space)? Explain why or why not.

   Which of these rights is most important to your partner?

   When was the last time you failed to respect these rights?

9. How do you demonstrate to your mate:

   a) Sacrificial love?
   b) Friendship love?
   c) Protective love?

10. When was the last time you demonstrated each of these three types of love to your spouse?

    a) Sacrificial love
    b) Friendship love
    c) Protective love

Notes

1. Leo Buscaglia, *Love* (Thorofare, N.J.: Charles B. Slack, Inc., 1972), 125.

2. This is based on the theory and works of Henry A. Murray as presented in Calvin S. Hall, and Gardner Lindzey, *Theories of Personality*, 2nd ed. (New York: John Wiley & Sons, 1970), 174-180.

3. George Burns, *Gracie: A Love Story* (New York: Signet, 1991), 15, 85.

4. Robert Fulghum, *All I Really Need to Know I Learned in Kindergarten* (New York: Villard Books, 1989), 19-20.

5. George Bach and Ronald Deutsch, *Stop! You're Driving Me Crazy* (New York: Berkeley Books, 1979), 55-130.

4

COMMUNICATION

The garden was perfect and the couple could do anything they wanted. They ran naked through the grass, played with the animals, and laughed until their sides ached. In the garden there was one rule...just one. It was simple and easy to understand: *Don't eat from the tree in the middle of the garden.* The husband and wife could do anything else they wanted, but like most people, they were drawn to that one tree. They stared at it, walked up to its trunk, ran their fingers over its bark. It didn't seem like a bad tree.

One day, while the woman was sitting beneath the shade of the tree, a serpent came by and told her it was a wonderful tree with delicious fruit. The woman picked one and turned it over in her hand, wondering what could be wrong with a tiny bite. She looked both ways and took a small bite. It was good. She picked another one and gave it to her husband. He also took a bite. Suddenly, everything changed. A wall rose between the couple as they grew fearful and embarrassed. They covered their nakedness and hid from the Master Gardener.

That evening the Gardener was walking through the garden, but he didn't see the carefree couple.

"Where are you?" he called.

"Hiding," the man and woman answered in unison. "We're afraid, so we're hiding."

"Have you eaten from the tree?" asked the Gardener.

"It's not my fault," said the man. "My wife gave it to me."

"It's not my fault," cried the woman. "The serpent told me it was okay."

The Master Gardener shook his head and a tear ran down his cheek.[1]

Communication breakdown is the most frequently mentioned difficulty among couples in my office. It's a problem now and has been since the beginning of human history. Breaking the rule of the garden damaged Adam and Eve's ability to communicate openly.

They covered themselves and hid from each other. They pulled back and slipped on a mask.

I watch couples do this all the time in my office. They cover their hurts and bury their feelings. They withdraw and say everything's fine, when they know it's not. They hide in their silence—lonely, hurt, fearful, and angry. They push their partner away when what they yearn for more than anything else is love and understanding.

When hiding failed, Adam and Eve resorted to blaming each other.[2] Again, their communication pushed them apart rather than pulling them together. Couples attack each other in many ways. It continues to amaze me how people can be so hurtful to those they love the most. They blame, demean, and dominate; they are critical, sarcastic, and insensitive. They cut each other down in public and in private—seemingly unaware of the potentially permanent damage a sharp tongue can do.

The tongue is dangerous. It can get us into a lot of trouble. One little word, said at the wrong time or with the wrong tone of voice, can explode into a wall of anger. James, the brother of Jesus, wrote, "A whole forest can be set ablaze by a tiny spark of fire, and the tongue is as dangerous as any fire, with vast potentialities for evil. It can poison the whole body, it can make the whole of life a blazing hell."[3] There's good reason to watch what we say.

In another place James summarizes God's view of communication: "Be quick to listen, slow to speak and slow to become angry."[4] Just as in many aspects of life, the theory sounds so simple, but the application is so hard.

PART ONE: QUICK TO LISTEN

Everybody wants to be heard. As a psychologist, part of my job is to be a good listener. People have sat in my office, pouring out their hurts and joys, and told me that I was the first person to ever truly listen to them. How sad. Listening is vital to a relationship. One of the greatest gifts we can receive from our spouse is the assurance they will listen with their undivided attention.

Listening adds at least three things to a marriage.

It encourages our spouse to talk. When someone is listening, it is easy to talk. The better we listen, the deeper our partner will share. After all, why should they talk if we aren't listening?

It helps us understand our spouse. Proverbs says, "Let the wise listen and add to their learning."[5] It is amazing how much you can learn by keeping quiet and listening. We gain new information this way, and it is through this information that we understand what our partner is thinking and feeling at the moment. If we don't listen, the relationship withers.

It draws a couple closer. Listening is an intimate act for it provides a peek into a partner's innermost being. The more we understand, the closer we feel. We build bridges with our partner when we listen attentively as they share their private world. Listening shows we care and exhibits respect. Sometimes a silent mouth and an attentive ear is the most loving thing we can offer.

It was the middle of the Civil War and Abraham Lincoln was under incredible pressure. There were many who thought he should issue a proclamation to free the slaves. There were also many who were furious that he would even consider such a proclamation. Lincoln wasn't sure what to do.

He wrote an old friend back in Springfield and asked him to come to the White House. The friend rushed to Lincoln's side and listened as the president talked for hours of the arguments for and against freeing the slaves. He explained the options, read articles, explored ramifications, quoted opinions, spoke of consequences, and described feelings. The friend kept listening. Hours later, Lincoln

Good listening skills do not come naturally; they take discipline and desire.

thanked him for all his help and the good friend traveled back to Springfield. He never took an opportunity to speak. What Lincoln needed most at this critical time was for someone to truly listen.

Good listening skills do not come naturally; they take discipline and desire. Let's begin by looking at five important aspects to listening.

STOP

Turn off the TV, put down the newspaper, and stop whatever you're doing. You may be able to work and listen at the same time, but it shows a lack of respect. Get rid of any external distractions that might keep you from truly listening.

The external distractions are obvious, but clearing the internal distractions can be more difficult. We start out listening, but our partner says something that reminds us of something else. Before we realize it, we're on a mental side trip and we have no idea what our spouse just said. Part of this problem is that we all have an internal monologue constantly running in our head. Through this monologue we are either agreeing or disagreeing with what we hear. Sometimes our internal monologue has nothing to do with what we have just heard. Rather, we're thinking about the weather, or how hungry we are, or the last fight we had with our spouse.

There are three other internal distractions that can undermine listening: defensiveness, assumptions, and preparing your response.

Defensiveness. Everyone becomes defensive at times, but men especially do. We feel accused and misunderstood. We wish to explain, justify, and describe the extenuating circumstances. Yet in our defensiveness, we can't be effective listeners.

Assumption. Another distraction is that we assume we have heard this before. Maybe you're right, but don't assume you know what your spouse is going to say. You may be wrong. Besides, such an assumption kills communication. One woman told me that her husband never said anything that surprised her because she knew him like a book, cover to cover. This was her excuse for not listening, but I encouraged her to listen anyway and try to get him to talk about subjects they had never discussed.

Preparing a Response. A major internal distraction is preparing our response. Listening is more than politely waiting our turn to speak. It is easy for our minds to race ahead. We finish their sentence in our head and know our response. This leads to the bad habit of interrupting our spouse. There is nothing so rude as a person who cuts others off in mid-sentence and then takes over the conversation. Slow down, wait, and take turns.

LOOK

Listen with your eyes. If you look at the person speaking, they will assume, correctly or incorrectly, that you are interested in them and in what they have to say. Conversely, they assume you are not interested if you don't look at them. In looking, watch their body language and facial expressions, but in particular, their eyes. The eyes provide a wealth of information—a flash of anger, a look of confusion, or tears. As you stop and look you communicate your love.

Giving full attention assures that you are interested, you do hear, and do want to understand. As you look at your spouse, try to sit still, lean forward, nod, and make other non-verbal motions to communicate that you are listening. Nothing is as flattering as full attention. True listening conveys, "Tell me," or even "Tell me more!" This encourages your spouse to talk and share their heart without fear or pressure. Don't listen with a critical or judgmental attitude. I work hard to be aware of my body language. We must be careful not to turn away, rub our eyes, clear our throat, yawn, sigh, or tap our foot. Such actions might communicate impatience or a lack of interest.

Sam and Elizabeth sat in my office on a sunny July day. Their marriage was crumbling and Elizabeth felt they had a communication problem. As she shared her background, Sam stared out the window. Whenever she mentioned anything especially painful about the marriage, Sam shifted his body so it was facing away from her. Finally in frustration Elizabeth said, "There he goes again, refusing to listen to me."

Sam turned his head toward her and said, "What do you mean? This is how I always sit."

"I know," Elizabeth cried, "that's the problem."

FOCUS

Paul Tournier says it is impossible to overemphasize the immense need humans have to really be listened to.[6] There are at least four ways we can deal with our partner when they talk to us.

We Can Ignore What They Say. This is most likely to happen when we are tired, stressed, angry, preoccupied, or simply on information overload.

We Can Pretend to Listen. My mother says, "It goes in one ear and out the other." She's right. Periodically, this does happen to me. Just the other day my wife gave me some instructions on how to care for the children while she was out for the afternoon. I stopped what I was doing, looked at her, and nodded my understanding at appropriate intervals, but I hadn't focused. As soon as she left, I thought, "What did she ask me to do?" I didn't have a clue.

We Can Selectively Listen. Most people hear about 20 percent of what is being said. We use a shortcut method: letting our minds wander and then checking in periodically to get the general flavor of what is being said.

We Can Truly Listen. Sometimes we think of listening as a passive activity, but it isn't. True listening requires close attention. It involves listening with our ears, eyes, brain, and heart. Concentrate on your mate. Focus on more than just the words they say; focus on their tone of voice, facial expressions, and body movements. Active, attentive listening says: "I am here for you. This time is yours. You have 100 percent of my attention because I really care about what you have to say." If you want a healthy marriage, give your partner at least fifteen minutes of undivided attention each day.

ABSORB

What our partner says tells us a lot about their frame of mind and who they are. Part of listening is absorbing their message. It is taking the time to think, and turn it over in our mind as we concentrate on what we heard. If we wish to know and love our spouse in a deep way, we must listen in a deep way.

Absorb Their Words. What did they really say? Listen to each word and phrase carefully. Repeat their words in your head to make sure you have them straight. Our partner's words allow us into their thoughts and through their thoughts we find their heart.

Absorb Their Meaning. What do you think they meant? Don't react or jump to conclusions, but contemplate what's between the lines. Sometimes words get twisted and phrases don't come out right. Sometimes we ram our foot so deep in our throat we can't dislodge it, and the harder we try the worse it jams. Then we are in trouble. There are times we need to look beyond the words and give our partner the benefit of the doubt. Remember, think the best.

Absorb Their Feelings. Observe them. How do they look? What are they feeling? Emotions create a context for what is said. When I am angry or hurt, I often overstate what I mean. Yet when I am fearful or anxious, I might understate myself. If we miss the feelings in a statement, we may miss the meaning.

Absorb The Need. You need to ask yourself, "What does my mate need?" Listen closely to hear what you can give. Listen with a sensitive, unselfish heart. Review the list of needs in chapter 3, then ask yourself if your partner currently has any of these needs. If so, reach out and seriously try to meet them.

CLARIFY

If we had perfect communication we would never need clarification. However, being human, our communication breaks down daily. This occurs when what we heard is not what was said.

One evening, as I was tucking my four-year-old son into bed, he asked if we could play. I explained that it was bedtime and we don't play at bedtime. He insisted that he wanted to play and he said he could do it quickly. He folded his hands, bowed his head, and said, "Dear God..." Then it hit me—he wanted to *pray*—not play. I had not heard clearly what he said.

Communication experts say there are at least four messages in every conversation.

- What was said.
- What you heard.
- What was meant.
- What the other person thought you heard.

So what you heard might be different from what was said, or what was said might not be what was meant. It's so easy for confusion and misunderstanding to happen.

When I was in college, I dated my boss's daughter. One afternoon I asked if I could come over that evening and visit his daughter. "Of course not," was his reply. It seemed like a strange response, but I took him at what he said and I didn't visit his daughter. The next day my boss confronted me and asked why I'd stood up his daughter. I repeated what he'd said the day before and he burst out laughing, "I was just joking. You can come over whenever you want." What he had said was not what he meant.

> *The listener remembers what they heard and the speaker remembers what was meant. Somewhere in-between is what was actually said.*

It is amazing how often two honest, mature, intelligent adults sit in my office and argue over a recent conversation. Both claim to remember what was said, but both remember it differently. So they come to me to determine who is lying. Well, neither is lying. This is usually a problem of perception. The listener remembers what they heard and the speaker remembers what was meant. Somewhere in-between is what was actually said. The solution to the couple's disagreement is clarifying the message. There are three aspects to this.

Ask for More Information. There are times my wife says something and it goes right over my head. Maybe I wasn't listening or I became distracted, but during these times I just don't understand what she's saying. I might smile and nod while my mind races to figure out where she's coming from. Sometimes I can figure it out, but at other times I'm lost.

The only way to fully understand is to ask. When we miss something that was said, we need to ask our partner to repeat it. We should ask for an explanation if we don't understand what is being expressed. Don't be afraid to ask and don't pretend to understand.

I have a client who has a wonderful way of asking for more information. She politely says, "Excuse me, but I just missed that. Would you please say it again in a different way?" Try it, it works.

Check Out Word Meanings. What we think our spouse means by a particular word might not be what they mean at all. Last week I had a young couple in my office and we discussed a misunderstanding over how much is a few and how much is several. They both assumed the other knew what they meant when they used these words, but they were wrong. The husband said a few meant seven or eight and that several meant between ten and twenty. The wife insisted that few indicated two and several were five or six. This confusion caused a great deal of frustration because neither had checked out the other's word meaning.

I pulled out my *American Heritage Dictionary* and looked up the two words. It defines few as "a small number" and several as "more than two or three, but not many." As we talked it through, the couple came to a shared meaning. In the future, a few would be three or four, and several would be between five and ten.

Paraphrase What You Hear. It is always a good idea to double-check what you hear to make certain it is what your partner means. The process is simple. The listener truly listens to absorb what they hear. Then they report back to the speaker, in their own words, what they heard. Next, the speaker either confirms the listener's accuracy, or clarifies the misinterpretation. This process is repeated until both partners agree on the message. In Norman Wakefield's book *Listening* this is called *reaching a shared meaning* and it is diagrammed this way:[7]

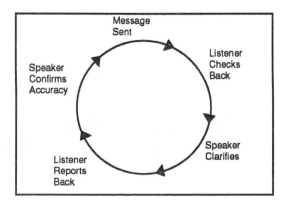

Listening is of no value if we misunderstand the message, but by paraphrasing we can make sure that both partners are on the same track.

In *Achieving the Impossible* Dr. Charles Sell writes, "It takes two good listeners to make one good marriage."[8] So if we want a good marriage, we must be good listeners. The steps are easy and should be memorized.

- Stop
- Look
- Focus
- Absorb
- Clarify

Now the next time our mate is conversing with us we will be ready to genuinely communicate. When they have finished and we have reached a mutual understanding, thank them for sharing with us. Once we have truly listened we are ready to speak, but be careful.

PART TWO: SLOW TO SPEAK

Words have an incredible power. Through words we can give our partner the greatest happiness or bring about the lowest despair. We have the ability to praise, affirm, and encourage our spouse, or we can hurt, humiliate, and destroy them. With the simple arrangement of twenty-six letters we can make or break our marriage. Words and sentences can be used for good or evil. The apostle Paul wrote, "Do not let any unwholesome talk come out of your mouths, but only what is helpful for building others up according to their needs, that it may benefit those who listen."[9] Our talk is either unhealthy or healthy. Unhealthy talk pulls a marriage apart, whereas healthy talk brings it closer together. So watch what you say.

> *Listening is of no value if we misunderstand the message.*

UNHEALTHY TALK

There is nothing so painful as painful words from the one you love. There are many ways to destroy communication in a marriage. Here are six ways to demonstrate poor communication.

Negative Statements. Negativity drives me crazy. I know a woman who finds something wrong with much of what her husband does. They have been married for twenty-five years but it's a dead relationship. Negativity killed it long ago. Some couples try to give one positive for each negative, hoping to balance the two, but it doesn't. It takes at least ten positives to make up for each negative.

Negativity is an attitude not limited to mere words: a sharp edge to your voice, a sarcastic tone, a rolling of the eyes, a stare, a harshness of expression, folded arms, a snort—all of these communicate criticism and disapproval quite effectively. All are deadly to a relationship.

We all blow it at times and we don't need somebody throwing it in our face. Maybe it was our spouse's fault this time, but next time it might be our own.

Thoughtless Words. There are few things more awkward than seeing a spouse be put down or ridiculed by their mate. My sympathy quickly goes to the victim and my anger flares toward the abuser. Years ago a man sat in my office and called his wife horrible names. When I confronted him with his disrespectful behavior he said, "She deserves it and besides, I'm not saying anything behind her back that I wouldn't say to her face." There is no excuse for name calling, regardless of what your partner has done. Besides, it usually tells more about the maturity and sensitivity of the one speaking than it does about the behavior or character of the one being attacked.

People say things in anger they later regret. They open their mouths and thoughtless words tumble out. When this happens we need to quickly seek forgiveness and not justify our inappropriate words. Yet some will say, "I was just speaking the truth," but truth without sensitivity is cruel. We must be careful of words that hurt or rub our partner the wrong way. Let's avoid trigger words that offend them or make them angry. When they ask us not to use certain words then, in love, we must strike those words from our vocabulary. Love has a kind tongue.

Blaming. Many men, including myself, struggle with accepting responsibility for our actions and reactions. We use "you" statements much more than "I" statements. We look for excuses or someone else to blame. Often we end up blaming the one closest to us and that person is usually our wife. It isn't always necessary to determine who's at fault. There are times when nobody's at fault, it's just the way things happen.

There is a wonderful scene in the 1991 movie *Regarding Henry* where the main character, played by Harrison Ford, is having breakfast with his family. He has a reputation for being cruel and ruthless, but he's just had a life-changing experience. During the meal his daughter spills her orange juice and the table is instantly silent.

"Oh, I'm sorry," she says, expecting her father to blow up and chastise her. Instead, he smiles.

"That's okay, I do that all the time."

"You do?" she says in amazement.

"Yeah."

Then he reaches forward and tips over his own juice. "See," he says. He grins and the tension breaks.

We all blow it at times and we don't need somebody throwing it in our face. Maybe it was our spouse's fault this time, but next time it might be our own. Let's not shame or embarrass our mate over spilled orange juice. Don't dwell on past or present mistakes, and don't bring them up unless there is an extremely good reason.

Overtalking. A husband and wife came to my office together in order to improve their communication. She did most of the talking and described the problem in vivid detail. The difficulty came down to the fact that the husband rarely spoke. When I saw him alone, I found he was both articulate and talkative.

"Why don't you talk with your wife more?" I asked.

He smiled and said, "Once she gets talking, there's no room

for anybody to say anything."

Some people are natural talkers. They get excited about what they have to say and don't leave much room for a response. They force their spouse into silence. I once saw a bumper sticker that put it this way:

I can't get a word in edgeways!

Try to avoid monologues and speeches. Stop every three or four sentences and ask for feedback. If we talk longer than that, we might be overtalking.

Exaggerations:. It's easy to stretch the truth. When my son was three, I was teasing him with some exaggerated fact. Finally he looked at me very seriously and said, "Daddy, you call that teasing, but it's really lying." Exaggeration is lying and it's something we do every day. We stretch the truth so we look better, get more sympathy, or make a situation sound worse than it really is. My grandmother used to warn me about "making a mountain out of a molehill." It's easy to create a crisis when one doesn't really exist.

Another way we fall into exaggeration is by using gunpowder words that can blow up in our face. Words such as *always, never, all, everybody, nobody.* We use these words in phrases that distort the truth: "You're *never* on time"; "You're *always* saying things like that"; "*All* men are insensitive"; "*Everybody* thinks you overreact"; and "*Nobody* is as rude as you." As soon as we make such comments with a gunpowder word, our partner thinks of an exception and up goes their defenses.

Manipulation. There are many means of manipulating our spouse. Manipulation is attempting to get our way dishonestly. Rather than being direct about our wants and needs, we become sneaky. We control one another through these five common methods:

- **Guilt**
  Reminding them of their failures, especially their greatest failures.

- Silence
  Depriving them of communication by refusing to speak to them.

- Emotionalism
  Using tears, anger, or depression to get our chosen response.

- Sexuality
  Depriving them of intimacy; using sex as a bargaining chip.

- Intimidation
  Threatening them verbally, non-verbally, or any other way.

Manipulation is underhanded and potentially cruel. In time, it creates resentment in your spouse.

There is nothing more painful than having unhealthy communication with the one you love. It is through communication that we connect and our spirits touch. If that connection becomes contaminated, it is only a matter of time before the whole relationship is poisoned. In the process of communication, wisdom is knowing what not to say rather than in what to say.

Words can heal and strengthen a relationship, and make you more attractive and appealing to your spouse.

For those of you who are abstract thinkers, you have read the above principles and are ready to apply them. However, those who are concrete thinkers would find a few specific examples helpful. Therefore, I gathered together some close friends and asked them what not to say to your spouse. Here is their list:

"I told you so."
"You're just like your mother [or father]."
"You're always in a bad mood."
"You just don't think."
"It's your fault."

"What's wrong with you?"
"All you ever do is complain."
"I can't do anything to please you."
"You get what you deserve."
"Why don't you ever listen to me?"
"Can't you be more responsible?"
"What were you thinking?"
"You're impossible!"
"I don't know why I put up with you."
"I can talk to you until I'm blue in the face and it doesn't do any good."
"I can do whatever I like."
"If you don't like it, you can just leave."
"Can't you do anything right?"
"That was stupid."
"All you ever do is think of yourself."
"If you really loved me, you'd do this."
"You're such a baby."
"Turnabout's fair play."
"You deserve a dose of your own medicine."
"What's your problem?"
"I can never understand you."
"Do you always have to be right?"

Now that you know what to avoid, it's time to consider how to communicate in a way that will demonstrate all the elements of unconditional regard.

HEALTHY TALK

Some called Major Evans the ugliest man in the world. He was born in England and died there in the 1920s. In spite of his horrible appearance, Major Evans frequently boasted that he could make any woman fall in love with him. He could make this boast because he possessed the gift of eloquence; being able to say the perfect word at the perfect time. He claimed he could make any woman love him, regardless of her beauty or high status, as long as she would close her eyes for a mere five minutes and listen. All she had to do was hear his words and he guaranteed she would be in love with him when she opened her eyes. [10]

I don't know if Major Evan's boast was ever proven, but I do know that sincere and loving words can soften the hardest heart. Words can heal and strengthen a relationship, and make you more attractive and appealing to your spouse. Proverbs says, "A word aptly spoken is like apples of gold in settings of silver." [11]

Here are five principles for speaking in a healthy way.

Speak from the heart simply, directly, and honestly, but always temper your words with love.

Be Direct. Think about what you want to say, then say it clearly and specifically. Don't beat around the bush. Hinting and ambiguity create confusion. It forces your partner to be a mind reader and most people are not good mind readers. Several years ago Ellen sat in my office weeping. She said, "I've been married only one year and I don't think my husband loves me anymore."

"What makes you think he doesn't love you?" I asked.

"He hasn't told me he does in over six months."

The next day I spoke to her husband, Craig, and asked how he felt about his wife. He smiled and said, "Ellen is the most wonderful woman in the world. I don't know what I'd do without her."

"Did you know Ellen wonders if you really love her?" I asked.

"That's ridiculous. I give her flowers and take her out to dinner. I try to show her how much I care about her every day." Craig was showing his love, but Ellen needed to hear it spoken more directly.

Years earlier a couple sat in my office and the wife told me how angry she was at her husband. He said he had no idea she was so upset. She turned to me and said, "I was so mad that I went into the kitchen last night and pounded on the pots and pans for a full hour."

This surprised her husband. He looked at her and said, "I thought you were just having trouble cleaning up after dinner."

Obviously the wife's message had not come across as clearly as she had hoped. Messages may not be understood if they aren't specific or direct. However, this does not give permission for one to be brutally blunt or insensitive. Too often I hear people justify their callous or cruel comments by saying, "I was just being honest." This is a poor excuse for hurtful communication. Speak from the heart simply, directly, and honestly, but always temper your words with love.

Be Vulnerable. We are all afraid of intimacy, yet at the same time we crave it. Over and over again, individuals tell me they are afraid that if their spouse really knew their deepest secrets and most embarrassing sins, they wouldn't love them anymore. So they put on a mask to hide behind for protection.

We don't like rejection so we keep our communication shallow, disclosing only what is necessary. However, one of the greatest joys and rewards in marriage occurs when we share our deepest selves—uncensored—and find acceptance for who we are, regardless of our flaws and failures. In John Powell's little book *Why Am I Afraid to Tell You Who I Am?* he identifies five levels of communication.[12]

Level One: Cliché Communication

This is the superficial, shallow talk we share with strangers. In some ways it's non-communication. It's a way of acknowledging somebody's presence without having to relate to them. We ask how the weather is, or how they are, and then don't even listen for their reply.

Level Two: Reporting Facts

We live in an informational age where we collect and dispense facts. For most couples it's easy to exchange data; this helps us to coordinate our lives. We talk about our schedules, work, house, car, and children, but it still doesn't involve a high level of risk.

If trust is the foundation of a relationship, then the desire to keep a secret becomes a more critical issue than the secret itself.

Level Three: Sharing Ideas and Opinions

Generally, facts are impersonal, whereas ideas and opinions are personal. Sharing how we think and what we believe provides a glimpse into who we are, and that can be frightening. When we discuss our relationship, faith, goals, and philosophy of life, we risk disagreement, conflict, and rejection. Yet we also risk understanding, growth, and closeness.

Level Four: Revealing Emotions

We are all emotional and that is good. Feelings prove we are alive. To not reveal feelings means one is either not in touch with them, afraid of them, or doesn't trust the relationship. A relationship without the expression of emotion is dying or already dead. We need to talk about our joys, fears, disappointments, and confusions. We need to laugh together, cry together, and even get angry at each other. Shutting down emotional disclosure, in yourself or your spouse, shuts down the heart of the relationship.

Emotions can be both wonderful and irrational. Since they are a crucial part of who we are as individuals, they're also a crucial part of who we are as husband and wife.

Level Five: Complete Personal Disclosure

The climax of communication is unrestrained openness and honesty. It is the total sharing of every fact, opinion, and feeling we currently have or ever did have. This can be threatening because we usually keep secrets about the wrong, embarrassing, or hurtful things we've done. However, there is a freedom when our partner is aware of our every sin, shortcoming, and secret, yet loves us anyway.

Secrets create problems and the lack of transparency is a form of dishonesty. If trust is the foundation of a relationship, then the desire to keep a secret becomes a more critical issue than the secret itself. (I realize there are healthy secrets, but the parameters must be defined and discussed by each couple.) Complete disclosure paves the way to complete togetherness. There is nothing as lonely as feeling you can't share your heart with your mate.

A couple sat in my office yesterday afternoon and both said they could talk about anything with each other. They had learned the importance of transparency the hard way; keeping secrets almost destroyed their marriage. She never told him of her frustration with the relationship; she grew cold. He didn't communicate how hurt he was with her coldness; he had an affair. If they had been vulnerable, this betrayal might have been avoided.

Ask Questions. As a psychologist, I spend a lot of my day asking questions. I'm a curious person and I like to learn about people. I ask my clients about their past, their family, hobbies, fears, and goals. Questions come easily for me, but with a little practice anybody can generate them. Questions accomplish at least three things in a relationship.

1. **Encourages Communication.**
   When a partner asks, their mate answers, and the conversation volleys back and forth, as with a friendly game of tennis.

2. **Shows Interest.**
   A question, especially a personal one, implies "I want to interact with you. You are interesting and I am interested. Talk with me."

3. **Gathers Information.**
   Questions can be superficial or profoundly deep. At their best they lead to an intimate, accurate, up-to-date picture of your spouse. As my wife answers questions, she reveals to me what she wants, thinks, and feels, and I discover her inner self. She is different from me and to assume I know her answers without asking is dangerous. I can't assume. I need to ask—not to interrogate or accuse—but to understand. As I ask thoughtful questions and listen, I learn more than I ever anticipated.

Speak Gently. "A gentle answer turns away wrath,"[13] King Solomon wrote. The opposite is also true—hard, cold, or loud answers stir up trouble. Some twenty years ago I heard the popular marriage and family therapist, Norman Wright, speak on communication. One of the things he said was that only 7 percent of a message consists of words. The rest of the message is 38 percent tone of voice, and 55 percent non-verbal behavior. We all need to watch our words, making them as kind and positive as possible.

Even more damaging than words is our tone of voice and non-verbal behavior. When frustrations increase, so does the loudness of our voice. Then our partner shouts to be heard above our voice, so we get louder to match them, and soon we are trying to out shout each other. The louder we yell the more frustrated and angry we get. It creates a crazy cycle. We need to make our tone of voice soft and caring. If firmness is necessary, we must do it without demeaning or shaming our partner. Assume a caring posture and don't reject or threaten with body language. A tender touch that shows affection or concern can make a world of difference. Most of us respond best to gentle communication: gentle words, gentle tone of voice, gentle non-verbal behavior.

Encourage and Build Up. We live in a world that chews people up and spits them out. At the end of the day most people feel burned out with exhaustion. Unfortunately, this is the time most couples interact and it's easy for communication to become impatient, irritable, and negative. We discourage instead of encourage each other.

A healthy marriage is a safe haven where we can relax and recuperate from the tensions of everyday life. We need to hear positive things from our mate. Just as I gathered together some friends to tell me what not to say to a spouse, so they also suggested what they would like to hear from their spouse.

"Good job!"

"You are wonderful."

"That was really great."

"You look gorgeous today."

"I don't feel complete without you."

"I appreciate all the things you've done for me all these years."

"You come first in my life, before kids, career, friends, anything."

"I'm glad I married you."

"You're the best friend I have."

"If I had it all to do over again, I'd still marry you."

"I wanted you today."

"I missed you today."

"I couldn't get you out of my mind today."

"It's nice to wake up next to you."
"I will always love you."
"I love to see your eyes sparkle when you smile."
"As always, you look good today."
"I trust you."
"I can always count on you."
"You make me feel good."
"I'm so proud to be married to you."
"I'm sorry."
"I was wrong."
"What would you like?"
"What is on your mind?"
"Let me just listen."
"You are so special."
"I can't imagine life without you."
"I wish I were a better partner."
"What can I do to help?"
"Pray for me."
"I'm praying for you today."
"I prize every moment we spend together."
"Thank you for loving me."
"Thank you for accepting me."
"Thank you for being my partner."
"You make every day brighter."

If we said these words more often, fewer marriages would be empty or terminated. We all need building-up and encouragement. If this can come from our partner, it's worth more than from anyone else.

Communication comes in two varieties: unhealthy talk and healthy talk. Unhealthy talk is easy—just open your mouth and let the words roll out. These hurtful words can ultimately kill a relationship. Although unhealthy talk is deadly, healthy talk brings new life to a marriage. It takes time, effort, thought, and self-control. It brings a husband and wife closer. Healthy talk comes when a person is slow to speak and thinks about what they say. It also helps if a person is slow to get angry.

PART THREE: SLOW TO ANGER

Scott had been upset for a long time, but when Lisa made a comment about his driving, all his anger came to the surface. In his rage he slapped her face and she immediately hit him back. When the police came, this normally rational and respected couple was screaming and throwing things at each other. Scott spent the night in jail and Lisa spent the night crying herself to sleep.

A week later, they both sat in my office embarrassed and apologetic. Scott sighed and said, "I really love Lisa, but I obviously have a problem. How can I handle my anger? And how can I make sure something like this never happens again?"

Whenever two people spend much time together, they will sooner or later get angry at each other. The challenge is to manage our anger in an appropriate way. Here's a little test. How would you respond?

- You work hard all day in the house or yard, and your partner never notices.

- You are talking to your mate and he or she doesn't answer you.

- While you are struggling to carry four cups of coffee to the table, your spouse bumps into you, spilling the coffee, and doesn't even apologize.

- You are to meet your partner at a particular restaurant, and he or she is forty-five minutes late.

- Your mate jokes and teases you about a sensitive area, and you ask him or her to stop. Your mate just laughs and asks, "What's wrong with you?"

- You accidentally take a wrong turn while driving, and your spouse yells at you.

- You are trying to concentrate, and your partner keeps making distracting noises.

- You are trying to tell your mate something very important to you, and he or she keeps interrupting.

- Your spouse forgets your birthday.

- You are in a hurry to get somewhere, and your partner is moving in slow motion.

Many of these situations trigger anger in a relationship. Anger isn't necessarily bad, as we'll see in chapter 5. It's bad only when it's misdirected, too frequent, too intense, violent, or lasts too long. Anger, as a feeling, is neither good nor bad.

The question Scott asked is important. "How can I handle my anger?" Let's look at five helpful steps.

ADMIT YOUR ANGER

Many people have difficulty being honest and direct about the emotion of anger. Before we can deal with it, we must stop playing games. Let's review four common games:

Denying. Everybody gets angry, but it amazes me how many people insist they are an exception. Often these people just call it by a different name. They are frustrated, irritated, ticked off, flustered, upset, bugged, or impatient, but they never get angry.

Several years ago a man sat in my office, slamming his fist on the arm of his chair and emphatically insisting, "I'M NOT ANGRY!" I asked what it was like for him to be angry and he said, "If you saw me angry, you'd know it. I start yelling, and cussing, and hitting."

What this man didn't realize was that anger comes in stages. Between mild and strong anger are many stages of anger. People don't often recognize their anger until they blow up. The subtle warning sign of a clenched jaw, a red face, a racing heart, or a raised voice doesn't register as anger to them. Anger is a part of life. Each day we feel it in one form or another. To deny our anger is to lose touch with how we feel.

Stuffing. This is pretending everything is okay when it's not; or that something really doesn't bother us when it does. It may seem nice on the surface, but it's dishonest. Not only that, but it can be highly destructive to both you and your relationship. The problem with stuffing is that anger doesn't always stay stuffed. Somewhere in our minds we have a mental closet. In this closet we stuff everything we don't want. We try to forget it when we slam the door shut. The problem is, sooner or later the closet gets too full and the door bursts open, throwing its contents all over our lives. Likewise, anger doesn't stay stuffed; it continues to accumulate. Even though we may have forgotten all about it, it will come back to haunt us through high blood pressure, heart attack, depression, stomach problems, or a number of other physical and/or psychological disorders.

Saving. One who saves their anger says to themselves, "I'm angry, but it's just something little. I'll put it in my collection and use it when I need it." They keep track of hurts and wrongs, usually bringing them up in the middle of an argument. Their anger becomes ammunition with which to gain control. They'll let you know "that's the fifth time you've done that in the past month," or "what you've just said reminds me of last summer when you..." Saving it is analogous to placing anger on the stove and letting it simmer. It doesn't blow up but it doesn't go away. It's just there whenever you want to throw it in somebody's face, and that somebody is usually your mate.

Displacing. When Teresa is angry at her parents, she tends to yell at her husband. She told me that her parents are frail and being mad at them would only make them feel bad. So she comes home with her anger and as soon as her husband does anything irritating, she blows up at him.

Rather than directing our anger where it belongs, we displace it by directing it toward an innocent, unsuspecting party, usually our partner. Maybe we're angry at the boss, a neighbor, a relative, or the family pet, but we end up directing it toward our spouse.

I saw a classic cartoon in college about displacement: a boss yells at a man, the man yells at his wife, the wife yells at her small son, who goes outside and kicks the dog.

When you're angry, be honest about it. Admit what you're feeling as soon as possible and direct it where it belongs. You can't handle your anger until you admit it and bring it out into the open.

EVALUATE YOUR ANGER

Asking ourselves questions helps us to understand our anger and keep us from reacting so quickly. A person's anger is very predictable once the pattern is found. Still, people tell me, "I can't control it. My anger just explodes before I even have a chance to think about it." It might feel that way, but it's not true. We can control our anger and asking ourselves these questions will help us get started.

- What triggers my anger?
  Frustration?
  Loss?
  Fear?
  Hurt?
  Injustice?
  Embarrassment?
  Disappointment?
  Confusion?
  Anxiety?

- When am I most likely to feel anger?
  When I'm late?
  Hungry?
  Tired?
  Overwhelmed?

- What am I telling myself about the person or situation I'm angry at?
  Am I jumping to conclusions?
  Am I exaggerating or overreacting?
  Am I taking it too personally?
  Am I giving them the benefit of the doubt?

- What can I do to reduce my anger?

CHOOSE YOUR PERCEPTION

Slow down and use the answers to the above questions to put the problem in perspective. Try to look at it from different angles. How might someone else view it? What one person takes offense at might not bother someone else. It all has to do with our perception. Talk to yourself about the situation in as positive a way as you can. Remember that negative self-talk can fuel the fire.

Focusing on the negative leads to overreaction. As a child, when I was in a huff about something, my grandmother would say, "What difference will this make in a year? In five years? In eternity? God is in control and in the big picture everything has a reason. Besides, it all comes out in the wash."

Years later, as I reflect on her advice, I try not to let things get to me. Most things that I get angry about won't amount to a hill of beans in a year, let alone eternity. God is in control, and my anger is usually a test as to how I will respond. I try to resolve my anger rather than feed it because I want to be healthy. The simple but profound Serenity Prayer says it so well.

God, grant me
The serenity to accept the things
  I cannot change,
The courage to change the things
  I can,
And the wisdom to know the
  difference.

In the midst of tense situations, remember that love sees the best in your spouse and is not easily angered.

CONTROL YOUR RESPONSE

Up to this point the focus has been on what is happening inside our heads, but as our anger builds there is a pressure to express ourselves. Some people lash out; others withdraw into silence. Some are explosive with verbal or physical abuse; others are subtle with razor-sharp sarcasm or passive/aggressive behavior. How we respond when we're angry has a major impact on our relationships. So as King David said, "In your anger do not sin."[14] Let me help you with the following four steps.

Calm Yourself Down. If your anger is getting out of control, lower your voice and breath deeply. If you still can't calm down, remove yourself from the situation. Tell your spouse you are starting to lose your temper and you need some space. Tell them where you are going and when you'll be back. Find a quiet place, sit down, have a drink of cool water, and try to relax.

Watch Your Words and Actions. When you're angry, it is easy to say and do things that you will later regret. Watch carefully what you say; once those words are out of your mouth, you can never take them back. Threats, put-downs, and thoughtless words cut sharp as a knife. Also, any form of physical abuse—hitting, slapping, pushing, twisting arms, grabbing, holding down, kicking or scratching—is inappropriate. These actions not only hurt the body, but hurt the spirit in a way that may never fully heal.

Poor communication skills condemn a relationship to either stagnation or dissolution.

Work Your Anger Out. Anger produces adrenaline and adrenaline seeks release. You need to work your anger out when you feel angry. Go for a drive, weed a garden, chop wood, paint a room, write a letter, punch a pillow, or take a walk.

About five years ago the mother of a teenage boy I was seeing in therapy gave me a call. She told me her son had gotten angry, ran out of the house, and was walking around the yard. I told her that is what I had suggested he do if he became angry. She hesitated and then said, "But he's been walking out there for over three hours." I guess he had a lot of anger to work out.

Talk About Your Anger. If you can, calmly talk about your feelings when you're angry. Tell your spouse what you're angry about and why. Take responsibility for your feelings. Be direct and honest without blaming or attacking your spouse. If you're overreacting, admit it. The better you can communicate about your anger, the more you can control it. Don't be afraid or embarrassed by your anger. As you learn about it, you learn about who you are. Sharing this difficult emotion with your partner also helps them learn about who you are.

DON'T LET THE SUN GO DOWN ON YOUR ANGER[15]

Commit yourself to resolving your anger as soon as possible. Unresolved anger turns into bitterness, revenge, or both. The sooner you handle your anger, the better. Anger not dealt with grows and takes on a life of its own that can undermine any relationship. When you discover your anger, don't let it build. Try to de-escalate it and come to some level of closure before the day ends. There is nothing more comforting than a peaceful night's rest; knowing that you and your partner have the security to express anger and the maturity to deal with it in a timely manner. We will deal with this in more detail in chapters 5 and 6 on conflict management and forgiveness.

If anger is denied, stuffed, saved, displaced, or allowed to blow up, it will grow. As it grows, it will take over both the person and the relationship. Angry feelings that are not dealt with will lead to angry behavior; unchecked angry behavior will develop into an angry personality. We think of such personalities as having a short fuse, being hotheaded, or quick-tempered. Their anger is not just something they feel, it now controls them. The final step of the cycle is the passing on of their angry behavior to their children who will also struggle with anger management.

A HAPPY HOME

Good communication helps to build a healthy marriage and a happy home. Poor communication skills condemn a relationship to either stagnation or dissolution. To be slow to hear, quick to speak, and quick to anger pushes people away.

Silas Marner by George Elliot was published in 1861. In this novel, Silas Marner is a sad, lonely, and angry man whose chief activities are weaving cloth and hoarding money. He lives in solitude and has no friends. He neither listens nor speaks to people unless it is absolutely necessary. When he does speak, his words are cold and his stare is frightening. He is a miserable man with poor communication skills. As the years pass by, Silas Marner's life narrows and hardens as his anger grows into bitterness. One day he finds a yellow-haired baby girl that nobody claims. He raises little Eppie and in the process, his life broadens and softens. He learns to communicate and resolve his anger.

The last paragraph of the book shows the wonderful

transformation that can happen to anyone willing to seriously work on their communication. Eppie turns to Silas and says, "What a pretty home ours is! I think nobody could be happier than we are."[16]

That's a statement I wish every married couple could make.

Discussion Questions

1. What is the most trouble your tongue ever got you into?

2. What external and/or internal things keep you from truly listening to your spouse?

3. When was the last time you did the following to your partner? Explain.

   a) Ignored what they were saying.
   b) Pretended to listen.
   c) Selectively listened.
   d) Truly listened.

4. What sort of miscommunication has happened in your marriage during the past three months?

   How did it start?

   How could it have been avoided?

5. Which of the following forms of unhealthy talk are you most likely to engage in?

   a) Negative statements   d) Overtalking
   b) Thoughtless words   e) Exaggeration
   c) Blaming   f) Manipulation

   Explain when, where, why, and how you use these forms of unhealthy talk.

6. How does your mate respond when you use any of the above?

   What do you think he/she feels when you use any of the above?

7. What is the nicest thing your spouse has ever said to you? Be specific.

8. At what level of communication is your marriage most frequently operating?

   a) Cliché
   b) Reporting facts
   c) Sharing ideas and opinions
   d) Revealing emotions
   e) Complete personal disclosure

9. How often do you get angry?

   What triggers it?

   How do you express it?

10. When was the last time you got angry at your spouse?

    How did it get started?

    How long did it last?

    How was it resolved?

11. Are there any unresolved issues of anger toward your mate that still need to be dealt with? Be specific.

12. On a scale from 1 to 10 (1 = excellent, 10 = poor) how would you rate yourself in the following areas?

    a) Quick to hear.
    b) Slow to speak.
    c) Slow to become angry.

Notes

1. Adapte Genesis 2 and 3.

2. See J. Grant Howard, *The Trauma of Transparency: A Biblical Approach to Inter-Personal Communication* (Portland, Ore.: Multnomah Press, 1979), 25-36.

3. James 3:6, Phillips.

4. James 1:19.

5. Proverbs 1:5.

6. Paul Tournier, *To Understand Each Other* (Atlanta: John Knox Press, 1976), 29. The actual quotation reads, "It is impossible to overemphasize the immense need men have to be really listened to...."

7. Norman Wakefield, *Listening: A Christian's Guide to Loving Relationships* (Waco, Tex.: Word, 1981), 61ff.

8. Charles M. Sell, *Achieving the Impossible: Intimate Marriage* (Portland, Ore.: Multnomah Press, 1982), 66 (italics mine).

9. Ephesians 4:29.

10. *The Heritage Club Sandglass*, Number 111:28, 1.

11. Proverbs 25:11.

12. John Powell, *Why Am I Afraid to Tell You Who I Am? (So We Can All Get to Know You!): 25 Guidelines for Good Communication* (Niles, Ill.: Argus Communications, 1969), 54-62 (commentary on each of the five levels is mine).

13. Proverbs 15:1.

14. Psalm 4:4, cf. Ephesians 4:26.

15. See Ephesians 4:26.

16. George Eliot, *Silas Marner: Weaver of Raveloe* (New York: Books, Inc.), 250.

5

MAKING PEACE

We live in a world torn with war and conflict. This morning's newspaper announced violent conflicts in Rwanda, Bosnia-Herzegovina, and Northern Ireland. There is a truce in the civil war in Yemen. Two days ago Israeli warplanes attacked a site in southern Lebanon, and tension over North Korea's nuclear program continues to escalate as the United States threatens sanctions. These conflicts will end, but new fights will take their place. Marriages are also sites of conflict but unlike international disputes, marital fights are not necessarily negative.

When was your last fight? This is one of my favorite questions to ask couples. If their last fight was too long ago, I worry about their honesty and communication skills. If it was relatively recent, I move to my next question: What was your fight about? Most couples turn silent and look sheepishly at each other. I reassure them that what they tell me is kept in complete confidence. I promise I will not tell their children, neighbors, friends, or pastor.

Many marital arguments are over stupid little things that are fairly irrelevant, but in the midst of the battle they seem so important. In a way they are important. Not because they are significant in themselves, but because they provide an opportunity to develop a deeper, healthier personality. This process should draw a couple closer together.

We face many difficulties in marriage. Difficulties from situations outside the relationship, from our partner, and from deep inside ourselves. In the book of James we read that these difficulties have a purpose. The theme of the first chapter is "Adversity Builds Character"where it tells us that difficulties:

1. Test faith.
2. Develop patience.
3. Build maturity.
4. Add wisdom.

5. Encourage prayer.
6. Force consideration of eternal values.

Conflict provides us an opportunity to develop in these six positive ways. In order to do so we must ask ourselves six corresponding questions about each conflict:

1. How does God want me to behave?
2. Am I being patient?
3. Am I responding maturely in thought, word, and deed?
4. What have I learned about my spouse and myself?
5. Have I prayed?
6. How important is this issue from an eternal perspective?

I hate these questions! Yet if I hope to have a positive marriage, I must deal with each one honestly.

Every couple fights. This is partially because each person is unique and sees situations differently. I think we should clean the kitchen as we cook; Tami thinks we should clean up after the meal. I think certain colors go together; Tami strongly disagrees. I have a certain landscape plan for our yard; Tami has a different plan. These are just a few of our differences; you and your spouse have your own. These differences give life variety and excitement. They also lead to disagreements that turn into conflicts. A conflict is an opportunity to express your perspective and understand your spouse's.

A conflict-free home is unrealistic. Conflict and making peace are hallmarks of true intimacy.

There are two different continuums to most conflicts—volume and time. Some conflicts are quiet and if you were a mouse in the corner you might not even know a fight was happening. Others are loud with yelling and crying and an intensity that tightens your stomach. In the second continuum there is also a polarity. Some fights are short—a difficulty

126

arises, is confronted, and it's over, never again to be mentioned. Others are drawn out and never are totally resolved.

A conflict-free home is unrealistic. Conflict and making peace are hallmarks of true intimacy. Two mature individuals try to live in harmony as a couple; though they realize that differences in personality will naturally lead to some level of conflict. Yet every healthy conflict ends in resolution and peace. The resolution might not be what you had hoped for, but only spoiled children insist on always getting their way. As a good spouse it is our challenge to be a peacemaker in a relationship that will have its share of conflicts. This is not peace without regard to cost. Rather, it consists of strength and sensitivity knowing that the husband and wife are not enemies. We are partners struggling to communicate, understand, and come close in spite of our fallen natures. Jesus said in the Sermon on the Mount, "Blessed are the peacemakers, for they will be called sons of God."[1]

CONTEMPLATING CONFLICT

Each year Tami and I have our annual vacation conflict. When I go on vacation I enjoy adventure and excitement. I want to go to new places and explore, especially places of historical significance.

Tami enjoys places she is familiar with where she can relax and do nothing. She enjoys vacations where she can lie in the sun. If we do go exploring, she is more interested in the animals and plant life of a region than its history. I'm more interested in a region's history.

Several years ago we went to Mexico and had our conflict. I wanted to explore the ancient Mayan ruins and Tami wanted to lie beside the pool and read a good book. We talked about our different goals and came to a compromise; on certain days we would explore, on other days we would relax. Both of us got some of what we wanted and we had a great vacation.

There are two unhealthy ways to deal with conflict. The first is to behave as a turtle. When turtles sense conflict they get out of the way and avoid it at all costs. Yet if a conflict gets too close, they pull their head and feet into their shell. They simply withdraw and refuse to deal with conflict. A person with a turtle attitude sees conflict as wrong and dangerous. They interpret harmony as avoiding conflict and pretending it doesn't exist. Rather than admit there is a difficulty, they stuff their feelings and withdraw into a polite, everything-is-fine sort of relationship. They choose to close their eyes to problems. What they don't see doesn't exist. This creates a situation where difficulties that might be easy to resolve are left with no closure.

Unfortunately, most unresolved difficulties will grow. They are analogous to a small infection in your thumb. If ignored, the infection will grow until the thumb is red, sore, and swollen. In time the whole hand is infected.

Conflict is not a contest or a game to be won by the more clever or ruthless partner. Even if you are right or your way is best, what good is it if you win the conflict and jeopardize the marriage?

The second unhealthy way to deal with conflict is to behave as a shark. When a shark senses conflict, it speeds toward it with razor-sharp teeth ready for attack. It sees every battle as something to win regardless the cost. It appears to enjoy conflict and delights in opportunities to prove its superiority. It forgets that if someone wins, then someone else loses.

For either spouse to lose in a marital conflict is unhealthy for the relationship. Conflict is not a contest nor a game to be won by the more clever or ruthless partner. Even if you are right or your way is best, what good is it if you win the conflict and jeopardize the marriage? Winning is not the goal of marital conflict. The best way to resolve any conflict is to create a situation where *both* partners win. Both turtle and shark attitudes can destroy a marriage.

As we contemplate conflict it's important to remember four basic facts.

CONFLICT IS NORMAL

A marriage dispute is not a sign of trouble. Conflict is natural and inevitable. Any two people who spend much time together are going to have their share of disagreements. However, a conflict is not the same as quarreling. A quarrel is negative, critical, and usually destructive. The book of Proverbs teaches that "a quarrelsome wife is like a constant dripping on a rainy day."[2] This is obviously true of a quarrelsome husband, too. Quarrels are exhausting; they wear you down and make you feel a little crazy. Quarrels tend to be circular—they don't seem to go anywhere. Conflicts move toward a conclusion and, if handled maturely, leave a couple better off than when they started.

MOST CONFLICTS ARE THE RESULT OF DIFFERENCES

As mentioned before, each individual has a unique perspective on life. Since opposites often attract, a husband and wife are likely to have different approaches toward many aspects of life and marriage. The following are some of the most common areas of conflict:

Parenting. Each parent deals with their children in their own individual style. One partner is usually more strict, with exacting expectations and discipline, than the other. One spouse will discipline with swats, but the other might feel more comfortable with time-outs or groundings. Some mates allow their children a lot of freedom, whereas others allow very little.

We either adopt similar parenting skills as our parents or we react against them by doing the exact opposite. If your father yelled at you as a child, you might follow in his footsteps and yell at your children. But if you believed his parenting style was unhealthy, you might do the opposite and insist that yelling not be allowed in your home. Everybody varies to some degree in their parenting style. The key is to work together as a team, not contradicting nor undermining each other.

Distribution of Home Chores. A century ago marital roles were clearly defined—the husband provided for the financial needs, maintained the yard, and did major repairs; the wife took care of the children, cooked meals, did laundry, and tended to the housework.

Today life is more complicated and marital roles are fuzzy.

Both spouses usually care for the children and, in many situations, they both work outside the home as well. Yet even if this isn't the case, who does what around the house can still result in conflict. Some spouses claim certain tasks as their own based on tradition, natural ability, or enjoyment. Others like to share tasks, working side by side or in tandem. Then there are the tasks that nobody wants to do, but they must be done. One facet of mature love is doing the dirty jobs around the house without complaining. Another is acknowledging your appreciation to your partner when they do those jobs. Taking your spouse's work around the house for granted is *never* a good idea.

Many couples solve the problem of how to distribute household chores by listing all that must be done and estimating the time required to complete each task. They divide the list based on interest. Whatever is left is split between the two of them, being careful to take into consideration outside employment and other obligations.

Relatives and In-laws. Most of us sense a certain obligation and family loyalty toward our own relatives. Even so, every family has that certain person who is difficult to love. One author calls these individuals "irregular" people. They have certain patterns of behavior that we would not accept in a friend. However, being relatives, we have learned over the years to be patient and accept them for who they are regardless of what they do. Our spouse, on the other hand, doesn't have this history and blood connection. They may not be so willing to overlook behavior they perceive as inappropriate. They may not understand our tolerance and might feel we shouldn't even socialize with them. I encourage couples not to put their partner in a position of having to distance themselves from their own relatives. However, if a spouse must decide between their mate and a family member, even their parents, they must choose their mate.

Communication Styles. Conflicts over communication usually involve either a lack of communication, self-centered communication, or destructive communication. All three of these difficulties create deep frustration that can easily explode into conflict. Rather than get defensive about our communication style, we need to go back to chapter 4 and review the principles of healthy and unhealthy talk. It is easy to fall into poor communication habits. True maturity admits poor habits and seriously works on changing them. If we are impacted by our spouse's poor habits, then we need to try to help them without nagging, belittling, or shaming them.

Money Management. Money can be a symbol of power, freedom, control, or security. Finances quickly become an emotional issue when one feels their freedom is being limited or their security is being threatened. It also becomes an issue of power or control when the husband and wife battle over who is in charge of the money. Most couples have what is called a "one-pot" system where all the money earned in the family goes into the family budget. This works best when the wage earners relinquish their money and treat it as "ours" with neither partner having the advantage over the other.

Some couples, especially those who have either married later in life or have been married before, have a two-pot system where there is a division between *her* money and *his* money. Still others have a three-pot system where money slips into *hers, his,* and *ours.* I believe the best system for most marriages is the one-pot system.

People handle money in many different ways. Some individuals are frugal; they live carefully within their budget no matter what. They take finances very seriously and know exactly what their assets and debts are. They save, tithe, and never use credit cards unless they can pay them off at the end of the month. Others are more liberal with their money management. They have no need for strict budgets and they rarely save. They are more carefree about how they spend, making purchases as needs and wants arise. Yet what one person believes is a need, the other might perceive as a want or even an extravagance. We all have different priorities.

I buy books and compact disks. Tami buys flowers for the garden and extra clothes. I think my priorities are more important than hers, and she believes hers are more important than mine. To resolve our problem, we learned to work together and manage our money in such a way that we can both buy what we want—clothes, books, flowers, and compact disks. Now we both win and we're satisfied, realizing that, even if we don't agree, we can still be sensitive to each other's wants.

Ultimately, money management comes down to paying bills. There are certain fixed expenditures in life such as housing, utilities, insurance, and food. Beyond this, every couple must answer a number of important questions:

- How much should we tithe?

- How much should we save, if any?

- Should we borrow? If yes, under what circumstances?

- How much should we spend on transportation, clothes, entertainment, gifts, hobbies, vacations, furniture, and anything else within this category?

After answering these questions, work together as a team being sensitive to each other's perception of finances. Remember, showing positive regard is more important than how you spend your money.

Expression of Affection and Sexuality. Affection and sexuality are very personal aspects of marriage. How they are displayed and received are equally personal. One field of psychology is called *Neuro-Linguistic Programming*. This program claims there are three major methods by which people think, learn, and relate: auditory, visual, and kinesthetic.

Auditory people prefer long conversations and music. They enjoy statements of affection and respond best to what they hear.

Visual people are drawn to attractive settings where they can gaze at their partner. They are watchers and respond best to what they see, such as pictures, scenery, movies, and face-to-face interactions.

Kinesthetic people enjoy touching and snuggling. They are impacted most by feelings even though they might not verbalize them very well. They crave closeness and physical comfort.

All three modalities are important but each person has their preferences. Just because a person is strong in one mode doesn't mean the other modes have no impact. Frequently, we assume that what we prefer in terms of affection and sexuality our partner will also enjoy; therefore, if we want back rubs, we give back rubs. If we enjoy candlelight lovemaking, we assume that's what our partner will also enjoy. Rather than listening and learning what their preferences are, we make presumptuous assumptions, then insist we are good lovers. Let your partner teach you how to love them. Listen to their likes and dislikes. Discover what is enjoyable, comfortable, and arousing to them. Take careful note of what they find uncomfortable and offensive. Don't argue or push. Respect their bodies. Some people want to be touched gently, others with a firm and more aggressive touch, and others simply don't want to be touched. Some people like wet, passionate kisses, others want light, tender kisses, and some don't enjoy kisses at all.

Friends provide a place to vent frustrations, check out perceptions, talk about things our partner has no interest in, and participate in activities our spouse doesn't care about.

Be a student of love. This beautiful area can easily become negative and painful. If this happens, talk through the problem; if you are at an impasse, speak to a professional. Don't let the frustration of differences steal away the warmth of affection and sexuality.

Friendships Outside Marriage. Friendship is an important aspect of life, but outside friendships can create stress in a marriage. Even as we learn to tolerate the bad habits of relatives, so we tolerate the bad habits of friends. Yet our partner might not be so willing. They might see friends as a negative influence or they might become jealous of the time and attention their spouse devotes to them. It is important that your spouse feels that they hold top priority in your life.

Your mate will feel threatened if your friend becomes too important to you. This is especially true if the friend is of the opposite sex. I am not saying that to have a healthy marriage one must eliminate friends. On the contrary, friendships are critical to a healthy marriage. A spouse cannot possibly meet all our social and interactive needs; to expect so puts an unfair burden on the relationship. Friends provide a place to vent frustrations, check out perceptions, talk about things our partner has no interest in, and participate in activities our spouse doesn't care about.

> *Friendship is special. Keep it that way and don't let friends undermine your character or your marriage.*

I play basketball with neighbors, go to concerts with my brothers, and discuss philosophy with my friend, Jerry. Tami has little interest in basketball, my style of music, or philosophical discussions. She doesn't want to do these activities but she encourages me to do them with my friends. However, if my involvement in these areas became more important than spending time with her, she would soon feel neglected and we would need to re-evaluate the situation. My principle is: Spend time with friends but *never forget your first love.* Your spouse must take top priority, though this shouldn't minimize the significance of friends. Don't ignore friendships and more importantly, don't ignore your spouse.

Unfortunately, certain friends create tension in a marriage in the following ways:

- As a negative influence,
- Demanding our time,
- Taking advantage of us,
- Lacking respect for our partner,
- Are of the opposite sex (especially if they are overly friendly).

These five difficulties must be taken seriously. We are usually more forgiving of our friends than our spouse is. This is because our spouse is more objective about our friends than we are.

If friends are a negative influence, discuss it with your partner and work out a solution that will be best for both of you. If friends are too demanding of your time or are taking advantage of you, set stronger boundaries. If friends are not respectful of your mate, defend your spouse and ask that they speak positively about them.

Friends of the opposite sex create special problems. They can trigger jealousies and become more intimate than what is healthy. Opposite-sex friendships are dangerous if they are not shared with your spouse. Be careful about spending a lot of time alone with the opposite sex, especially doing recreational or fun activities. Even though a situation is totally innocent, it can have the appearance of evil. Besides, innocent situations can easily escalate into not-so-innocent situations. Don't take foolish risks with your marriage. One safeguard is to openly share with your spouse *everything* you say or do with a friend of the opposite sex. If there are any hesitations to do this, you might be crossing a dangerous line.

Friendship is special. Keep it that way and don't let friends undermine your character or your marriage.

Most conflicts are the result of differences. Some are the result of expectations. We think life should go smoothly and always be fair. At times we insist, in some unrealistic corner of our brain, that our spouse should always be competent, industrious, patient, self-giving, and completely perfect. When things are not this way, we become frustrated and a conflict is born.

Another reason for a fight is our own selfish desires. We ignore the needs and feelings of our partner in order to do it our way. Sometimes we don't even care what they want. We are going to do it our way no matter what. This selfish part of us is stubborn and capable of all sorts of hard-hearted thoughts and deeds. Don't let your expectations or selfish desires destroy a healthy conflict.

MOST CONFLICT IS NOT DEALT WITH OPENLY

We all tend to sweep too much under the rug. At first, most of us have the turtle attitude, but if the frustration of individual differences is held long enough, our secret shark behavior emerges. Not dealing openly with conflicts is destructive to any relationship. The consequences of unresolved conflicts are myriad.

- Emotional distance/Neglect

- Hurt/Bitterness/Negativity

- Stress/Depression

- Loneliness/Social withdrawal

- Physical problems (headaches, stomach problems, high blood pressure, hives, heart problems, cancer)

- Phobias/Obsessive-Compulsive Disorder/Paranoia

- Spiritual dryness

- Addictions

- Adultery (emotional and/or physical)

- Divorce

- Death

Obviously there are other causes of these factors, but unresolved conflict can cause all of the above. If the problem of conflict is not dealt with openly, individuals and couples risk one or more of the above symptoms.

CONFLICT PROVIDES AN OPPORTUNITY FOR GROWTH

The purpose of conflict is to resolve difficulties that normally arise between two people. Yet in the process of this resolution a lot more can be accomplished. A disagreement is an opportunity to be honest about your feelings without being hurtful or abusive. Through a conflict you come to understand your mate better; their likes and dislikes, what is important to them, in what areas they are sensitive, and what they believe. This can be an exciting interaction, for as each of you understand these areas of your lives you move closer together in your marriage.

Conflict does not need to drive a wedge between you and your spouse; it can actually weld you together through closer understanding. Proverbs says, "As iron sharpens iron, so one man sharpens another."[3] If a conflict is approached with a healthy attitude, then both partners are sharpened. Each spouse respects the other when the disagreement is resolved. Both will have grown in their relationship. Yet this only occurs if fights take place in a context of love with each partner agreeing to fight fair.

HOW TO HAVE A HEALTHY CONFLICT

The inability to manage and resolve personal conflicts can destroy a marriage. A healthy conflict, where growth occurs, is contingent upon learning to fight with love and integrity. I encourage couples to fight on a regular basis for clarity, understanding, and closeness; nevertheless, a positive fight is not to be rushed into without a proper attitude. Like most important things in life, quality preparation is critical for success. A good fight consists of three parts: the preparation, the encounter, and the resolution.

> *Conflict does not need to drive a wedge between you and your spouse; it can actually weld you together through closer understanding.*

THE PREPARATION

To start a fight without preparation is risking a painful disaster. Several years ago I tore my Achilles' tendon playing racquetball. It was incredibly painful. The doctor at the emergency room placed a hard cast on my leg from my thigh to my toes, and I was on crutches for eight weeks. My physician told me I injured myself because I hadn't stretched out enough before playing the game. He informed me that if you don't prepare the muscles for playing, you risk physical damage. This principle also holds true for conflict. The following three steps are essential in preparing to fight:

Get in the Right Frame of Mind. A mature attitude is necessary when approaching a conflict. You might ask, what does maturity have to do with a fight? My answer is: *Everything*. If you can't fight maturely don't fight at all.

Before fighting find a quiet place to pray for wisdom and God's will. Seek his help in answering the following questions:

- What does God want in this situation?

- Does my attitude and behavior truly glorify God?

- How would Jesus respond in my situation?

When I asked these questions of a friend of mine he gave me a disgusted look and said, "But that isn't fair. It's impossible to respond like Jesus. He is God and I'm human." That is true, but as Christians we are to be as Christlike as possible. Once you get yourself right with God, examine yourself further with the following questions:

- What am I so upset about?

- Is this the real issue or am I frustrated about something else?

- Am I overreacting?

- What do I want? What would make me happy?

- How important is this issue to me?

- Am I being insensitive, selfish, or stubborn?

These questions help you to focus on what is happening within you, rather than on what your spouse has done or not done. The issue at this point is inner preparation and making sure your heart is ready for a positive battle. Another area to explore is your irrational beliefs connected with conflict. Four common beliefs are as follows:

- I must get what I want to be happy.

- Things have to go right (and I define what is right).

- I must be in control or something bad will happen.

- I cannot change.

All four of these beliefs are lies and clinging to them will block us from understanding our spouse's position. Admit it if you hold any of these irrational beliefs. (After all, we all have certain beliefs that are irrational.) Talk to your partner about them and where they might have come from, then dispute the irrational belief by stating the opposite:

- I can be happy, even if I don't get what I want.

- Things in life don't have to go right and they probably won't.

- I don't have to be in control. Ultimately, God is in control and things are much better in his hands than mine.

- I can change and the more I change, the better I will be.

Holding on to these rational beliefs will make your conflicts much healthier.

Schedule the Time and Place. Choose a time and place where both of you feel free and comfortable to discuss the issue. If the other person brings up the issue at a bad time, tell them you are willing to work on the conflict seriously and suggest a better time. Be sure to avoid conflicts when you first come home from work and at bedtime.

During homecoming the working partner is tired and is transitioning from job to home. Using this time to initiate a conflict risks them associating coming home with tension and sets a negative atmosphere for the rest of the evening. Allow them to relax and plug back into the home before introducing the conflict.

It is not wise to save conflict until bedtime. When people are tired they become impatient and irritable. Instead of resolving your conflict, it could cause it to escalate. Besides, don't fight in the bedroom—keep that room as your refuge. Save it for relaxation and romance.

As a couple, identify other terrible times to avoid fights; but remember that postponements can be dangerous. Resolving a conflict as quickly as possible is usually best.

Not only must you find the right time, but you must also find the right place. The primary concern with location is to maintain privacy. Don't fight in front of others for this might embarrass or humiliate your partner. Also, don't seek allies or involve others; this frequently does more to complicate a conflict than resolve it. However, if you do become stuck and decide you need a witness, mediator, or counselor, find someone you *both* agree can help.

Organize Your Concerns. Don't jump to conclusions. Think through the difficulty, distinguishing fact from opinion. At this point it might be necessary to investigate and collect more data. During this process try to identify the real difficulty. Remember, the apparent issue isn't always the real issue. Overlook minor factors or petty differences and determine how important this issue is to you. Is it really worth fighting for? If it isn't, drop it. If it is, focus on the core issue and your emotions regarding it.

Next, consider how your partner feels about the issue. Here is a check list to help you be properly prepared for your encounter:

- Keep an open mind and think of the issue from your partner's point of view.

- Jot down the central issues to be addressed.

- List the words and topics to avoid.

- List the words that best describe your feelings.

- Detail your suggestions and preferences for a solution.

- Plan what you want to say and write out your words.

Now that you are organized, you are ready for the encounter.

THE ENCOUNTER

With proper preparations made, it is now time to confront your partner, talking face-to-face, using the best communication skills from chapter 4. This encounter can be exciting, though it may also be intense. Don't let this frustrate or intimidate you. A conflict is the process of working toward a resolution. This process involves defining the difficulty, agreeing on "fight rules," and discussing possible resolutions.

Instead of blaming, identify your contribution to the conflict. Then define areas of agreement and disagreement. You might find you agree on more than you thought.

Defining the Difficulty. State the issue at hand simply and clearly as you see it without raising your voice or exaggerating. Be careful about either overstating or understating the situation. Overstating a difficulty can come across as an attack, and trigger a defensive stance or a counterattack. Understating a difficulty suggests that it's not important and isn't worth a conflict. So it is stuffed away and left unresolved. To keep the difficulty in perspective it is often helpful to determine exactly what type of difficulty it is. There are at least four types.[4]

- **A Difference.** Two people see a situation from individual and possibly opposing perspectives.

- **A Problem.** Something isn't working as it should. There is a solution; it needs to be found and applied. Problems are solved and there may be more than one solution.

- **A Predicament.** This situation is more intense than a problem and there are no easy or satisfactory solutions. Every choice seems flawed. It feels like whatever you do, the result will be negative. At times it even feels as if your choices will make things worse than the original difficulty.

- **A Crisis.** This is a very large predicament with a sense of urgency. It looks like an emergency and appears that action must be taken immediately or something terrible will happen.

A conflict gets out of control when a couple thinks of every difficulty as a crisis. Very few situations are a true crisis. Though our conflicts feel major at the moment, they are usually something less urgent than a crisis.

Talk about the specifics of the situation, backing up each statement with facts. It is easy for facts to get lost in vague generalities. The more specific the statement the better. Be careful to distinguish facts, opinions, and feelings. Far too often, when we feel strongly about something, we make statements of opinion or emotion sound factual.

Stick to the truth but make sure to communicate truth in love. Truth is not a club, it's a shepherd's staff; therefore, use it to guide rather than to beat your spouse. Discuss difficulties with gentleness. Instead of blaming, identify your contribution to the conflict. Then define areas of agreement and disagreement. You might find you agree on more than you thought. Don't be discouraged by your areas of disagreement; view them as challenges to work through in a healthy way. Some basic guidelines will help.

Agreeing on Fight Rules. Conflicts can quickly escalate from an opportunity to grow to something ugly where harmful things are said and done. The purpose of a fight is to enhance a relationship, not damage it. To accomplish this, many couples have developed "fight rules." These are guidelines to follow to keep a conflict under control. Below are some of the rules that couples have found helpful.

1. Show Respect. God is more concerned with whether you fight fair than whether you are right. Too many people have won their argument and lost their marriage. The process is more important than the result. Hundreds of times couples have sat in my office and told me about a huge fight. They can't remember what it was about or how it was resolved, but they remember vividly what was said or done. That memory replays over and over in their mind, building a wall of hurt and mistrust between a couple who once committed themselves to love and cherish each other.

Always remember the following two principles of respect:

- Attack the problem, not the person.
- Never hit below the belt.

The first is self-explanatory but let me explain the second. In boxing, a punch below the belt is considered unfair. It is taking advantage of a weakness and is called *fighting dirty*. Everybody has an emotional belt line but it is different for each person. Some people have a low belt line and most things don't bother them. Others have a high belt line and are very sensitive. We all have sensitive areas that trigger pain or defensiveness. Avoid these areas, especially during a conflict. Respect does not call names or take cheap shots. It does not make negative references to relatives or in-laws. It does not put down your spouse's appearance, competency, or character, even if it's just a joke. Respect is treating your partner as if they are the most attractive, intelligent, successful, godly person in all the earth.

2. Stick to One Issue at a Time. Dealing with too many issues at one time creates confusion and problems are seldom resolved. Focus on the initial difficulty and don't confuse it with other issues until the original issue is resolved. Deal with difficulties one at a time in an intelligent and orderly fashion. If your mate confronts you with an issue you don't like, don't try to get back at them or change the subject by saying: "Well, what about...?" or "What I did wasn't as bad as what you did." This game of one-upmanship doesn't resolve anything, it merely leads to hostility. If you discover you have strayed from the main issue, apologize and get back on course.

3. Stay Focused on the Present. Don't bring up the past. When you confront your spouse with what happened a day, a week, or even longer ago, they are at a disadvantage because they may not remember. Even if they didn't forget, both of you are at a disadvantage because your memories distort what happened in the past. Everyone remembers differently. You selectively remember what you want and forget the rest. The further you are removed from the incident, the more difficult it is to accurately report what happened. Be careful about opening up old wounds that time has healed. If it was talked about and resolved in the past, then don't bring it up again. Becoming trapped in the past doesn't allow for change.

Even as the past presents dangerous waters, so does the future. None of us can know what tomorrow holds. It's counterproductive to say "I'll never change," "I'll always do that," or "I won't do this." This sort of talk can set up a self-fulfilling prophecy that discourages your spouse.

Leave the past in the past and the future in the future. Stick to the present and your conflicts will go smoother.

4. Speak Only for Yourself. Don't presume to know what your mate thinks, feels, or even wants. Talk about what *you* think, not about what *they* think. You don't truly know what they think unless they tell you. Make "I" statements, not "you" statements. Say, "I think," "I heard," "I feel," or "I want." State your perspective as yours and not as the one and only perspective. When making feeling statements, take responsibility for your emotions. Say "When _____ happens, I feel angry," not "You make me so mad." Also, if you want something let your partner know by clearly stating your wants. *Ask* them what they want—don't *tell* them what they want. To presume is demeaning and tends to intensify a conflict.

5. Don't Interrupt One Another. Interruptions are rude. People usually interrupt if they are afraid they won't be heard, or they will forget the great point they want to make. Interruption is a symptom of impatience; though it might also be a sign that the speaker is monopolizing the conversation by talking too much.

A strategy that stops both interrupting and overtalking is the *five-plus-five rule*. It works this way: Your mate gets five uninterrupted minutes to state their perspective while you listen. Put yourself in their shoes and listen carefully to understand how they perceive the conflict. If they state a criticism, find the truth in it (even if it's only a tiny kernel) and agree with it. When they are finished or their five minutes are up, whichever comes first, paraphrase back what you heard to their satisfaction. Now you get five minutes to state your perspective, which is then paraphrased by your spouse. Share what you heard or saw, what you thought, what you felt, and why you felt that way.

When your time is finished, both of you share exactly what you would desire in an ideal situation. During this process, bite your tongue when your partner is speaking. The five-plus-five rule allows both of you to have your say without interruption, and without fearing your spouse will monopolize the talk. If one five-plus-five isn't enough, add another; however, be cautious about not dragging out explanations and "I" statements. Conflicts are exhausting and it's best to resolve them as quickly as possible without rushing or railroading either one of you.

6. Use Signals and Time-Outs. Don't let your conflict get out of hand. Agree on some signal to use when you or your partner break the rules (such as calling foul or raising your hand). If you see your spouse using the signal, stop immediately. If you break a rule, call a foul on yourself.

Unfortunately conflicts can escalate. When this happens you might need to go beyond a signal and take a time-out. Any hint or threat of violence is grounds for an immediate time-out. Violence is never acceptable during a marital conflict. If a situation looks as if it's moving out of control, take a break from each other for ten to twenty minutes to calm down and reflect on the conflict. When you need a time-out don't just walk away, tell your spouse you need some space and that you will be back soon to continue resolving the conflict. Time-outs should never be used to pout, manipulate, or punish your mate. They are a legitimate and sometimes critical way of maintaining control when tensions flair.

7. Pray Before and After the Conflict. Prayer draws you and your spouse together and reminds you that God is watching your every move. As a child I once heard a sermon that said everybody in heaven would know everything. This sent my imagination reeling and soon I thought of heaven as filled with movie theaters playing complete, full-length, unabridged, unedited versions of everybody's life. This thought frightened me, but it also caused me to carefully weigh all I said and did. If you thought the world would know every detail of your conflict, how would you fight? Deep, honest praying sets your conflict in context. When you pray, sit down and hold each other's hands.

Before a conflict, ask that God's will be done and that you will both treat each other with respect. After a conflict pray for forgiveness if your behavior was unbecoming and ask for this encounter to bring you closer together.

Take these rules, or make up new ones, and review them regularly. You might also want to write them out in simple form and stick them to your refrigerator door as a constant reminder to fight fair. The fights will come. When they do, will you be prepared to handle them with love and maturity?

Discussing the Options. The more creative a person is, the more options they can generate to resolve any given difficulty. In your next conflict, *be creative!* Brainstorm as many ways as possible to deal with the situation. Start with the obvious but don't stay with safe ideas. Open the discussion to divergent directions. Consider all alternative solutions.

- Even if you've tried it before.
- Even if it sounds absurd.
- Even if it seems too hard.
- Even if it seems too easy.
- Even if you heard it doesn't work.
- Even if it frightens you.
- Even if others might not agree.

Let your only limitations be legal, moral, and safety issues. Once you have finished your list, start narrowing down the options. Rate which options each of you likes best. Evaluate the short- and long-term consequences of each option, asking yourselves:

- What might happen if we applied this option?
- How would we feel if this did happen?
- Can we live with the consequence?

Now that you have gotten this far, you are ready for resolution.

THE RESOLUTION

The positive aspects of most conflicts are not evident until the resolution phase. During the preparation phase there is often anxiety as you wonder what is going to happen. During the encounter phase, emotions reach a peak when hurt, frustration, and anger overcomes you. Now, in the resolution phase, you feel relief because the conflict is finished; excitement because reconciliation is at hand; and, hopefully, peace because you have worked through a potentially damaging situation in an honorable way. Resolution is the goal of every conflict for it is here that closure and clean-up take place. To not reach resolution is to fail in your conflict. The following three steps make sure resolution leaves a couple in better shape after a conflict than before.

Resolve to Resolve. Determine to bring a mutually acceptable closure to the situation. There are three major choices.[5]

- "I'll change."
  This is called *accommodation*.

- "I accept the fact that you won't change."
  This is called *acceptance*.

- "We will both change."
  This is called *compromise*.

If you can't make a permanent resolution, then make a temporary one. Agree that it's okay to do it this way for now, but renegotiation needs to come soon. Once you have made your resolution, no matter how temporary, decide how to implement your plan. Focus on your goal and consider its possible obstacles. Then discuss strategies to overcome these potential obstacles. Next, develop four achievable action steps that will help you reach your goals, creating a deadline for each step.

At this point, Ken Sande, in his book *The Peacemaker*, suggests you review what you have resolved by asking each other the following closure questions:

- What issues were resolved?
- What actions will be taken?
- Who is responsible for each action?
- What are the dates by which each action should be completed?
- When and how will the results of this agreement be reviewed? [6]

Answer these questions together; then follow through on your resolution, patiently and consistently taking one step at a time. Once your agreement is made, keep your word and don't complain.

Evaluate Your Fight. Once the resolution is made and the agreement understood by both, it is valuable to critique how each of you handled yourself during your encounter. Below are ten areas of evaluation.[7] Sit down together and each of you mark how you felt after your fight. There are no right or wrong answers. Just be as honest as possible.

Fight Evaluation

	YES	NO
1. Increased commitment to relationship		
2. Decreased hurt		
3. Increased understanding of mate		
4. Increased feeling of being understood		
5. Decreased fear of mate		
6. Increased trust of mate		
7. Increased respect of mate		
8. Increased self-worth		
9. Decreased tension		
10. Increased intimacy		

When the evaluation is finished, talk about how each of you marked your questions. Yes means you handled the situation in a healthy way. No means you need improvement. Note your areas of agreement when you both answered the same. Congratulate each other on the positive answers and discuss what went wrong and why, on the negative answers. Circle those areas where one marked yes and the other marked no.

These cross responses indicate different perceptions and need to be discussed. The more cross responses, the more emotionally out of touch you are with each other. Don't get defensive or discouraged at cross responses. Merely step back and look at the situation through your spouse's eyes, using their personality, definitions, history, and current emotional state. The purpose of this evaluation is not to shame or reprimand you, it is to improve your conflict style and point out possible blind spots. Use it to improve your fights and help you be more sensitive to how your actions are perceived by your spouse.

As Christians, we need to go beyond merely resolving conflict because we are called to make peace.

Make Up. When Tami and I were first married we had a running joke that we loved to have a good fight because it was so much fun to make up. Tami even claimed that at times she would fake a fight just to make up because when we made up, we really made up. It was fantastic! The bigger the fight, the greater the making up. This is the key to a good fight. First of all apologize, if appropriate, for wrong thoughts, attitudes, words, or actions. Then both initiate positive, loving behavior.

Don't wait for the other to initiate the apology. Too many times a husband or wife waits for the other to start. They will say they initiated last time, or the other didn't fight fair, or the whole fight was really their spouse's fault so their spouse needs to make up. Aren't these terribly feeble excuses? If you love each other, show it. Keeping track of who should or shouldn't initiate is silly. Grow up and make up.

Encourage each other and say nice things. Conflict can be exhausting and leave a person feeling fragile. Take care of each other. Do something fun and relaxing and enjoy your time together as you reconnect. Be gentle and compassionate. One of the best ways to end a fight is with a hug. Not a forceful, sexual, or halfhearted hug, but a genuine tender I-love-you-with-all-my-heart hug. A genuine hug is a symbol of emotional and physical reunion, and brings closure to the conflict.

Resolution is often the most difficult aspect of marriage. If you don't learn how to face conflict and deal with it, your marriage will not last. Truthfully, every couple I know that has ever divorced has done so because they could not resolve their issues. Divorce was their resolution. As Christians, we need to go beyond merely resolving conflict because we are called to make peace.

CONTEMPLATING PEACE

Most couples want peace. Resolved conflict leads to peace, but unresolved conflict leads to chaos and possible divorce. A lack of peace drives you crazy and weakens your marriage. Peace is an agreement to resolve any fight that crops up in your relationship. It is much more than the absence of conflict; it's the best of all times in your marriage. Yet peace is an illusive visitor. Life seems to move too fast. There is so much to do, to know, and to experience. I feel in a constant state of overload and I'm always one step behind. Peace seems like an alien concept; something I dream about but can rarely capture. It doesn't fit into today's techno-paced hyper-kinetic information age. On vacation we even rush away from the rush. Thankfully, there are times and places where we stumble into a peaceful moment such as a day at the seashore, a walk through a secluded forest, or a lazy afternoon on a quiet lake. Yet peace is much deeper and stronger than the place we experience it. It's a state of mind and a satisfying feeling. It's a sense of relaxation and contentment where there are no concerns.

Lately my children have been marching around the house singing "Hakuna Matata." It's a catchy little song from Walt Disney's 1994 movie *The Lion King*. The phrase means *no worries*. An aspect of peace is that you set aside your worries and enjoy life. When you are at peace you can let your guard down and be yourself. There is a tranquillity of spirit that engulfs your entire being.

Paul wrote the following in his letter to the Philippians:

Do not be anxious about anything, but in everything, by prayer and petition, with thanksgiving, present your requests to God. And the peace of God, which transcends all understanding, will guard your hearts and minds in Christ Jesus.[8]

Marriage bonds grow tougher and stronger as you work successfully through conflicts. This doesn't mean you will perfectly resolve every difference; it does mean you will try to talk them through and work on them. It also means you will fight for peace. As a couple, let peace be your goal. Strive for a peace that allows you to relax and escape the craziness of this hectic world. Make your marriage a refuge of love and peace, but realize the odds are against you. Modern narcissistic culture is a powerful undertow that threatens to sweep away your peace. To stand against this current, a couple must cling to their faith in God. This is the only source for a true and lasting peace. Jesus said:

Peace I leave with you; my peace I give you. I do not give to you as the world gives. Do not let your hearts be troubled and do not be afraid.[9]

Fear and anxiety chase away peace but faith chases away fear and anxiety. As you grow in God's peace, your relationship with each other will blossom. His inner peace will work its way throughout your life and your marriage. Conflicts will become less selfish and more gentle. Resolutions will come quicker and be more satisfying.

We all need peace and if we don't have it as individuals, we won't have it as a couple. A marriage in conflict may appear fine on the outside, but its soul is dry and in turmoil. A relationship without peace will have only temporary and superficial resolution to its inevitable conflicts.

The pastor of the church our family attends closes the Sunday morning services with the following words from the Old Testament book of Numbers:

May the Lord bless you and keep you;

may the Lord make his face to shine
upon you and be gracious to you;
may the Lord turn his face toward you
and give you peace.[10]

Discussion Questions

1. What is the last conflict (big or small) that you had with your spouse?

   Was it loud or quiet?

   Was it short or long?

2. How often do you and your partner fight?

3. Which of the following areas do the two of you conflict the most? In which do you tend to agree?

   a) Parenting
   b) Distribution of home chores
   c) Relatives and in-laws
   d) Communication styles
   e) Money management
   f) Expression of affection and sexuality
   g) Friendships outside marriage

4. When it comes to conflict, are you a turtle or a shark?

   Which is your mate?

5. Have you and your spouse ever prayed before a fight?

   What impact did it have on your attitudes?

6. Which one of the four irrational beliefs are you prone to engage in?

   a) I must get what I want to be happy.
   b) Things have to go right.
   c) I must be in control or something bad will happen.
   d) I cannot change.

7. What was the worst time and place for you to discuss a difficult issue?

   What was the worst time and place for your partner?

8. Thinking back on your relationship, try to describe an example of each of the following:

   a) A difference   c) A predicament
   b) A problem   d) A crisis

9. What three fight rules would you like to adopt in order to make your conflicts more positive?

   a)
   b)
   c)

10. Which type of resolution happens the most frequently in your conflicts?

    a) Accommodation (I'll change.)
    b) Acceptance (I'll accept the fact you won't change.)
    c) Compromise (We will both change.)

    How do you feel about this pattern?

11. On a scale from 1 to 10 (1 = positive, 10 = negative) how well do the two of you handle and resolve conflicts?

Notes

1. Matthew 5:9.
2. Proverbs 19:13.
3. Proverbs 27:17.
4. Paul Weller, *How to Help a Friend* (Wheaton, Ill.: Tyndale House, 1978), 51-71. These difficulties are a modified version of Dr. Weller's work which is *Problem, Predicament, Crisis, and Shock.*
5. Charles M. Sell, *Achieving the Impossible: Intimate Marriage* (Portland, Ore: Multnomah Press, 1982), 128-9.
6. Ken Sande, *The Peacemaker: A Biblical Guide to Resolving Personal Conflict* (Grand Rapids: Baker, 1992), 193 (Adaptation mine).
7. George R. Bach and Peter Wyden, *The Intimate Enemy: How to Fight Fair in Love and Marriage* (New York: Harper, 1974), 19. Comments are loosely based on the concepts presented in their book.
8. Philippians 4:6-7.
9. John 14:27.
10. Numbers 6:24-26 (author's paraphrase).

6

FORGIVENESS

Early one morning a stranger walked into Joseph K.'s house and arrested him. Subsequently he was taken to a courtroom and put on trial. Throughout the proceedings, Joseph K. repeatedly tried to find out what the accusations toward him were, but nobody would tell him. Ultimately, he was found guilty on the evening before his thirty-first birthday. Around nine o'clock, Joseph K. was taken to an abandoned gravel pit outside of town and executed.[1]

The Trial by Franz Kafka is a strange novel but its message is clear: We are all guilty and deserve punishment. This is also the message of our Christian faith that says, "All have sinned and fall short of the glory of God."[2] *The Trial* ends with hopelessness, but the Bible offers hope founded on forgiveness.

In marriage, we are all guilty of wounding our mate and for that we deserve punishment. Without forgiveness our relationship sinks into a sea of hurt and guilt. Hurt undermines your marriage but forgiveness shores it up again. Without forgiveness the relationship dies.

WHAT IS FORGIVENESS?

The argument was intense and Mark spoke without thinking. As soon as he opened his mouth he knew he had gone too far, but the words were out and he couldn't take them back. Cindy's face went pale and tears pooled in her eyes. She stood in silence unable to believe what she had just heard. As she reeled from the pain of the remark, her heart stung, not only from the words, but that they came from someone she trusted not to hurt her. She withdrew, unable to remain in the presence of her new husband. She felt betrayed. Mark also withdrew, driven back by shame and embarrassment, amazed that such hurtful words could come from him. Alone in separate corners of their small apartment, they both wondered whether the relationship would ever be the same.

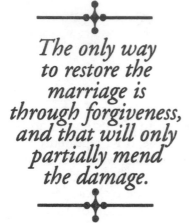

The only way to restore the marriage is through forgiveness, and that will only partially mend the damage.

When we hurt our partner, the relationship changes. A wounded heart and a broken trust test a marriage. The only way to restore the marriage is through forgiveness, and that will only partially mend the damage. Forgiveness and time may heal the pain, but there are always scars. Some scars are hardly noticeable whereas others are so deep they may never fade. Without forgiveness we are trapped, but to activate forgiveness we must understand what it is and what it is not.

IT IS NOT IGNORING

Some think forgiveness means closing your eyes to an injury and pretending you don't hurt. The philosophy is that if you don't think about it, the pain will magically disappear. In reality just the opposite is true; to ignore a hurt allows it to fester and grow the same way the thumb infection did in the last chapter. The longer it is ignored, the redder and more painful it becomes.

George and Elaine came to my office after being married thirty-eight years. They said if I couldn't fix their relationship they would go straight to a divorce attorney. When I asked how long they had struggled with a particular problem, they both agreed that it began thirty-eight years ago on their honeymoon.

"Why have you waited so long to deal with this hurt?" I asked.

"I thought if I ignored it, it would go away," said Elaine. "But I guess I was wrong because it's just gotten bigger and bigger over the years."

If we hurt, we hurt. Wishing it away doesn't work. In fact, when we don't confront the pain, our partner may not realize what they have done and continue to repeat the painful act. Forgiveness requires confrontation, not ignoring.

IT IS NOT EXCUSING

Excusing and making excuses are two different things. Excusing says, "That's okay, it's not that big of a deal," or "What you did wasn't really wrong." It minimizes the pain and doesn't allow the offender to see the seriousness of their actions; therefore, it has the same effect as ignoring. The offender might continue repeating the painful act and be oblivious to the damage being done.

Making excuses tries to reduce or eliminate the offense by providing more data: "I didn't mean it," "It was an accident," "Everybody talks that way," or "I came from a dysfunctional family and I'm simply doing it the only way I know how." All of the above might be true, but it doesn't take away the offense. There are explanations but there are no excuses.

We need to have some understanding of the why's, but a hurt is still a hurt. It may not have been intentional but the pain is the same. Years ago a Greek philosopher wrote, "The boys threw stones at the frogs in play; but the frogs did not die in play, they died in earnest."

Excusing is the opposite of forgiving. We excuse others when they are not guilty, but when people hurt us they are guilty. They need to take responsibility for their actions whether or not they were intentional. Forgiving is saying, "What you did was wrong, regardless of the how's and why's, but God forgave me so I will forgive you." An excuse leaves one with their guilt whereas forgiveness can remove guilt and allow a couple to grow in spite of it.

IT IS NOT FORGETTING

Forgiving someone does not require forgetting the hurtful act. Actually, forgetting is sometimes impossible. Our brain is like a computer. Whatever happens to us is stored in our memory and will always be with us in some form. There are at least two ways of remembering: reliving or recalling.

To relive a memory, the hurt is so vivid that it still affects us and our relationship with our spouse. Even if the hurt occurred twenty or thirty years ago, it feels as if the pain just happened. It eats away at us and controls us by keeping us up at night, affecting our health, and preoccupying our mind.

To recall a memory, the hurt is simply a fact of history. It is a part of who we are, but it is resolved and belongs to the past. It no longer controls us or blocks our relationship with the one we love.

Forgiveness asks us to face our hurt and not let it control us. We may not be able to forget the pain, but we don't need to relive it. Forgetting would be nice, but it isn't a requirement for forgiveness to be genuine. In a way, forgetting may cheapen our forgiveness, for to forgive as we remember our pain makes it a more difficult task and, therefore, a more valuable gift. Yet it is easier to forget after we forgive. Over time, with God's help, the details get blurry and the pain fades into the background. Forgiveness doesn't mean you have forgotten the hurt, it simply means you have chosen not to focus on it. We remember what happened, but our relationship is more important than clinging to our hurt.

IT IS A DECISION

Forgiveness is a decision based on reality and love. Reality deals with the hurt honestly and directly; it refuses to ignore, excuse, or forget. Love stares at the hurt and is willing to trust again, even though trust has been broken. It risks being hurt once more in order for the relationship to grow. This is why some say that forgiveness is love's toughest work.

> *Love stares at the hurt and is willing to trust again, even though trust has been broken. It risks being hurt once more in order for the relationship to grow.*

Life is full of hurts. Every day, in a hundred random and thoughtless ways, people who claim to love each other inflict pain on one another. To love one another you must risk getting hurt.[3]

There are at least six types of hurt; three are considered minor offenses and three major. We will deal with the three minor offenses first.

Annoyances. These are the smallest of the hurts. Some call them irritations, others simply call them bad habits. I drive my wife crazy by using the remote control to check every channel on the television set. She annoys me by stretching a simple short story into a full-length novel. We all have frustrating behaviors that our partners would do almost anything to change, but if we take every annoyance and turn it into a battle, our relationship becomes a war zone. One spouse is constantly hurt and the other is afraid to say or do anything for fear of making the situation worse.

Slights. These are words or actions that make us feel ignored, forgotten, or simply not important. They are usually unintentional and should not be taken personally. Yet we all have times when we are hypersensitive. We know things shouldn't bother us but they do. At such moments my mother will say, "Don't get your nose out of joint." I sometimes feel slighted when Tami forgets something that was important to me, or spends more time with the children than with me. Slights are more often reminders of our own insecurities than indicators of our partner's wrongdoing. It's best to shrug off a slight.

Disappointments. Years ago I saw a poster that read, "Blessed are those with no expectations, for they shall not be disappointed." The poster was correct, but we all have expectations; some are realistic and fair and some are not. When we marry our spouse we have special expectations of them. These expectations come from our family of origin, our culture, our faith, and numerous other places. It is not possible for our partner to meet all our expectations, just as there is no way we can meet all of theirs. As a result, we both feel disappointed, let down, and cheated. Often a person isn't aware how important a specific expectation is to their partner. If we clearly

> *We all have tender areas where a minor offense can pierce to the heart and become a major hurt.*

communicate our expectations there are usually fewer disappointments.

These three hurts are minor offenses. The offender should seek
forgiveness, but the offended should forgive whether asked or
not. However, if these are repeated (especially on a regular basis)
they can quickly become a major offense.

An annoyance that's identified as especially bothersome, yet is
continued without regard to the spouse's wishes, soon becomes
something greater. A persistent slight or a stubborn disappointment where the offender is cavalier or insensitive about their
partner's feelings can exaggerate the size of the hurt. We all have
tender areas where a minor offense can pierce to the heart and
become a major hurt. Now let's examine the three major hurts.

Disloyalties. Psychologists love surveys and I'm no exception. I
asked a hundred people to define disloyalty. They came up with
three interlocking concepts.

- Being false to one's word.

- Being faithless to one's commitment.

- Failing to defend, protect, honor, and cherish one's mate.

In Psalm 78 the poet describes disloyalty as being "as unreli-
able as a faulty bow."[4] Disloyalty is passive; it is not doing something we should have done. We had an opportunity to demonstrate our love and commitment to our spouse but we did nothing. This is not forgetting, it is choosing to act as if our partner is
unimportant. It is treating our mate as if they are a stranger. The
apostle Peter said he loved Jesus, but when put to the test he
acted as if he didn't even know him.[5]

We are disloyal when we break a promise, speak disrespectfully,
let other things or people take priority over our love, or simply
ignore that our commitment is total and timeless.

Betrayals. These are more painful than disloyalties. Betrayal is
active. It is from a Latin word that means *to give over to the enemy.*
It is an action planned and premeditated out of anger, greed,

selfishness, or lust. We betray our spouse when we set out to do something we know will hurt them. Judas betrayed Jesus for thirty pieces of silver. His own desires were more important than his relationship with Jesus.

A betrayal involves treating our spouse as an enemy. It happens when we either try to hurt them, or don't care if we hurt them. Betrayals leave our partner in shock. They shatter trust and create a desire to escape. The marriage is no longer safe and the victim wonders whether it will ever be safe again.

Cruelties. These are the most painful of all hurts because there is a brutality and violence about them. They take place when we assault, attack, or abuse our partner. Cruelties are not just blackened eyes or broken noses; they can be degrading insults, forced sex, or severe intimidation.

Someone once said, "We are to love people and use things, but in this mixed-up world we use people and love things." We are cruel when we treat our partner as an object, something to be used, then discarded. There are four arenas of cruelty:

1. **The Physical Arena.** When we hit, slap, push, bite, scratch, or in any way do bodily damage to our partner.

2. **The Verbal Arena.** When we use words, tone of voice, or volume to inflict pain.

3. **The Emotional Arena.** When we use humiliation, intimidation, and/or manipulation to harm our spouse.

4. **The Sexual Arena.** When we attempt to force, overpower, or manipulate our spouse into sexual activities that they do not desire.

Cruelties are the most difficult to forgive. The Jewish leaders who ordered Jesus to be beaten and crucified were cruel. Yet even in the midst of this brutality Jesus looked down from his cross and prayed, "Father forgive them; for they know not what they do."[6] With God's help even a forgiveness that feels impossible can be given.

Forgiveness is a decision to let go of these six types of hurt.

One does not pretend they don't hurt, that the wrong doesn't matter, or that it is easily forgotten. Forgiveness looks through the hurt and chooses to give love instead of hatred; patience instead of punishment; understanding instead of anger and revenge. It is a decision to look forward instead of back. Ken Sande, author of *The Peacemaker* writes that letting go involves four promises.

- "I will no longer dwell on this incident."

- "I will not bring up this incident again and use it against you."

- "I will not talk to others about this incident."

- "I will not allow this incident to stand between us or hinder our relationship."[7]

These promises do not come easily, but without them we are trapped by our pain. Forgiveness brings a husband and wife back together as friends rather than as enemies. We need each other's forgiveness. We need each other's love and acceptance. We need each other.

GRANTING FORGIVENESS

Forgiving allows us to grow beyond our pain and closer to one another. This is difficult sometimes because God has made each one of us different. Some of us are Teflon people—hurts just don't stick and forgiveness comes easily. Others of us are sponge people—hurts soak in deep and forgiveness takes time. These differences are neither good nor bad, but they can lead to difficulties. Two common problems are forgiving too quickly and forgiving too slowly.

GRANTING TOO QUICKLY

On the surface, to forgive quickly seems positive and even admirable; however, speed can result in a forgiveness that is not genuine. Remember, forgiveness involves facing the reality of a hurt and choosing to love.

Sometimes we forgive quickly just to get it behind us. We yearn for reconciliation and rush past our pain in order to heal the relationship. But it's a superficial healing—similar to placing a Band-Aid on a wound without properly cleaning out the infection. Three reasons we might forgive too quickly are as follows:

Fear. We are afraid if we don't forgive quickly our partner might become angry, even reject or abandon us. So we sweep our hurt beneath the carpet and get back to normal as quickly as possible.

Loneliness. We can't stand the distance that is caused by the hurt, so we are willing to do anything to have everything the way it used to be. We ignore the pain and embrace our partner.

Propriety. We want to do the right thing and be a good person, so we move quickly. We know that forgiveness is important; therefore, we assume the faster we give it the better.

GRANTING TOO SLOWLY

Sometimes our forgiveness is blocked and we can't move forward. An obstacle appears too great; even if we want to forgive it seems impossible. Yet each of the following six obstacles can be overcome. They are the blocks to forgiveness:

Pain. The more we trust, and the deeper we're hurt, the more difficult it is to forgive. Sometimes the hurt feels too great. We never thought someone we trusted so much could hurt us this way. The pain overwhelms us and it feels unforgivable.

Fear. Great pain produces great fear. Sometimes we think we can never trust our mate again. We say to ourselves, "If I forgive it will happen again." Therefore, our fear creates distance and that distance is our protection.

Anger/Revenge. Hurt turns into anger and anger can easily turn into revenge. They hurt us and we want them to suffer. I know a wife who cut her hair against her husband's wishes. The next day he shaved his head against her wishes. Tit for tat.

The ultimate goal to healthy forgiveness is bridging the chasm of hurt so the two sides can come together again.

Justice. Sometimes the way our mate treats us seems so unfair. We don't deserve to be treated that way. We have a hard time forgiving until we see that they have changed their ways.

Expectations. We all have expectations of our partner. We want them to come to us, acknowledge our pain, understand how deeply they hurt us, or make some form of restitution. These are all reasonable expectations but they don't always happen. Sometimes we need to let go of what is reasonable and forgive anyway.

Depression. Hurt and anger held inside turns into depression. We say to ourselves that we must be worthless or unimportant for them to treat us that way.

JUST RIGHT

Somewhere between forgiving too quickly and forgiving too slowly is the "just right" category. This is where we take the hurt seriously without becoming stuck. The ultimate goal to healthy forgiveness is bridging the chasm of hurt so the two sides can come together again. There are five steps to this sort of forgiveness.

Admit Your Hurt. Be honest and don't minimize the pain; also be realistic and don't exaggerate the situation. What exactly was the hurt? Walter Wangerin, Jr. writes, "When the heart is hurt, the eyes are blurred by tears, and the world itself is distorted."[8] Sometimes an annoyance can feel like a disloyalty, or a slight as a betrayal. Something that has happened once or twice feels as if it always happens and a single hurtful act becomes a character trait.

Exaggerations help us feel more justified in our pain; it makes our mate more guilty. Love sees the best in our spouse. It admits the hurt without imagining the worst. It also admits whatever role, big or small, we might have had in the hurt. Did we, in any way, contribute to or antagonize our own hurt?

Remember how God has forgiven you. That alone should motivate all who consider themselves Christians to forgive.

Confront Your Partner. Whether you go to your partner or they come to you, it's important to confront them with your pain. Be open and direct without attacking. Don't let your partner dismiss, deny, or minimize the hurt. Stand your ground, calmly expressing your perspective and feelings. They need to know they hurt you and that the hurt was deep. When finished, carefully listen to their perspective and feelings. They will undoubtedly add to the picture and even though this might not reduce the pain, it might make it easier to forgive. Try to understand why the situation happened. It's easy to jump to conclusions, but what we see on the surface is usually only a small portion of the picture. The deeper we dig the better we understand. An old French proverb says, "To understand all is to forgive all."

State Your Forgiveness. If you do not forgive, why should your mate forgive you? Just as your spouse has hurt you, so you have hurt them. This time they need your forgiveness, but next time you might need theirs. We all need forgiveness. Remember how God has forgiven you. That alone should motivate all who consider themselves Christians to forgive. Yet sometimes forgiveness feels impossible and we don't know how to override those feelings. These are times we must allow God to forgive through us.

In *The Hiding Place* Corrie ten Boom writes about being imprisoned in Nazi concentration camps during World War II. Her father and sister, Betsie, died in these camps, but Corrie lived and learned to forgive:

It was at a church service in Munich that I saw him, the former S.S. man who had stood guard at the shower room door in the processing center at Ravensbruck....

He came up to me as the church was emptying, beaming and bowing. "How grateful I am for your message, Fraulein," he said. "To think that, as you say, he has washed my sins away!"

His hand was thrust out to shake mine....

I tried to smile, I struggled to raise my hand. I could not. I felt nothing, not the slightest spark of warmth or charity.... Jesus, I cannot forgive him. Give me Your forgiveness.

As I took his hand the most incredible thing happened. From my shoulder along my arm and through my hand a current seemed to pass from me to him, while into my heart sprang a love for this stranger that almost overwhelmed me.

So I discovered that it is not on our forgiveness any more than on our goodness that the world's healing hinges, but on him. When he tells us to love our enemies, he gives, along with the command, the love itself.[9]

Let Go. When we are hurt, ultimately, one of three things happens: we blow up, hold in, or let go.

When we blow up we feel immediate relief, but we can easily do long-term damage to our marriage. The following actions are associated with blowing up:

- Yelling
- Screaming
- Violence
- Gossip
- Abusing

- Revenge
- Sarcasm
- Humiliation
- Attacking
- Profanity

When we hold in we stuff our anger and potentially poison our physical, mental, and spiritual health. By holding in we sometimes hide our anger from both ourselves and our spouse. These actions are associated with holding in or stuffing:

- Withdrawal
- Hatred
- Anxiety
- Resentment
- Depression

- Silence
- Disgust
- Bitterness
- Rumination
- Grudges

The best way to deal with hurt and anger is to let go. This means we release our anger and refuse to allow it to control us. One way of letting go is by focusing on the positives in our spouse. In that classic passage in Philippians it is written, "Finally, brothers, whatever is true, whatever is noble, whatever is right, whatever is pure, whatever is lovely, whatever is admirable—if anything is excellent or praiseworthy—think about such things."[10] Practicing these positives keeps us from holding onto our hurt and anger. In doing this we redirect our focus and are able to truly let go. Thus, we can move on to the final step of healthy forgiveness.

Reconcile. The previous four steps pave the road to reconciliation. Without those four steps, the step of reconciliation cannot happen. To reconcile means to come together again and make the relationship right. There may still be scars and consequences, but the focus is on the future rather than the past.

Reconciliation is a process that takes time, energy, and direction. The direction involves an agreement to work on the following:

- Renew our trust.
- Restore our love.
- Recommit our vows.
- Re-establish our togetherness.

These four tasks are not easy, but with them come a healing and rebirth of the relationship.

Late one afternoon Denise received an anonymous phone call from a distraught woman.

"I just have to tell you that I've been having an affair with your husband for the past three years and I can't deal with the guilt anymore."

Denise was stunned. She thought her marriage would never survive this crisis. At best, she thought it would be a damaged relationship that would limp along, intact, but never fully satisfying. Yet with God's help she learned to admit, confront, forgive, let go, and reconcile. The process took over three years, but now she says that her marriage is deeper, stronger, and better than it ever was before. Denise is in love again and she is glad she forgave.

Unfortunately, not every story has a happy ending. There are times when we forgive, but the offense doesn't stop or the offender doesn't act remorseful. There are also times when we have to protect ourselves and forgiveness must be granted from a distance. There are still other times when the trust is too badly broken and the heart too deeply wounded for a couple to fully reconcile. Remember the four A's?

1. Abandonment
2. Abuse
3. Addictions
4. Adultery

Nevertheless, whether a spouse stays or separates, forgiveness is possible. It's harder doing it alone, but God can always do it through us.

Granting forgiveness is a step into the world of mercy. It is giving a spouse something they don't deserve. They have hurt you and they deserve anger and punishment, sharp words and silence. They deserve a little of their own medicine—an eye for an eye, a tooth for a tooth. But no, you surprise them with mercy. They give you pain and you give them love.

When Jesus was asked how many times one should forgive, he said, "I do not say to you, up to seven times, but up to seventy times seven."[11] We say to ourselves, "That is too many. Maybe I can forgive once or twice, but if my partner continues...." So we ask again, "How many times should I forgive?" The answer is the same—seventy times seven. We hang our heads. We have our limits. There is only so much one person can take. Why should we have to put up with this? Then we remember all the times God has forgiven us. When we add it all up, the sum equals something in the ballpark of seventy times seven.

SEEKING FORGIVENESS

Seeking forgiveness is difficult for some of us. It involves admitting we have failed and are accepting responsibility for our failure. President Harry Truman had a plaque on his desk that read, "The buck stops here." He was willing to swallow his pride and accept responsibility.

These days nobody wants to accept responsibility. Seeking forgiveness is not popular. It takes maturity and sometimes we aren't mature enough to own up to what we have done, even if we did it unwittingly.

Many of us, especially men, get defensive and make all sorts of excuses. Our defensiveness keeps us from seeing the truth, traps us in our own self-protectiveness, and dishonors our partner. Worse than all of that, it keeps us from being forgiven. Seeking forgiveness is similar to granting forgiveness in that it faces the same two dangers—seeking too quickly or too slowly.

SEEKING TOO QUICKLY

Seeking forgiveness too quickly may seem noble and good. Some might even say the faster one is forgiven the better, but things done quickly may not be done properly. If we absent-mindedly say we are sorry and move on as if we never have hurt our mate, then we are insensitive and superficial. Forgiveness must be sought with sincerity and vulnerability.

We ask forgiveness too quickly when we focus more on our comfort than our partner's pain. Asking involves deferring to the other. Our partner doesn't have to forgive us. Also, they may not be ready to forgive when we first seek their forgiveness. We must be careful not to be selfish in our asking. Our request must be based on honestly facing our action and genuinely regretting what we have done. To seek forgiveness too quickly is to ask without thinking through the ramifications and consequences of our behavior. Feeling their hurt will soften our heart. Racing past their feelings does not allow us to absorb their pain. We forgive too quickly when our main goal is to:

Get It Over. We wish life would return to the way it was before the hurt and we want it to happen as soon as possible. The wall between us and our partner is inconvenient and uncomfortable. If they need an apology, we'll apologize—anything to make the relationship right again. Whether or not we see our wrong is not our primary concern. Our concern is getting life back to normal, to bandage the hurt, to quench the anger—not because we take

Guilt is not a bad or shaming emotion. It is the recognition that we live in a moral universe where there are rights and wrongs.

responsibility for it, but because it is bothersome.

Erase Guilt. Our guilt makes us feel bad and drives us to seek forgiveness. We wish to feel good and forget our offense, but we can't absolve ourselves. We need our partner to forgive us for the hurts we have caused. We recognize what we have done and we may even take responsibility for it, but we seek forgiveness for personal reasons. We are focused on *our* pain, not our partner's. We seek forgiveness through selfish eyes; thus, we lack the ability to feel our partner's hurt. Our quickness has not provided the necessary time to feel deep remorse and contemplate full repentance. It is a hollow apology.

SEEKING TOO SLOWLY

Why do we avoid seeking forgiveness when it's so critical to a healthy relationship? We all need forgiveness but we take so long to claim it. There are many blocks to asking forgiveness, but each block contains some combination of pride, ignorance, and insensitivity. Five of the most common blocks are as follows:

Denying. I didn't do anything wrong. There is really no problem here. My partner is just having a hard day; everything is really okay.

Ignoring. I know I hurt my mate, but if I pretend the hurt doesn't exist it may go away. I will simply not acknowledge the problem and hope my spouse will forget it ever happened.

Minimizing. What I did wasn't really that big. Maybe it was an annoyance or a slight, but certainly nothing more than that. My spouse wears her heart on her sleeve—she's always been hypersensitive. She should be able to just drop it and move on with life.

Blaming. It wasn't my fault. It was the neighbor's fault, the government's fault, the in-laws' fault, my parents' fault, God's fault, everybody else's fault, but it certainly wasn't my fault.

The 40/60 Rule. I admit that I'm partially responsible for this situation. In fact, I might even be forty percent responsible, but sixty percent of the fault belongs to my spouse. That means he is more to blame than I am, so he should come to me seeking forgiveness.[12]

JUST RIGHT

Seeking forgiveness is just as important as granting forgiveness. In marriage we need to do both frequently. The following steps should be helpful.

Acknowledge Your Guilt. We must face what we have done, whether we did it on purpose or accidentally. It is easy to justify our words and deeds, but when we do wrong we are guilty. Employing strategies to manipulate around the guilt does not eliminate it. Guilt is not a bad or shaming emotion. It is the recognition that we live in a moral universe where there are rights and wrongs. Hurting our partner is wrong. To think otherwise diminishes the relationship.

There are two ways of dealing with guilt. Either we change our value system, making our behavior acceptable, or we change our behavior. The most sincere change in behavior involves remorse and repentance. Remorse is feeling regret and sorrow for what we have done. We recognize the hurt on our spouse's face and it brings us pain.

Repentance is more cognitive. It means to come to our senses

> *You asked for forgiveness because you needed to ask; not to strong arm or manipulate them into giving it to you. Your job is to ask, whether this means getting it or not.*

173

and change the way we think. We have offended both God and our mate. Admitting that to ourselves is the first step to seeking forgiveness. As we feel our guilt, which leads to remorse and repentance, we humble ourselves before God and ask his forgiveness. In making things right with God, we clear the way to making things right with our spouse.

Confess Your Wrongs. The first step was largely an internal process, but this step is mostly external. It involves finding the right time and place to go to your mate privately when no other person or distraction can interrupt. Go to them humbly and state your wrongdoing. Be specific and complete. Tell them why your actions and words were wrong. Then go one step further and confess any sinful attitude that might have contributed to your behavior: pride, selfishness, ingratitude, jealousy, bitterness, laziness, resentment, insensitivity, self-righteousness, dishonesty, or stubbornness. Now pay attention because the next four words are very important. *Acknowledge your partner's pain.* It is amazing how this alone can reopen a closed heart.

Next, apologize for causing their hurt and don't make excuses. Excuses minimize the other person's hurt. Instead, express genuine sorrow and regret for hurting them. Share how you wish you had handled the situation differently, and how you plan to change so you will not repeat your offense.

Ask Forgiveness. This goes beyond simply saying you are sorry, which admits that what you did was not right. It is humbling yourself and asking, "Will you forgive me?" This shifts the emphasis to the other person. It publicly communicates your own guilt and gives your partner power. With these words you take responsibility for your actions and submit yourself to your spouse's mercy. It risks being open and vulnerable, admitting you have failed and are not perfect. This simple question is a vital act of humility, responsibility, and vulnerability.

There is a critical warning at this point. Do not pressure your spouse for immediate forgiveness. In fact, don't expect it. You asked for forgiveness because you needed to ask; not to strong arm or manipulate them into giving it to you. Your job is to ask, whether this means getting it or not. Some people can grant forgiveness easily and others need time to work through their thoughts and feelings. You may have asked with sensitivity and sincerity, but your partner may simply not be ready to forgive. Be patient and pray for them.

Change Your Behavior. The old saying is irritatingly true. Actions do speak louder than words. Sometimes our intentions are so good and our promises sound so sweet, but our follow-through is sorely lacking. Our actions should demonstrate the sincerity of our remorse and repentance. Our partner is waiting and watching to determine whether or not we are true to our word. A change is expected and needed. Without it, we are liars. With it, we regain our partner's trust and prove we are trustworthy. To change anything, at least four components are necessary:

- Make a plan. Keep it simple, realistic, positive, specific, and measurable.
- Start now.
- Be accountable to someone you respect who will be tough on you if that's what it takes.
- Lean on God.

Make Restitution. Once you have hurt your mate you can never totally erase that hurt; but you can provide a token of your love that shows you understand the seriousness of your act. As a wedding ring is a symbol of love and commitment, so restitution is a symbol of remorse and repentance. Restitution says, "I owe you more than I can ever pay. Thank you for your forgiveness. Please allow me to give you something in gratitude for your mercy."

Determining what to give is often awkward. Be careful about asking your partner for suggestions. They might suggest something you aren't ready to give, and your reluctance might be perceived as minimizing your offense. Give from your heart, but remember that this gift should cost you something. If it is too small, your spouse might be offended thinking you take your offense lightly. On the other hand, it should not be overwhelming. If it is too great, they might be embarrassed or think you simply want to buy them off. The third danger is if you offer nothing at all they might question the sincerity of your forgiveness. Simply put, be balanced in your giving.

More will be presented on the art of giving in the next chapter.

Forgive Yourself. We all blow it. We are all imperfect and in need of forgiveness. This does not justify our hurtful words or deeds; it is simply a fact. To think that our sins are unforgivable shows either arrogance or lack of faith. The apostle Paul writes, "There is no one righteous, not even one."[13] Later he writes that God "forgave us all our sins."[14] If God forgives us, we need to forgive ourselves. Yet there are situations when that is very difficult.

- When the pain was caused by ignorance, irresponsibility, or maliciousness.

- When the person wronged is extremely hurt or angry.

- When the hurt was sexual, physical, financial, or social.

- When our spouse cannot or will not grant forgiveness.

These situations often make it more difficult to forgive ourselves; but regardless of what we have done, God will forgive us if we seek his forgiveness. All we have to do is ask with a humble heart. Yet even when God has forgiven us, there are times we cannot forgive ourselves.

If you feel stuck, ask yourself:

- Do I recognize the wrong in what I have done?

- Do I feel sorrow for what I have done?

- Have I approached my partner and apologized?

- Have I asked forgiveness?

- Am I making a sincere effort not to repeat my wrong?

- Have I made adequate restitution?

We have all done things we wish we could forget—things we wish we had never done. Repentance is not forever beating ourselves for past actions. Forgiving ourselves is letting go of the past. If we don't, it haunts us the rest of our lives.

Years ago someone told me an old story about Sir Arthur Conan Doyle, author of the Sherlock Holmes mysteries. They said that Doyle was quite a prankster and on a foggy London night he thought of a rather mischievous prank. He sent telegrams to five or six of the most influential people in the city and each message read the same:

I'VE DISCOVERED ALL STOP FLEE LONDON IMMEDIATELY OR EVERYTHING WILL BE PRINTED IN TOMORROW MORNING'S NEWSPAPER STOP

Early the next morning Doyle set out to visit the individuals who had received his telegram. None of them were home, for during the night each person had mysteriously slipped away from the city.

To be forgiven you must seek forgiveness from God, your mate, and yourself. God will always forgive and your mate will sometimes forgive; but in order to forgive yourself, you must seek forgiveness from both God and your mate every time.

Seeking forgiveness opens the door to freedom and togetherness. If you don't seek you may not be forgiven, and you could become trapped in your guilt—a guilt that grows over time and ultimately can destroy you. The antidote to guilt is forgiveness. Without the antidote, guilt will grow and undermine relationships, health, and possibly even sanity.

Mary had held her secret eight years and finally couldn't stand it any longer. She'd had an affair with her husband's best friend, gotten pregnant, and had an abortion. She was strongly pro-life but believed that if her husband discovered the pregnancy it would end the marriage. So she ignored her beliefs and tried to hide the evidence of her unfaithfulness.

> *If you don't seek you may not be forgiven, and you could become trapped in your guilt—a guilt that grows over time and can ultimately destroy you.*

For eight years her broken vows and unborn child haunted her. She avoided her husband and was distant from her children. The shame was intense and the self-hatred overwhelming. The guilt ate at her until she broke.

When I first saw Mary she was in the psychiatric unit of a local hospital, banging her head on the floor and crying, "Stop it, please stop it."

"What do you want to stop?" I asked.

"The heart. Can't you hear it? It keeps pounding, pounding, pounding. My baby's dead, but his heart won't let me sleep."

She went on to tell me her story and that she could hear her baby's heart everywhere she went. As we talked I suggested she seek forgiveness from her husband. Mary paled and said he would kill her.

During the next year Mary faced her actions and guilt and found God's forgiveness. As she grew healthier, she was released from the hospital and returned home to her husband.

Forgiveness is taking out the garbage. If we don't grant and seek forgiveness on a daily basis, it starts smelling up our entire marriage.

It was on a warm August night that she finally told her husband about her unfaithfulness and the baby she aborted. The words cut deep and the pain caused him to tremble. He reached out to her, held her close, and together they wept.

"Of course, I forgive you," his voice broke. "I still love you. I just wish you hadn't gone through eight years of torment because you were afraid to come to me."

It took time, but the relationship and the hurts were healed. Mary and her family still feel the scars of those eight lost years, but the craziness is gone because forgiveness was sought and granted. Now the relationship can grow again.

WHY IS THIS SO IMPORTANT?

Forgiveness is our only escape from the trap of our guilt. Without it we shrivel and die, both as individuals and as a couple. With it we feel the freedom to draw close and love again. Forgiveness forces us to face our humanity and see how broken we are. At times we all wound and are wounded. We wound others out of human weakness and sin. We wound because we have been wounded by our spouse, our parents, or others. C. S. Lewis said "we live in a broken world" and I must agree.

As we forgive our mate and they forgive us, we reflect God's forgiveness. If we don't forgive our spouse, why should they forgive us? Or more significantly, why should God forgive us?

Forgiveness is love in action. It raises the questions:

- How big is your love?
- How much can it forgive?
- What are its limits?

Without forgiveness a relationship is doomed. A couple may stay married, but their relationship becomes one of tolerance or torture, rather than one of joy. In his book *Forgive and Forget* Lewis B. Smedes said, "When we forgive we ride the crest of love's cosmic wave; we walk in stride with God."[15] I'll take this one step further and say, to walk with God, one must forgive.

Unforgiveness stymies your marriage. Gifts become meaningless, togetherness a fruitless effort, romance a sham, and ministry difficult. The team is broken and the marriage is dead.

Forgiveness renews your original commitment to love one another for better or worse. It is a coming together after the injury. For when our partner hurts us, or vice versa, the pain becomes a wall between us. Ultimately, forgiveness removes the wall allowing us to come together again. The marriage gets a second chance and this time, with God's help, we will do better. Forgiveness provides hope and a chance to experience the reality of grace.

TAKE OUT YOUR GARBAGE

In the late 1960s folk singer, Arlo Guthrie, wrote a song entitled "Alice's Restaurant." It tells the story of Alice who lives in the upstairs of an abandoned church. Alice decides that since the sanctuary isn't being used, she won't take her garbage out any-more—she'll just dump it downstairs. However, a year later, the garbage has grown and it stinks up the whole church.

Forgiveness is taking out the garbage. If we don't grant and seek forgiveness on a daily basis, it starts smelling up our entire marriage. Every day we injure each other. The majority of these are minor offenses, but what is minor to us may not be minor to our spouse. Even minor offenses, when multiplied over months or years, can accumulate into a giant mess.

Some of us have saved our garbage and it's piling up in our marriage. Old hurts have not been taken care of, and when we get too close to our partner we have to hold our nose. The moral is simple: If you want a sweet-smelling relationship, take out the garbage.

Discussion Questions

1. When your partner hurts you, do you:

   a) Ignore it?
   b) Excuse it?
   c) Forget it?
   d) Work through it?

2. Give an example of each of the following from your marriage.

   a) An annoyance
   b) A slight
   c) A disappointment

   How did you handle each one?

3. How would you define being disloyal to your mate?

   What does it look like in a marital relationship?

4. Betrayals and cruelties between spouses are frequently very difficult to talk about. What impact do such acts have on a marriage? Be specific.

5. Which of the following four promises is easiest for you to keep?

   a) I will no longer dwell on this incident.
   b) I will not bring up this incident and use it against you.
   c) I will not talk to others about this incident.
   d) I will not allow this incident to stand between us or hinder our relationship.

   Which is the most difficult? Why?

6. Are you more likely to forgive too quickly or too slowly? Why?

7. When is it most difficult to do the following:

   a) Admit your hurt?
   b) Confront your partner?
   c) State your forgiveness?
   d) Let go?
   e) Reconcile?

   When are these most difficult for your partner?

8. When was the last time you asked your partner to forgive you? Describe the situation?

9. When you know you have hurt or offended your mate, on a scale from 1 to 10 (1 = all the time, 10 = not at all) how would you rate your tendency to change your behavior?

   Are these changes easy or difficult for you?

   What motivates you to make these changes?

10. Is it easier for you to forgive your spouse or to ask them to forgive you? Why?

Notes

1. Franz Kafka, *The Trial* (New York: Knopf, 1937).

2. Romans 3:23.

3. Lewis B. Smedes, *Forgive and Forget: Healing the Hurts We Don't Deserve* (New York: Pocket Books, 1984), 31-37.

4. Psalm 78:57.

5. Matthew 26:69-75.

6. Luke 23:34, KJV

7. Ken Sande, *The Peacemaker: A Biblical Guide to Resolving Personal Conflict* (Grand Rapids: Baker, 1991), 164.

8. Walter Wangerin, Jr., *As for Me and My House: Crafting Your Marriage to Last* (Nashville: Nelson, 1987), 97.

9. Corrie ten Boom with John and Elizabeth Sherrill, *The Hiding Place* (New York: Bantam, 1974), 238.

10. Philippians 4:8.

11. Matthew 18:21-22, NAS.

12. Sande, op. cit., 80 (author's paraphrase).

13. Romans 3:10.

14. Colossians 2:13.

15. Smedes, op. cit., 192.

7

GIVING AND RECEIVING

I love Christmas.

When I was a child, my father would bring home a six-foot Douglas fir several weeks before that special day. We dressed the tree in ornaments, lights, and tinsel until it shimmered before our eyes. My brothers and sisters and I anxiously counted off each day, eagerly awaiting Christmas Eve. As the days passed, brightly wrapped packages appeared beneath our beautifully decorated tree. These gifts were tied up in ribbons and bows of every imaginable color. The closer we got to Christmas, the more presents were tucked beneath the tree.

Early in the morning, before my parents were awake, I would tiptoe into the living room and stare at the gifts. They were in all shapes and sizes. I edged closer and ran my fingers over the wrapping paper, looking for those presents with my name on them. Once found, they were poked and turned over, shaken, and rattled. Then I sat back and dreamed of all the marvelous toys I hoped were wrapped in those fancy packages.

Giving and receiving bring equal pleasure. In giving to others, their pleasure becomes ours and in receiving, our pleasure becomes theirs.

Oh, the magic of Christmas and the mystery of gifts. We all have memories of the excitement and anticipation. The childlike part of us still can't wait to see what is so carefully concealed under the Christmas wrap. I eagerly break the ribbons and rip off the paper to discover the hidden surprise. I also like to watch the joy on other faces as they open gifts I'm giving.

Giving and receiving bring equal pleasure. In giving to others, their pleasure becomes ours and in receiving, our pleasure becomes theirs.

THE ART OF GIVING

A spirit of generosity and sharing bring magic to a marriage. When we give to our partner, we stretch beyond ourselves. When we stop giving, the magic fades. After twenty years of marriage to Tom, Carol sat in my office and said the relationship was finished.

"How do you know it's over?" I asked.

"He doesn't give anymore."

"What do you mean?"

"When we were first married," she explained, "he gave me a kiss every morning and told me he loved me every night. He gave me cards every holiday and roses on our wedding anniversary. Somewhere along the line he stopped giving and the marriage went downhill from there."

What went wrong with Tom and Carol's marriage was more than just the lack of giving, but that was an important piece of the puzzle. When we don't give, something dies in both of us. Both partners need to give, for it is in giving that we remind ourselves of our ongoing commitment. Giving brings us together and, over time, keeps us together.

Some people are givers and others are takers. My wife is a giver. She looks for opportunities to give. Her gifts come in all shapes and sizes. Some are tangible, others are intangible. She also gives little presents. At unexpected times and places I will find a card saying, "I miss you," or a batch of chocolate-chip cookies, or a new shirt. Tami gives great gifts and she is constantly looking for creative ways to give. A few weeks ago I was at the grocery store and saw the brand of dry-roasted peanuts she likes. So I bought them. It wasn't a special occasion and Tami hadn't asked for them. I purchased them because they would make her happy.

I'm not bragging, but I gave again today. Tami sent me to the store for snacks and I thought, "What would Tami like best?" Ice cream was the immediate answer. So I went to the cooler and picked out a half-gallon of Heavenly Hash, my favorite. Then I stopped and thought, *Maybe this gift would be more meaningful if I purchased her favorite flavor rather than mine.* I replaced the Heavenly Hash with Cookies 'n Cream. I knew my gift would be greatly appreciated, not only because it was ice cream, but because it was a flavor I wouldn't have chosen for myself. This gift was totally for Tami.

Giving is an art. To understand it properly, we need to answer the same questions a journalist does when writing a news story: who, what, where, when, why, and how.

It's obvious that the *who* in a book on marriage would be the couple reading this book. Each of you are to give to the other. Now we will see the different ways giving can be done.

WHAT SHOULD WE GIVE?

Giving good gifts takes time and effort. Most of us want the recipient to enjoy and appreciate the gift we give. We want our gifts to mean something. Yet we often assume that what we appreciate and find meaningful will have the same impact on our loved one. This is not necessarily true. If we sincerely want to give good gifts, we need to do a little research and ask a few questions.

- What type of gifts does your partner like the most?

- What is the best gift they have ever received? Why?

- What is the most disappointing gift they have ever received? Why?

When we finish our research, we should have a better sense of what is a meaningful gift to our spouse. Don't fall into the trap of considering only tangible gifts for there are other ways to give. Giving falls into at least three categories.

Presents. Traditionally, this is what we think of when we wish to give—something you can see and touch, such as a book, a sweater, or a piece of jewelry. Some people think if they can't give something big, they won't give anything. Yet more often little presents are stunning in their elegant simplicity and that is as powerful as big presents. So don't underestimate the meaning of a single rose, a card, or a magazine tied with a bow. In fact, sometimes the little gifts are more memorable.

My grandmother's eyes twinkle when she tells of the cup of coffee my grandfather brought to her in bed each morning. A young woman said she knew her husband loved her because he gives her two chocolate truffles every Saturday. Little gifts send a strong and clear message of love.

James and Della know how to give presents. O. Henry celebrated their art of giving in his classic short story *The Gift of the Magi*.[1] It was the day before Christmas and Della didn't have enough money to buy her husband, James, a gift. She knew what she wanted to give him, and that it would please him so much.

James had a very special gold pocket-watch. It was passed down from his grandfather to his father, and now it belonged to him. There was only one problem with this precious family heirloom. The watch was attached to an old leather strap. The perfect gift would be a simple but elegant platinum watch chain that she saw in a local shop.

Della was an attractive young woman with beautiful brown hair that reached below her knees. The only way she knew to get the money she needed was to cut off her lovely curls and sell them, which is exactly what she did. That evening she was so excited when she presented James with the sparkling watch chain. But the watch was gone. James had sold it so he could buy a set of tortoise shell combs with jeweled rims for Della's beautiful hair.

My great-grandmother gave poems to those she loved. My grandfather gave wooden boxes and bird houses. A woman at our church gives tomatoes. My wife gives me cookies and clothes. So what can I give to my wife? This book is a gift to her. Publishers say books on marriage are not very marketable and that I should spend my time on a project that would have broader appeal. However, Tami wants me to collect my thoughts on marriage, so this is for her.

Compliments. Mark Twain once said that he could live for two weeks on nothing but a good compliment. Everybody likes to receive compliments. They are all valuable but are not all equal. There are compliments of appearance, when we say someone is handsome, or beautiful, or attractive. There are also compliments about possessions such as, "I love your sweater," or "You have a fantastic car." Most compliments fall in the two categories of appearance or possessions, but these are not the most desired compliments. People like to hear compliments for performance. We all enjoy hearing we have done a good job and are appreciated. Even more meaningful are compliments about our character. Compliments that look to the heart of who we are.

Sometime in the early 1960s a junior-high math teacher had her class list the names of all the students in the room and write down the nicest thing they could say about each of their classmates. The next day the teacher wrote the name of each student on a separate piece of paper. Then she listed what everybody else had said about that person. When she returned these papers, the class was surprised. Few of them believed that other students had thought such nice things about them.

Yes, it was the old list where the teacher had written all the good things the soldier's classmates had said about him. His father turned to the teacher and said, "Thank you so much for doing that."

Years passed and the teacher forgot all about her little exercise. Unfortunately, the next time she saw many of those math students was at the funeral of one of their former classmates who lost his life in Vietnam. After the funeral, most of the classmates met at the home of the young soldier's parents. His father sought out the teacher and showed her a wallet that belonged to his son. They found it in the pocket of the fatigues he was wearing when he died. Opening the wallet, the father pulled out two worn pieces of notebook paper. They were yellow with age and mended with tape from being folded and refolded so many times. Yes, it was the old list where the teacher had written all the good things the soldier's classmates had said about him. His father turned to the teacher and said, "Thank you so much for doing that."

A group of the classmates noticed the list and gathered around the teacher. One by one, each thanked the teacher for their wonderful gift. One fellow said he kept his list in the top drawer of his desk at home; another kept his in his wedding album; a woman saved hers in her diary. One classmate summed it up for everyone as she pulled her tattered list out of her wallet. "I think we all saved our list." The teacher had given a wonderful gift and years later it was still treasured. Compliments are special gifts, especially compliments of character.

Periodically I ask a husband or wife, "What do you appreciate about your partner's personality?" It usually catches the person off guard. It is easier for us to think of negatives than positives. To make this question easier, I have listed one hundred compliments of character. Read through the list and circle those which apply to your spouse. Then during the next week use these as compliments. Put your arms around your mate and say, "Thank you for being so practical," or "I appreciate how understanding you are." Here's the list. Try the assignment.

Accepting	Diligent	Likable	Romantic
Adventurous	Disciplined	Logical	Secure
Affectionate	Efficient	Loving	Self-aware
Ambitious	Encouraging	Loyal	Self-controlled
Appreciative	Enthusiastic	Mature	Sensitive
Assertive	Fair	Mellow	Serious
Attentive	Faithful	Merciful	Sincere
Brave	Flexible	Non-judgmental	Sociable
Calm	Forgiving	Objective	Spiritual
Caring	Friendly	Optimistic	Spontaneous
Cheerful	Fun	Organized	Straightforward
Compassionate	Generous	Patient	Strong
Concerned	Gentle	Peaceful	Structured
Confident	Graceful	Persuasive	Supportive
Conscientious	Grateful	Playful	Tactful
Consistent	Happy	Polite	Teachable
Content	Honest	Practical	Tender
Cooperative	Hospitable	Precise	Thoughtful
Courteous	Humble	Principled	Thrifty
Creative	Independent	Punctual	Trustworthy
Curious	Innovative	Reassuring	Understanding
Decisive	Insightful	Relaxed	Visionary
Deep	Intelligent	Reflective	Warm
Dependable	Intuitive	Respectful	Well-mannered
Determined	Kind	Responsible	Wise

Self. Walt Whitman, the American poet, wrote, "When I give, I give myself." In a sense, all gifts involve giving ourselves, but here are those intangibles that require time and attention. The giving of self builds security in our spouse. It involves those little messages of caring such as a smile, a look, a phone call, or an "I love you." Sometimes it involves touch and tenderness, when we hold hands, kiss, rub a back, or give hugs. Other times it's as simple as turning off the television or putting down our newspaper and truly listening. It involves risking our innermost thoughts—our dreams, our fears, and our secrets.

Another aspect of giving ourselves is volunteering. This includes doing those things our spouse would appreciate, maybe even doing it without them asking us. Some of these things are fun, such as a trip to the beach, or the mall, or the zoo. It may also be going on a walk, or spending an evening at a movie. Another aspect of volunteering involves having a helping spirit. This includes washing the dishes, cleaning the car, and doing the laundry even when it isn't our job. Doing these things without complaining is a wonderful gift. Tami says a gift I give her is getting up in the middle of the night when the children want a drink of water, have to go to the bathroom, or are frightened by nightmares.

Giving of ourselves involves being there, and being there is not passive. It means sacrificing our preferences. When a child cries out at 3:00 A.M., I would rather ignore it and hope Tami would handle the problem. But I don't. I sacrifice my preference by going to the child's room and taking care of the problem. In this small way I try to return to Tami the hundreds of self-gifts she gives to me each day. Ultimately, this is the most powerful of all gifts. When we give of our time and energy, we give from the very essence of who we are. There is no other gift so deep or meaningful.

WHERE SHOULD WE GIVE?

Real estate agents say the three major factors in buying property are location, location, and location. Giving also takes place in a location and these locations are important.

About five years ago, two of my brothers and I were hiking along the Oregon Coast, when we came across an exceptionally beautiful spot. We hiked across a narrow ledge and carefully made our way to the face of a cliff high above the crashing waves of the Pacific. The scene was rugged and the view breathtaking. As the three of us sat on the edge of the world, we decided to share this location with our wives. We gathered wildflowers, hid them in the bushes, then went to get our wives at the cabin.

Half an hour before sunset we blindfolded them and led them down the narrow path to the face of the steep cliff. As the sun began to sink into the ocean, we presented our wives with bouquets and removed their blindfolds. The six of us huddled close together and watched one of the most spectacular sunsets I have ever seen. The location was perfect. Tami threw her arms around me and we kissed until the light faded from view.

The answer to where should we give seemed so obvious that at first I skipped over it. Most of us know that we should give everywhere and anywhere we are. Yet if this answer is so obvious, why don't we do it? Let's explore both the obvious and the unusual locations.

At Home. A residence is more than a place to eat and sleep. It is a place to seek shelter from the battles of a pressurized world. Give what you can, big or small, in every room of your home. Fill it with a spirit of love and generosity. Give your gift in the bedroom when you first wake up; or at the front door when either of you leave for work or return home. Give in the kitchen as a meal is prepared, or in the dining room as you sit to eat.

Give throughout your house as you or your partner deal with the children. Give in the living room, on the back porch, the deck, or wherever your spouse relaxes. Give in the garage, laundry room, or yard when your mate is doing the everyday chores around the house. At the end of the day, return to the bedroom and give one final time as you both bring your day to a close.

At Work. Very few partners work at the same location, but this shouldn't stop your giving. Show up unexpectedly and take them to lunch or tell them how much you love them. Bring them a favorite candy bar, tickets to a movie they want to see, a hug, or anything that would give a lift to their day. Drop them a note. Give them a phone call. Send a card. Order their favorite pizza and have it delivered. Recently, when I moved into a new office, Tami sent me a beautiful flower arrangement. Don't let distance block your giving.

Sometimes it takes planning ahead. A friend surprised her husband at work one day by coming in as a scheduled noon appointment under the assumed name of "Mrs. Whitman." To do this she had to call his secretary ahead of time to have her new identity entered into his calendar. At the appointed time, Mrs. Whitman arrived. When his secretary ushered his wife in, he was surprised and delighted. He was so happy to be going to lunch with his love instead of having to hold a noontime meeting with a stranger.

Be creative. It's fun and it builds wonderful memories.

Out and About. Much of life goes on beyond home and work. A healthy marriage also stretches beyond these important locations. Ask yourself what you can give your partner as you sit in the car or go on a walk. We forget that giving can take place anywhere: at a grocery store, restaurant, church, mall, park, or theater. Part of the gift might be the location itself. The other part is the "what" that I referred to earlier. Giving is easy when you are in a pleasant location, such as on a vacation, at a concert, a sporting event, or enjoying some scene of natural beauty. On the other hand, giving in tough locations is frequently appreciated even more. Give the gift of your patience in a long line that isn't moving; a glass of cold water in a hot stuffy room; a compliment in an embarrassing situation; a hug in a hospital room; sympathy in a funeral chapel.

A couple's young son lay in a hospital bed gravely ill with meningitis. The young mother spent her days at her child's side. After work, the father would meet her at the hospital to give her a break and spend some time with his son. One evening, before the child's condition began improving, he brought his wife a gift. It was a small book of poetry to divert her troubled thoughts and lift her weary spirit. The mother said the fact she got a gift brightened her day; that it was poetry added to her pleasure.

True giving is not limited by location. Wherever you are becomes the perfect place to give.

In Secret Places. It had been a long trip and I was far from home. As I was at my hotel unpacking, I found a note from Tami tucked between my shirts that read, "Wish I were there." I smiled and wished she was with me too. That night I discovered another note in the book I was reading. It said, "Thinking of you." The next morning I ran into a note in my sports jacket wishing me "Good Luck," and one in my wallet saying, "I love you." I found another one in my brief case seducing me with, "I can't wait until you get home." In all there were ten notes hidden throughout my luggage, keeping Tami close to me. She told me, "I'm proud of you," "You're the best," and "I'm missing you." As I found each message, I'd smile and set it on the night stand by my bed. I love surprises! Gifts hidden in secret places are special to any marriage.

I know a husband who left a note on his front door directing his wife to the kitchen. In the kitchen a note sent her to the bedroom where she was pointed to the garage, then guided to a neighbor's house. There she found her husband who surprised her with the keys to the car of her dreams.

Most of us can't provide such extravagant gifts, but we can hide smaller gifts in all sorts of secret places. What about under their pillow, on the dashboard of their car, in their pocket, between their underwear or lingerie, under their dinner plate, or in their Bible? Tape a favorite love song both of you claim as "our song," and at the right spot insert a love message from your heart, then finish taping the song. Put it in the cassette player of their car with a self-stick note saying, "Play me." Let them discover your love for them as they negotiate traffic.

Let creativity do its magic and surprise your spouse today with a gift hidden in some secret place.

Let creativity do its magic and surprise your spouse today with a gift hidden in some secret place.

At Special Romantic Places. What special place did you go to on dates to talk and dream, and be together? For some it is a park or restaurant, for others it might be a bowling alley, church, discotheque, or even a particular street corner. Every couple has their special romantic place that brings back wonderful memories— places where they first met, dated, kissed, and proposed. Other locations trigger special memories too. The place of your honeymoon, a great vacation, a certain Valentine's day, an embarrassing evening, an intimate conversation, a fun time, a point of forgiveness, an act of tenderness. Remember special places and return to them. Enrich those memories by filling those places with gifts. Part of the gift is just remembering the special events that occurred there. The world is full of special places. Go to those old places and celebrate memories of togetherness. Look for new places to create memories and traditions. Search for special locations to give gifts and stretch your love creatively.

WHEN SHOULD WE GIVE?

This sounds like an odd question, but I find that if I don't plan my giving, it doesn't happen. My life consists of schedules and timetables. If events don't make it into my calendar, they are forgotten. When a couple is dating, giving is easier and it comes more often. Once the wedding is over, the demands of everyday life seem to numb the brain. We become slothful, distracted, and absentminded. Time moves more quickly. Days and weeks run into months. Suddenly the question hits us: "When was the last time I gave something special to my love?" Jesus said, "Give, and it will be given to you."[2] So, when should we give?

When It's Expected. There are five critical holidays that every married person should have memorized. If you don't, there is potential trouble. Oh, your partner might be kind and say they understand, but you have sent a damaging message that will come back to haunt you. These holidays require gifts of some kind—they must be acknowledged. To forget them, ignore them, or choose not to celebrate them could be interpreted that your spouse is no longer special to you. However, to use these five red-letter dates as opportunities for giving will send a message that you love and treasure your mate. Mark the following red-letter dates in your date book:

- Christmas
- Spouse's Birthday
- Your Wedding Anniversary
- Valentine's Day
- Mother's or Father's Day

The giving on these days need not be extravagant, but one should be aware of expectations because unmet expectations lead to hurt and disappointment. Everyone has different expectations. My wife expects a card and a neatly wrapped gift for her birthday. A nice dinner at a fancy restaurant is appreciated, but it doesn't meet expectations. An unwrapped gift, or a gift given two days late is also a disappointment. For me to be a loving husband I need to be aware of these expectations. I want my wife to know she is special and for me to communicate that message I must package it in a way that is meaningful to her. The right gift in the right way at the right time is my goal.

195

Unexpected gifts don't need to be complicated or expensive. Their value comes not from the gift itself, but from the caring heart that thought of it.

Plan for these days and mark them on your calendar. Make them special. Now sometimes, because of finances or timing, a couple decides not to celebrate one of these critical holidays. Beware! Why cancel an opportunity to say, "I love you!"? Don't let anything stop you. During our last anniversary money was short, but that didn't stop Tami from buying me my favorite chocolate-covered blueberries, wrapping them in beautiful paper and presenting them with a romantic kiss. It was a small gift costing a little over two dollars but it was just as meaningful as a gift costing two hundred.

When It's Unexpected. French psychiatrist, Paul Tournier, wrote, "The more unexpected and personal the gift, the more it touches the heart."[3] We all like surprises and gifts for no particular reason. The challenge in a good marriage is to be constantly looking for excuses to give when it's neither requested nor required.

The Adélie penguins live in Antarctica where there are few gifts to give in that frozen wasteland. However, the male penguins are resourceful. They search the ground until they find a smooth pebble, then they waddle to their mates and present them with their spontaneous gift.

Unexpected gifts don't need to be complicated or expensive. Their value comes not from the gift itself, but from the caring heart that thought of it.

Unexpected giving can happen every day. Its only limitation is your own creativity. For those who require more structure, think of what you might give your mate on these "non-critical" holidays:

- New Year's Day
- President's Day
- St. Patrick's Day
- Easter

- Memorial Day
- Flag Day
- Fourth of July
- Labor Day
- Columbus Day
- Halloween
- Veteran's Day
- Thanksgiving

Better yet, make up your own special days to celebrate the unique person that God created for you.

When It's Needed. At times we all have practical needs. Useful gifts may not be as exciting as frivolous gifts, but they are certainly just as appreciated. Some hesitate to give practical gifts, thinking they are boring and unimaginative. These givers want to give something fun or impressive. Therefore, they ignore the practical need because of their own pride.

Others don't meet the need because they don't know about it. The one in need is hesitant to ask, thinking that if their spouse truly cared, he or she would know the need. Throughout Scripture it talks about the importance of asking. To have someone give before we express our desire is special, but to give after being asked does not invalidate the gift. I've heard people say, "If you have to ask, it doesn't count." I strongly disagree. Most of us are terrible mind-readers, especially men. We must be told when there is a need or a desire for something special. I suppose if we were more observant or sensitive, we would figure it out on our own. Even though the gift received was requested, it is still a gift. After all, it is much better than a requested gift not received.

Still others struggle with the fact that they want to give a gift that is a surprise. They enjoy that look of shock and joy when the gift is something totally unexpected. They ignore their partner's request and get something else. Now the giver is accused of insensitivity, stubbornness, or simply not listening. If the surprise factor is important to you, why not do both? Give what is needed, then give something totally unexpected.

> *The real question isn't when should we give, but when can we afford not to give? Giving fortifies a marriage, providing the inner strength for it to last a lifetime.*

The real question isn't when should we give, but when can we afford not to give? Giving fortifies a marriage, providing the inner strength for it to last a lifetime.

WHY SHOULD WE GIVE?

This also seems to be obvious, but it surprises me how many people, especially men, do not understand the value of giving gifts. Too often it is seen as another assault on the budget. Maybe the following seven points will help answer the question of why we should give gifts.

To Get. Yes, I know this sounds selfish and it probably is, but it is a fact that the more we give, the more we get. Generosity is contagious. When Tami gives me a compliment, I want to return it. When she does something special for me, I want to do something special for her. I know the pattern well—if I am giving, I will receive. Modeling a spirit of giving may generate a reciprocal attitude in our spouse if that is an area of weakness.

To Show Appreciation. Sometimes gifts are tokens of gratitude. It may be a verbal "Thank you," a special meal, or a small gift. When we appreciate something, it's important that we find a way to communicate our pleasure. Our partners do so much for us that we often take things for granted. It's sad that we rarely see the value of someone until it's too late. We live in a culture of negativity and as a result we often focus on what our spouse does not do; exaggerating and generalizing to the point that we forget all the fine things they do accomplish. We need to regularly give them tokens of appreciation, large and small, for all they do to improve our lives.

To Apologize. Every day we say and do things that are insensitive, hurtful, and selfish. Because our mates see us at our worst—when we're tired, hungry, upset—they are frequently the target of our most ungodly words and behavior. Whenever this happens, we owe them an apology and sometimes even restitution. Apologies may be in words as long as they are sincere and meaningful; but if our wrong causes pain, then restitution may be due. During these times a present or an act of kindness is more appropriate. To hurt our partner without heartfelt apology and some form of restitution deepens their pain, thus risking permanent damage to the marriage.

To Encourage. The apostle Paul commands us to "encourage one another and build each other up."[4] If we are to encourage our neighbors and friends, then how much more we should encourage our spouse.

Living with me can be tough. My hours are long, people call me at all hours of the day and night, and I am often speaking someplace in the evening. Tami needs my encouragement. She needs to hear me say that she is a great wife, a special friend, a loving mother, and a great woman. She needs my gifts of encouragement especially when she feels frustrated and exhausted after a full day of caring for our three children. I need to encourage her more often.

> *For if giving is the coinage of love, then not to give will ultimately lead to bankruptcy.*

To State Our Love. Giving is romantic—especially to women. It's a symbol of how special, cherished, needed, and unforgettable our partner is. It draws us close and is a reaffirmation of our original commitment to one another. Walter Wangerin, Jr. says that a gift "is the dearest, clearest way to say, all wordlessly, 'I love you.'"[5] He's right! Every gift to our partner is a statement of our love. Do not be stingy or miserly with these statements. Some give only small gifts or no gifts at all. We must remember that to not give risks the loss of love. For if giving is the coinage of love, then not to give will ultimately lead to bankruptcy.

To Keep Our Hearts Soft. Those who don't give, grow hard-hearted and cold. They become self-centered and absorbed in their own pleasure. To give stretches us beyond ourselves. Over and over again we are warned in Scripture not to grow hard-hearted;[6] it kills relationships and ultimately destroys us. When the desire to give grows cool, it is a sure sign of danger that loss of affection, emotional distance, and possibly even divorce is not far behind.

To Improve Our Marriage. I guarantee that giving will improve your marriage. Why? Because giving increases our love and love increases our giving. The circle builds on itself and with each consecutive rotation, the husband and wife grow closer. This giving leads to a togetherness that is one of the most fulfilling aspects of any marriage.

To honestly look at why we should give, it is important to understand why we don't give. There are many reasons, but here are seven:

Fear
We are afraid our giving will be rejected.

Anger
We are so hurt and upset that we don't believe our partner deserves our giving.

Stress
We are so anxious that all our attention is focused on survival. We don't have the energy or ability to give.

Depression
Our world seems dark and hopeless. We can't give to ourselves, let alone our partner.

Loss of Love
We don't care about giving because we no longer care about our partner.

It's Not Important
We are very busy and there are other things more demanding and important to us than giving to our partner.

Don't Know How
We grew up in a family where giving wasn't taught and now we aren't sure how to start.

If any of these seven issues block your giving, please seek help and do it immediately. Talk to your pastor, a counselor, or someone you respect. Don't ignore this problem. It may not be creating difficulties in your marriage now, but sooner or later it will. By the time it blows up in your face, it may be too late.

For those of you who give, increase your giving. Focus on the seven reasons to give and stretch yourself. Now we can look at our last question.

HOW SHOULD WE GIVE?

It seems to me that there are three types of gifts: selfish, shallow, and sincere. Each gift has its place, but the sincere gift is the one most valued. Under the right circumstance, selfish and shallow gifts might be acceptable, but if they are the pattern, there is a problem.

Selfish Gifts. Giving a gift that is something we want more than they want is selfish. A friend gave his wife a super-deluxe gas barbecue for Mother's Day and she was not impressed. She knew this was something he had desired for months and giving it to her was merely an excuse for buying it. If I bought my wife a compact disc I want to listen to, or a book I wanted to read, it would be selfish. She might appreciate the gift, but she would know there was a hidden agenda.

Frank and Elizabeth had marital problems. She had moved out of the house and was considering a legal separation. He wanted her back. One Saturday night Frank showed up at her apartment with two beautifully wrapped packages. Elizabeth couldn't believe her eyes. This was so romantic. It wasn't like Frank. She invited him in and excitedly opened her gifts. The first was a pair of basketball tickets. Elizabeth hates basketball. The second was a sexy silk negligé. The couple had not been sexual in three months. Elizabeth was furious. She threw Frank and his gifts out the door as she yelled, "All you care about is sports and sex. When will you care about me?" Frank's gifts were selfish—they had strings attached. He wanted his wife to go to a game and afterward go home and have sex with him. He placed his needs above hers, then wrapped them up as a gift.

Shallow Gifts. People appreciate gifts that take time and effort because it increases the gift's value. A gift with little thought or planning might communicate that your partner is worth very little to you. I learned long ago that when I get flowers for Tami, roses or irises are the most appreciated; when I buy her clothes, I look for pastels; and when looking for candy, stick with chocolate. Tami spends all year looking for the best gifts to give to me, then she hides them, waiting for the perfect occasion. Gifts purchased at the last moment from a convenience store don't make good impressions.

Most men are not good at giving cards. The problem is that most women love cards—they set them on shelves, save them in drawers, and years later will read them again. I have an idea for men who struggle in this area. Go to a large card store and spend an hour. During this time, buy twenty cards your wife would love for every occasion. Then whenever you think about it, pull the appropriate card from your little collection and surprise her. You can mail it to her, set it on the bed, or put it in her car. She will love it, in part because it's a card, and in part because you took the time to select it especially for her.

Sincere Gifts. Why are some gifts kept and treasured, when others are quickly discarded? Suzy's husband gave her a fishing pole ten years ago. It has hung unused in the garage ever since. James received a beautiful gold-edged diary from his wife fifteen years ago. It is stored somewhere in the bottom of a box and has never been opened.

What went wrong with these two gifts? Other women might love Suzy's fishing pole and other men would write prolifically in James's diary. The problem is Suzy's and James's partners didn't do their homework. A sincere gift is personal. It takes into consideration a person's character, tastes, and interests. They watch and listen to see what a person enjoys. They inquire of their partner's friends and colleagues for ideas. When giving a gift it will bring a smile if it is exactly what the person wanted. The more we love someone, the more careful we are to choose a very personal gift.

Another aspect of a sincere gift is creativity. Making his favorite dessert or writing her a love letter are examples of giving with imagination. Tami goes beyond the ordinary with her creativity. There have been notes in my car, a candle-lit bedroom for our anniversary, concert tickets to one of my favorite musicians, "I love you" written across the bathroom mirror, and many more. These ingenious gifts are sincere and they leave lasting memories of love. Beware of selfish or shallow giving. Make your gifts as sincere as possible, for the sincere gift enhances both the one who gives and the one who receives.

The art of giving is an attitude. The what, where, when, why, and how simply provide a structure, but it is love, determination, and commitment that provide the spirit. There are times I don't feel like fueling my car with gas, but I have learned that not doing it has certain consequences. I might claim I forgot, or my gas gauge is broken, or I couldn't find a service station, but the consequences are still the same—no gas, no movement. Marriages are the same—if we don't give, we don't move. We end up stuck by the side of the road, wishing we had gotten gasoline several miles back. Don't wait until it's too late. Give and your marriage will continue to operate smoothly.

The quality and quantity of giving is often dependent upon your reactions. Rejecting your partner's gifts decreases the chances of future gifts.

THE ART OF RECEIVING

How do you receive a gift you don't really want or a compliment you don't believe is true? What do you say when you had your heart set on a certain gift and your partner, with a smile on their lips, gives you something totally different? How do you respond when your partner gives you selfish or shallow gifts? The art of receiving is often just as important as the art of giving. There are five ways to receive a gift and our mastery of this art may be what either kills or kindles the future giving of our mate.

REFUSING GIFTS

Abbey had placed three simple items on her Christmas list. They were things that were important to her, easy to get, and relatively inexpensive. She looked forward to Christmas morning and the opening of her anticipated gifts. Her husband surprised her by getting nothing on her list. He bought her gifts that were extravagant, but not what she wanted. In disappointment, she told him she didn't want his gifts and placed them in the back seat of his car. He felt rejected and the two did not speak for over a week.

Refusing a gift is cruel and self-centered. It's a slap in the face to the giver and almost always creates distance. The giver feels rejected and withdraws out of embarrassment, disappointment, or hurt. Maybe the gift was lacking, but the very fact it was given provides something on which to build. Gently educate your partner in terms of the gifts that bring you the most pleasure and pray that the next gift will be more sincere. Encourage your partner to continue their giving and over the years it will improve. The quality and quantity of giving is often dependent upon your reactions. Rejecting your partner's gifts decreases the chances of future gifts.

CRITICIZING GIFTS

"He never touches me anymore," the wife complained. "He used to give me marvelous back rubs, but he hasn't done that in years." I asked the husband why and he replied, "She said I was too rough, so I tried to be gentle; then she said I wasn't hard enough. Whatever I did was wrong, so I gave up." We give with the hope of pleasing our partner. To be told our gift is defective, inadequate, or wrong causes us to cringe. We begin thinking, why should we give if we can't please?

To criticize a gift is to criticize the giver. Yet often we are critical without even realizing it. Remember the tongue is a powerful tool. Proverbs says that "pleasant words are a honeycomb,"[7] but James warns us the tongue is a small spark that can set a great fire.[8] Critical words can do great damage. Consequently, we need to watch for negative comments and responses that slip into our conversation.

One of the worst offenders is the "yes, but" syndrome. We say, "Thank you for the flowers, but I wish you hadn't spent that much money," or "I really appreciate you watching the children, but I wish you'd done some laundry, too." In these statements the "but" invalidates the positive, thus making it a criticism. Now that was probably not the intention of the speaker, but that is often how it feels to the listener.

Love sees the best. The gift may have been selfish or shallow, but it is a gift. I wonder how often God looks down on the gifts we give him and shakes his head. So try to look beyond the gift, to the heart of the giver, reforming it into something positive. Every gift, no matter what it is, can be a stepping stone that brings us closer together.

IGNORING GIFTS

For many people, receiving gifts is difficult. They are not sure what to say when complimented, or how to respond when given a present. Therefore, they say or do nothing. The danger is that silence can be interpreted many ways. Is it rejection or criticism? Does it mean the gift is not wanted? Maybe the gift has merely left the receiver speechless? It is important to acknowledge gifts. Recognize and comment on the thoughtfulness of the gift and the giving. To do otherwise makes you appear critical and ungrateful. In the gospel of Luke, the story is told of Jesus healing ten lepers. After this gift, Jesus sent them to the priest in order to verify the cure. Later one of the former lepers returned to acknowledge the gift. Jesus' response was, "Were not all ten cleansed? Where are the other nine?"[9] When we receive a gift, big or little, are we one of the nine who ignore the giving or are we the one who acknowledges the gift with appreciation?

APPRECIATING GIFTS

As a giver, we need to be concerned about the gift, but as a receiver, the gift is secondary. What is important is that the gift given is a symbol of our partner's love and affection. Giving proves that our spouse cares and everybody wants to know that someone cares about them. Therefore, whether it is a kiss, a telephone call, a great meal, a bouquet of roses, or a trip to Tahiti, it all means the same—*you are loved!* All the gifts that come from the same heart, at least theoretically, are of equal value.

When we show appreciation for a gift, we are actually showing appreciation for the giver. To internalize this truth will take us a long way. When I praise what Tami gives, I am really praising who she is: her sensitivity, generosity, creativity, and desire to be the best wife she can possibly be. I'm celebrating her. Her gift is proof of her love. It communicates that she thinks I'm worth the time, energy, and money it took for her to give to me. If I don't appreciate that, there is something wrong. So I need to demonstrate my gratitude by words, attitude, and how I treat her. To do less would be rude and self-centered. The more I show appreciation, the more my wife wants to give. Therefore, I thank Tami regularly for all the special things she says and does.

TREASURING GIFTS

As a child I had a small box where I kept all my most valuable treasures. I hid my box under the stairs where nobody could steal its precious contents. These items might not have looked like much to anybody else, but to me they were priceless. There was my Roy Rogers's autograph, an 1899 silver dollar from my grandfather, a piece of genuine fool's gold from Uncle Walt, a slingshot, a blue stone from a neighbor, a secret message ring, a pocketknife from Yellowstone Park, and a strange assortment of smaller items. Each of these was priceless to me and each had its own story. These were my treasures.

In the same way we should treasure the gifts from our partner. Every year they give us thousands of gifts, each one precious in its own unique way. If we could cut out one gift each week, pack it away in our own treasure box and review the contents once in a while, we would all be happier couples. Usually, we don't reflect on what we have received until it's too late. So stop right now and think through some of the gifts you have received from your spouse over the years. Bask in the memories and treasure each one. Here is a partial list to get you started:

- Walks
- Hugs
- Surprises
- Vacations
- Presents
- Photographs
- Christmas
- Romance

- Compliments
- Special moments
- Children
- Good meals
- Cards and letters
- Courtship
- Everyday chores
- Togetherness

Take each of these gifts and place them in that treasure box deep inside your memory. Next time you and your partner are not connecting as well as you would like, pull out your box and remember how much you treasure both who they are and what they have given you.

Giving is critical, but so is receiving. It is an art which many of us ignore. Be careful about rejecting gifts. You don't want to stifle your partner's desire to give. Be sensitive about criticizing gifts; you may be doing more of this than you realize. Ignoring a gift may seem harmless, but it is the same as ignoring the giver and that is never harmless. Appreciate every gift and communicate your appreciation in personal and creative ways. Lastly, treasure each gift, carrying the memory of them with you wherever you go. For as you become a good receiver you will motivate both you and your mate to be better givers.

A WORLD WITHOUT GIFTS

A marriage without giving is a loveless relationship and a world without gifts would be miserable. Imagine for a moment what it would be like. Christmas and birthdays would not be the same. There would be no Valentine's day. Cards and letters would not be sent. Hugs and kisses would not exist. Romance would be impossible. Charities could not help others. Compliments would never be spoken. Courtesies would never be practiced. Smiles and kindness would be suppressed. Love would be outlawed. Hope would be stifled. Even our faith would not exist, for Christianity is based upon God's great Gift to us.

A world without gifts is difficult to comprehend and a marriage without gifts is impossible. If we don't give of ourselves, our commitment is meaningless and marriage, as we desire it, can't exist.

Discussion Questions

1. On a scale from 1 to 10 (1 = excellent, 10 = poor) what type of giver are you?

2. What type of gift does your spouse like the most?

   What is the most unusual gift you've ever given him or her?

   What is the most romantic gift you've ever given him or her?

3. When was the last time you gave your partner a compliment in the following areas?

   a) Appearance
   b) Possessions
   c) Performance
   d) Character

   In which area do you give the most compliments?

   In which do you give the least?

4. List three compliments that you wish to give your mate.

   a)
   b)
   c)

5. Where was the last place you gave your spouse a gift?

   What was his or her response?

6. What special romantic places have you enjoyed in your courtship and marriage?

7. What did you give your partner during the following five red-letter dates?

   a) Christmas
   b) Birthday
   c) Wedding anniversary
   d) Valentine's Day
   e) Mother's or Father's Day

8. What examples of the following three types of gifts have you given your mate?

   a) A selfish gift
   b) A shallow gift
   c) A sincere gift

9. Are you better at giving or receiving gifts? Why?

10. Have you ever refused, criticized, or ignored a gift from your spouse? Explain.

11. How do you show appreciation for a gift your spouse gives you?

12. Considering your whole marriage, what five gifts received from your mate do you treasure the most?

   a)
   b)
   c)
   d)
   e)

Notes

1. O. Henry, *The Best Short Stories of O. Henry* (New York: The Modern Library), 1-7.

2. Luke 6:38.

3. Paul Tournier, *The Meaning of Gifts* (Richmond, Vir.: John Knox, 1961), 43.

4. 1 Thessalonians 5:11.

5. Walter Wangerin, Jr., *As for Me and My House: Crafting Your Marriage to Last* (Nashville: Nelson, 1987), 241.

6. See Mark 3:5, 16:14; Hebrews 3:15, 4:7.

7. Proverbs 16:24.

8. James 3:6-7.

9. Luke 17:11-19.

8

TOGETHERNESS

January 20 was cold. Freezing rain had made roads slippery the night before and threatened to do so again. I didn't even care. The events of that evening had been planned months before and uncooperative weather would not hamper the festivities. As the seven o'clock hour approached, the church filled with guests. Those present had either not heard the forecast or didn't care.

Candlelight and violins welcomed our guests who were ushered to their appropriate seats. It was a serious ceremony with admonitions and vows. It was also sentimental with songs sung by close friends and special thanks to both our parents. Yet one symbol summed up the meaning and power of the whole wedding for me.

To the side of the wedding party—beyond the bridesmaids and groomsmen, even beyond the candelabras and flowers— stood a small table covered with a simple white cloth. On it were three candles. The one large, solid candle stood unlit between two thin, fragile tapers with flames flickering brightly. Shortly after Tami and I exchanged our vows and rings, we stepped up to this table. Together we picked up

Before the wedding we were an engaged couple, at the ceremony we became partners for life.

the two lit candles and joined our flames to the wick of the third candle. The purpose of this ritual, and indeed the whole marriage ceremony, was to communicate a single message: The two have become one.

This ceremony was the true beginning of our togetherness; everything up to now had been practice and dress rehearsal. Before the wedding we were an engaged couple, at the ceremony we became partners for life. Something new was born—a togetherness that continually needs protection and nurturing. If our togetherness is not properly cared for it will undermine every aspect of the marriage. The sweetness will turn sour and the strength will become brittle. Healthy togetherness is one of the greatest benefits and joys of marriage. Thousands of years ago wise King Solomon wrote:

> Two are better than one.... If one falls down, his friend can help him up.... Also, if two lie down together, they will keep warm. But how can one keep warm alone?"[1]

Togetherness is not the loss of our individual identity. It is the sharing and interfacing of personalities in such a way that both individuals are better and richer for the interaction.

Togetherness is a joining of two, regardless of how different. Togetherness is not the loss of our individual identity. It is the sharing and interfacing of personalities in such a way that both individuals are better and richer for the interaction. Togetherness comprises a she, a he, and a we. All three are critical. What togetherness represents is a balance. If the we overpowers the individual identity of one or both partners, it threatens the marriage. Likewise, if either the he or the she is over-emphasized, the marriage is off center.

Togetherness is a broad concept so we are going to divide it into eight categories.[2] Each of these is critically important.

EMOTIONAL TOGETHERNESS

Being tuned into each other's emotional wavelength is more difficult for some than others. When couples come into my office for marriage counseling one of the first questions I ask is, "How is your relationship?" Frequently one partner will respond with, "Fine, I'm not sure what the big deal is. We have our little squabbles, but nothing out of the ordinary. I really don't think we need to be here."

I ask the other the same question and they say, "I can't stand it. If something doesn't change very soon, we're not going to make it. I figured I had to see a lawyer or a psychologist and I thought we'd try you first."

I scratch my head and wonder how can two people be so out of touch with each other. I see this scenario repeated again and again. Maybe the real question is, why is it so hard for two people to connect emotionally?

Everybody's internal emotional world is different, based upon an interaction of genetics and environment. The differences frequently fall into at least one of the following categories:

Emotional Depth
Certain people feel emotions deeper and stronger than others.

Emotional Spectrum
Certain people have a broader spectrum of emotion than others.

Emotional Awareness
Certain people are more in touch with their emotions than others.

Emotional Comfort
Certain people are more at ease with the acceptance and/or expression of emotion in themselves and others.

In many relationships it is the last two categories that cause the most marital frustration.

Dave was having a terrible time with emotional awareness. He grew up in a strict Norwegian family where emotions did not exist. Mary was his opposite. She had strong emotions and was very much in touch with them. When this couple first came to my office I gave Dave an assignment. Each evening he was to write three feelings he thought Mary might have felt during the day. At the end of each week Mary would check Dave's list and indicate how accurate it was. After about a month he became very good at knowing where she was emotionally.

Mary was ecstatic and reported that she felt better about the relationship than she had in years. Dave did not agree. He said, "This is just too hard, I can't keep doing it." During the next few months Dave drifted back to his old habits. Mary felt abandoned and within a year they divorced.

Debbie and Jerry had the opposite struggle. She was fully aware of her husband's emotions and didn't feel comfortable with them—especially if they were strong emotions. In her family of origin, her father's anger meant loss of control and violence, whereas her mother's crying meant manipulation. Therefore, when Jerry was loud or emphatic, Debbie retreated in fear, but if he wept she became annoyed. Jerry finally realized there were only certain emotions he could express in Debbie's presence. This built an emotional wall between them until they entered therapy.

As they sat in my office I reviewed the following unhealthy ways to deal with emotions.

Ignore
"I didn't notice you were feeling that."

Deny
"You don't feel that."

Moralize
"You shouldn't feel that."

Ridicule
"What's wrong with you for feeling that?"

Attack
"Stop feeling that or I'll..."

These ways of dealing with feelings destroy emotional togetherness. To connect emotionally a couple needs to recognize, acknowledge, accept, understand, and affirm each other's feelings. This is difficult, but the rewards are worth it. Emotional togetherness strengthens the bonds of the relationship and deepens the intimacy.

INTELLECTUAL TOGETHERNESS

Sheldon Vanauken, in his book *A Severe Mercy*, tells of the commitment he and his wife had to intellectual togetherness. They shared their thoughts, ideas, opinions, and beliefs. They earnestly desired to stay mentally close. A symbol of this togetherness was that if one read a book that had impact on them, the other would also read it.

When I mentioned this concept to a wife who was feeling out of touch with her husband, she took the challenge. She said, "My husband is constantly reading Louis L'Amour novels. Since he won't crawl into my world, I guess I'd better crawl into his." Then she went home and asked her husband what his favorite Louis L'Amour novel was. He told her and she read it. Later she told me the book had opened hours of discussion about the Old West.

After reading a book, watching a movie, or hearing a sermon, talk about it. Share your thoughts. What impacted you? What did you like or dislike about it? Let your questions dig deep. I heard someone say that the average person stops thinking new thoughts when they stop going to school. If this is true, it is sad. Questions keep us alert. We can learn more about one another by asking questions. In the glove box of our car lies a dog-eared paperback entitled *The Book of Questions* by Gregory Stock.[3] As we travel down the highway it is not unusual for my wife to pull it out and ask me one of its thought-provoking questions:

- What is your most treasured memory?

- Would you accept a million dollars to leave the country and never set foot in it again?

- What would constitute a perfect evening for you?

As we share our personal perspectives we plunge deeper into intellectual togetherness.

Exposing our thoughts and opinions encourages growth. It sometimes stimulates a chain reaction where Tami's idea triggers a new idea in me, which leads her to another idea. This is the beauty of a true interchange—she gives to me and I give to her. Together we have intellectually stretched beyond what either could have done alone.

This was the discovery of Will and Ariel Durant during their sixty-eight year marriage. Both loved history and, though Ariel started as Will's writing assistant, he soon found that she was instrumental to his creative process. As their thoughts and interpretations wove together, Will could no longer credit himself as the solitary writer of the monumental history *The Story of Civilization*. Consequently, the last five volumes have Will and Ariel listed as co-authors.

Intellectual togetherness doesn't mean there must be agreement. It simply requests that both be honest and sensitive. The truth is, we are all unique. We don't need to feel threatened by differing perspectives or attempts to conformity. Actually, disagreement challenges one to go deeper than the superficial and to learn who the other person really is.

AESTHETIC TOGETHERNESS

Beauty and artistry encompass us. Yet we race through life only half noting our surroundings. We need the beauty of life to pull us above the difficulties and drudgery of our everyday existence. If we let it, beauty touches our soul. It also provides a type of togetherness that lifts us beyond the ordinary.

Such fine books as *Walden* by Henry David Thoreau and P*ilgrim at Tinker Creek* by Annie Dillard remind us to look deeper into nature's unique and awesome beauty. Nature's artistry may envelop us, but there is so much we see without really absorbing. As I write, it is springtime. The dogwood and apple trees fill my window with their snowy white and pink blossoms. The forsythia stretches out with its vibrant yellow. The rhododendrons stand above the azaleas as they take on every color of the rainbow. The world is a place of beauty. Absorb it.

A friend of mine once took a class to study the art and meaning of the Japanese tea ceremony. It took place in a beautiful Japanese garden. To prepare for the ceremony, each student was instructed to focus on a tree. I mean really focus...for a full hour. They were to study its size and shape; follow its outline and notice its symmetry; examine the trunk, limbs, and leaves; consider the texture and color of each part, noticing the various hues and shadings. All these little things we skim over without seeing in detail. My friend told me that the first five minutes of this assignment was boring, then he became absorbed in the intricate detail and infinite beauty of this one simple specimen.

God's creation is awesome. Notice it. Share it. When I see a sunset, a deer at the edge of a forest, or the colors of autumn in the countryside, I long to share it with Tami. Viewing it together gives it more impact and draws us closer. I am the sort of person who constantly says "Look at this," or "Did you see that?" If we see beauty together, it somehow makes it even more special. Nature's beauty not only draws us closer together, it also draws us closer to God. God created this beauty for us to enjoy and it reflects his majestic nature.

King David stared up at the sparkling night sky over Jerusalem and wrote, "The Heavens are telling the glory of God; they are a marvelous display of his craftsmanship."[4] I love to sit with Tami on our deck on a clear evening and watch the night sky. The stars twinkle and the moon shines brightly. We are so small and God is so great. We huddle closer together sharing our warmth and thanking God for each other.

Another aspect of aesthetic togetherness is the celebration of the artistic. Art has many mediums. Music, theater, movies, literature, dance, photography, paintings, pottery, and sculpture are a few. My dictionary defines *art* as "human works of beauty." Enjoying art side by side creates a cultural connectedness.

Art also builds memories. I vividly recall the pleasure of sitting next to Tami as we enjoyed the stage performances of *South Pacific* with Robert Goulet, and *Camelot* with Richard Harris. For those brief hours a wonderful blend of visual and auditory beauty enveloped us. We were carried back to Bali Hi and King Arthur's England as we suspended our disbelief.

Reading a poem or a well-written piece of prose aloud is another form of aesthetic togetherness. As Tami and I flew home from a psychological convention in San Francisco, I was lost in the beautiful language of George MacDonald's *Phantasies*. Whenever I read a line that was particularly moving, I had to repeat it to her. Somehow sharing it tied us together.

Now the problem with cultural beauty is taste. What I find beautiful, my wife may not and vice versa. Certain music and paintings that I find awe-inspiring, Tami finds unmoving. Appreciation of various art forms require cultivation. My wife loves ballet and though I acknowledge its beauty, I find it difficult to enjoy for any longer than a minute or two. Yet, I need to learn to relax and give it a chance.

There are times I will go to a concert or a play simply because I love Tami. My going is my gift to

There are many opportunities to share beauty that both partners will find rewarding. These sometimes take time and energy to discover, but once discovered, you achieve a wonderful togetherness.

her. I would never go to these events alone. I go for Tami and to share the experience with her.

In spite of differences in taste, two people can still draw together aesthetically. New experiences pull us beyond our comfort zone. A client of mine asked her husband to join her on a specific cultural outing. He held her hand and said, "I went with you last year, do you really want me to go again?" After discussing it, they came up with another aesthetic experience that neither had tried. They went and loved it. There are many opportunities to share beauty that both partners will find rewarding. These sometimes take time and energy to discover, but once discovered, you achieve a wonderful togetherness.

RECREATIONAL TOGETHERNESS

Several years ago I was teaching a series on marriage to a group of seminary students. They were a very responsive group until I asked, "What do you and your wife do for fun?" They all just stared at me with large question marks on their faces. Finally a courageous young man raised his hand and asked, "What does this have to do with marriage?"

Couples need to relate together in fun and play. We take life too seriously. Many of us grew up in families who held to serious mottoes. Which one of the following did your family espouse?

- Work hard.

- Get while the gettin's good.

- The early bird gets the worm.

- Don't waste your time.

- The idle mind is the devil's playground.

- If at first you don't succeed; try, try, and try again.

These mottoes have a way of keeping us always moving; we don't seem able to slow down and relax.

Some have grown up in families that were full of pain or abuse.

Because life was difficult, it forced them to grow up quickly causing them to miss childhood play. As adults they find no time for fun. Both groups miss out on a significant piece of marriage.

An important aspect of love is playfulness. It helps us relax and reduce the stress of life. Yet, many either feel guilty for playing or they just don't know how to play.

One hot afternoon our neighborhood had a water fight. The couples from three houses stretched their garden hoses out to the street and sprayed each other. The children ran about with buckets and squirt guns. We laughed and played and had a wonderful time. Then Sam came home from work. As he drove past us and into his driveway, he gave us a disgusted look. His scowl told us to grow up! Sam's look impacted all of us so we gathered up our children and hoses. It was no longer okay to play. We needed to move on to more serious activities, but it sure was fun while it lasted!

Fun and recreation are critical for a marriage. Sometimes you do it side by side as you watch a movie. Other times you do it face to face as you play backgammon. Either way, it's important to interact by talking, laughing, and touching. Remember you are together and having fun.

There are thousands of fun things to do. The only limit is your imagination. Anything can be fun if you have the right attitude. Here are fifty activities that might be fun to do together. If they don't sound enjoyable, make your own list.

1. Go to the park.
2. Play board games.
3. Take a hike.
4. Visit a pet store.
5. Make cookies.
6. Go roller skating.
7. Fly a kite.
8. Watch a movie.
9. Take a swim.
10. Walk in the rain.
11. Draw a picture.
12. Ride a carousel.
13. Sleep in the back yard.
14. Play tennis.
15. Collect rocks, shells, or whatever.

16. Plant flowers.
17. Explore.
18. Go to the zoo.
19. Watch a parade.
20. Ride bikes.
21. Ride horses.
22. Tell jokes.
23. Tell scary stories.
24. Eat at an unusual restaurant.
25. Go to a sports event.
26. Walk barefoot in the sand.
27. Create something with clay.
28. Go fishing.
29. Go window shopping.
30. Take a train ride.
31. Read a book aloud.
32. Play volleyball.
33. Take pictures.
34. Look at the stars.
35. Make up a song.
36. Feed the ducks.
37. Watch people.
38. Exercise.
39. Shoot off fireworks.
40. Ride on a swing.
41. Ride a Ferris wheel.
42. Play croquet.
43. Fix a gourmet dinner.
44. Watch cartoons.
45. Throw a Frisbee.
46. Play video games.
47. Build a model.
48. Go bird watching.
49. Go bowling.
50. Take an adventure.

Create an adventure. Make a picnic lunch together, climb into the car. Start driving nowhere in particular. At the first cross street she decides to go left, right, or straight. At the next cross street he decides to go left, right, or straight. Continue taking turns until you agree on a place to stop and enjoy your picnic. Not knowing where you will end up makes it a wonderful, carefree adventure. That is recreational togetherness.

WORK TOGETHERNESS

Every marriage consists of common everyday tasks and chores. Albert Schweitzer once said that much of life consists of taking out the garbage. It is comprised of hundreds of little irritating projects that keep piling up: dishes in the sink, dust in the corners, weeds in the flower beds. Clothes get dirty, light bulbs burn out, cupboards become cluttered. Certain things demand our attention and it is a lot easier to do them together.

I hate to make the bed alone. We have a queen-size bed and trying to make it by myself is awkward. Moving back and forth between the two sides is also time-consuming. It's so much easier with two people. Spreading the blankets, smoothing the wrinkles, evening everything up, and tucking it in goes quickly with a team approach.

Doing these common tasks together provide opportunities for real closeness. I have warm childhood memories of my grandparents standing at the sink washing and drying the dinner dishes as they discussed the events of the day.

Some therapists believe that the area of greatest conflict in marriage is the division of household chores. Who cleans the bathroom? Who cares for the lawn? Who does the ironing?

A hundred years ago, who did what in a marriage was a lot easier to determine. These days, roles are a lot more flexible and often a lot more confusing. One solution to this dilemma is to do more of these domestic chores as a team. Cooking, paying bills, parenting, washing the car, and many other tasks are done more effectively with two. This produces one more area of unity and togetherness, and avoids unnecessary arguments over who does what.

CRISIS TOGETHERNESS

Life rarely goes the way we plan it and marriage is no exception. Years go into dreaming of the perfect wedding ceremony and many months are painstakingly spent orchestrating every detail. When that special day finally arrives, friends and relatives gather, filling the church. Then inevitably something goes wrong. Every wedding I have ever attended has had its unplanned moments—babies wailing, flower girls or ring bearers refusing to cooperate, brides fainting, groomsmen tripping, soloists losing their voice, candelabras crashing to the floor, even electrical outages. With that we begin our marriage. Trying to plan perfection we ultimately have to face the fact that life rarely goes as we plan.

Marriage is full of unexpected crises. These traumas either destroy a marriage or make it stronger.

- Bankruptcy
- Infertility
- Severe depression
- Cancer
- Natural disasters
- Car accidents
- Nervous breakdowns
- Thefts
- Unstable economy
- Birth defects
- Rape
- Alcohol or drug abuse
- Death of a child

As I finished this list, Brittany came into my office.

"I love you, Daddy. What are you writing?" She looked over my shoulder and pointed to *Bankruptcy* and *Birth defects*. "These words start with 'B' just like my name."

I smiled and told her how much I loved her. She scampered off to her room, leaving me pondering my list and thanking God that none of these difficulties have attacked our little family.

I think of close friends who have struggled with great pain. There's Gary and Alice who would be such good parents, but are unable to conceive. Then I think of Doug and Susan who have moved thousands of miles away in hopes that a different environment will improve Susan's disabling allergies. I don't understand why bad things happen to good people, but they do. Unfortunately, these bad things often tear marriages apart.

Couples frequently seek professional help when they are in the midst of a crisis. Not long ago a couple came to me grieving the loss of their six-year-old son. He was their only child. A hit-and-run accident in front of their house killed him instantly. Their pain was overwhelming. The husband held his grief inside, refusing to talk about it or accept help. He had built a wall around himself. He no longer socialized or joked. When his wife tried to comfort him, he pulled away. When she broke into tears or begged his forgiveness for somehow not stopping the accident, he simply stared into space. The harder she tried to connect with him, the more distant he grew. Three months after the accident, the room remained as the child had left it. When his wife mentioned the need to straighten it up, he flew into a rage.

Leaning on each other is so much healthier than bearing the burden alone. Don't let the heartaches of life pull your marriage apart.

Six months after the accident, this couple was even further apart. In frustration, she left. He did nothing. She telephoned and begged him to communicate with her. He said he couldn't and hung up. A year later the couple divorced.

A crisis does not have to undermine a marriage. Gary and Alice have spent months talking about and grieving their infertility. They took a class on adoption and have now adopted a wonderful little boy. Their original dream was blocked, so together they built a new dream.

Doug walked close with Susan as her health deteriorated. When Susan improved during a vacation to Florida, the two discussed whether a move would help. They made a second trip and again, Susan's condition improved. Together they decided to leave their hometown and relocate their family. This is crisis togetherness. It was a hard move. Starting over is never easy.

These two married couples work as a team; when one hurts, so does the other. They share their pain and allow their crisis to bring them closer together. Leaning on each other is so much healthier than bearing the burden alone. Don't let the heartaches of life pull your marriage apart.

SEXUAL TOGETHERNESS

Sexuality is much more than erogenous zones and intercourse. It's a physical closeness that goes beyond just the physical. Its essence is emotional, social, and spiritual. Sexuality falls into three levels of intimacy.

Touching. We all need to be touched. Our skin craves it. Children without it become emotionally disturbed and can even die. Adults without it become irritable and often depressed. Every couple needs to touch. Holding hands, an arm around the shoulder, a pat on the back, sitting close, a hand on the leg are all messages of affirmation and a means of telling our spouse how special they are. These touches are critical to a healthy marriage, and they can happen anywhere, from walking through the mall to sitting in church.

Cuddling. This is more intimate than touching. It includes hugging, back rubs, kissing, and non-erogenous caressing. The intensity has increased. These activities are more private and personal. Unfortunately, many see cuddling as merely a prelude to lovemaking. Though it may lead to intercourse, cuddling can be an end in itself. It is sad to realize that many spouses yearn for cuddling, but avoid it because they think they know where it will lead.

To enhance romance, I will have a couple set up special cuddling nights. I instruct them to hug, kiss, and caress, but not to make love. This keeps cuddling pure and helps each partner to see this activity as an event that is special and satisfying in itself.

Lovemaking. Quality lovemaking is positive, relaxed, romantic, arousing, plus physically and emotionally satisfying for both partners. To achieve satisfaction in lovemaking requires communication, time, planning, and work. But the payoff for both partners is worth it.

Communication is the first step. Someone once gave terrible advice when they said, "Don't talk about it, just do it." A couple *needs* to talk about their lovemaking. Yet, when the subject comes up, many are embarrassed or anxious. Others fall into a joking bravado. Either way, honest and open communication doesn't take place. Here are a few of the questions that need to be discussed:

- Who initiates lovemaking and how?

- If one is not in the mood for whatever reason, how do they communicate it without hurting or offending their partner?

- Do you prefer passive or aggressive foreplay?

- What is most arousing to your spouse in the areas of vision, touch, sound, and smell?

- What is sexually offensive to your spouse in the areas of vision, touch, sound, and smell?

- How much time do you both desire to spend in foreplay?

- What types of birth control do you both feel comfortable with?

There are many other important questions, but these make a good beginning toward understanding each other and building sexual togetherness.

For over twenty years of marriage, lovemaking was not emotionally fulfilling for either Robert or Linda. Linda had not been orgasmic since her wedding night. Her gynecologist said there were no physical abnormalities. Because Robert sensed her sexual frustration it undermined his desire. Years had passed and neither spoke of their sexual needs.

As they sat in my office, I asked Linda what would constitute the perfect evening of lovemaking. She listed twelve things she thought would improve their sexual enjoyment. It surprised Robert. She had never mentioned these things to him. He loved his wife and certain things he had done were offensive to Linda. Other things that were arousing to her, had never happened.

At home that evening, Robert and Linda walked through her list. For the first time in over twenty years she was orgasmic. All they needed was communication, time, planning, and work.

I hear many complaints about sexuality. The most common frustrations are as follows:

Not enough touching.
"My spouse touches me only when interested in lovemaking."

Not enough cuddling.
"My spouse doesn't like to cuddle."

Not enough lovemaking.
"My spouse has a lack of sexual desire and is seldom interested in lovemaking."

Lack of context.
"We have not been getting along and my spouse wants to make love."

Foreplay too short.
"My spouse wants to move right into lovemaking without enough romance and arousal."

Too rough and/or aggressive.
"My spouse is not tender and sometimes hurts me."

Poor hygiene.
"My spouse's lack of cleanliness makes it difficult for me to enjoy lovemaking."

Too tired.
"We always make love at the end of the day and I'm just too exhausted for it to feel like quality time."

Poor communication.
"My spouse doesn't know what arouses me."

Too tense.
"It is hard for me to relax and really enjoy myself during love making."

Generally, sexual togetherness doesn't just happen. It's a process of sensitivity and fine tuning. If a couple takes the time, their sexual relationship will grow richer. If they do not, it will become an area of disappointment and irritation.

SPIRITUAL TOGETHERNESS

This is the strongest and most important aspect of togetherness. However, this area of intimacy is elusive to many because spirituality appears so abstract and personal. The word *spiritual* points us to the invisible core of who we are—our spirit, our soul. It also points us to a supernatural world that has its own set of rules. Like sexuality, some people feel comfortable with their spirituality and others don't. However, as we all have a sexual part, so we also have a spiritual part.

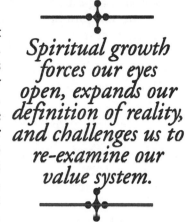

Spiritual growth forces our eyes open, expands our definition of reality, and challenges us to re-examine our value system.

Psychologists frequently divide it into two components. *External spirituality* looks spiritual on the surface. All the rituals and activities are followed perfectly—church involvement, Bible study, and tithing. Still, this person's faith is lacking. It does not integrate into who they are. There is no spiritual depth or vibrancy.

Internal spirituality defines who the person is and impacts their beliefs, decisions, and behavior. They may be involved in the same rituals and activities as the externally spiritual, but they look to God for ultimate truth and direction.

Focusing on God pulls us out of our selfishness. As two develop their spiritual dimension, they draw closer to God and closer to each other. Concepts of eternity and infinity provide a different perspective on a world we would like to revolve around us. Spiritual growth forces our eyes open, expands our definition of reality, and challenges us to re-examine our value system. Internal spirituality for either the individual or the couple has three levels.

Sensing God. This is the awareness that we live in a supernatural universe and are in the midst of a spiritual battle. Some are more in touch with this battle because they have a keen sense of good and evil. They move beyond the natural and tangible. In the classic *Lord of the Rings* J. R. R. Tolkien describes this struggle where the dark forces are trying to destroy the light.

In a different situation almost three thousand years ago, the King of Syria sent a great army to Dothan, sixty miles north of Jerusalem, to capture the prophet Elisha. Early one morning Elisha's servant awakened him in a panic. The Syrian army had surrounded the city and cut off escape. "Don't be afraid!" Elisha told him. "For our army is bigger than theirs!" His servant must have looked perplexed because the next thing Elisha did was to pray. "Open his eyes and let him see!" Before the servant's eyes a ring of blazing angels appeared surrounding the city and protecting them from the Syrian army.[5] That day Elisha's servant learned that sensing God involves looking beyond what his eyes could see.

In its essence, sensing God is facing truth. Every day we are deceived and distracted by hundreds of lies, big and small. We lie to ourselves and to each other. Pilate asked, "What is truth?"[6] The question still lingers two thousand years later.

Looking for truth and ultimate meaning together bonds a couple in a way that words cannot describe. Viktor Frankl, the existential psychotherapist, wrote that the search for meaning is the basis for mental health.[7] Truth and meaning are spiritual issues, and unless we sense God we are trapped in a limited, narcissistic world that leaves no room for togetherness of any form.

Begin building spiritual togetherness by talking about this dimension. Discussing truth and meaning forces a deeper examination of life. To those who are honest, it leads to an awareness of God. To sense God's presence in an ancient forest or a modern cathedral is an awesome feeling. To shiver at evil and applaud good draws us closer together.

> *The only way to defeat the enemy is to know the enemy. Ignoring it and hoping for the best will not save the marriage.*

Seeking God. Seeking God is like sensing God in that both are an attitude, but the actual seeking process requires action. First one asks, "Who is God?" As two dig deep to answer this question they develop a spiritual unity. The struggle both to *know* God and to know *about* God is a transcendent journey. Being fellow travelers lifts a couple beyond the natural tangible universe. This involves exploring creative ways to grow closer to God and encouraging each other in a devotional life. Seeking God takes many routes. Adam and Eve walked with God in the cool of the evening. Moses faced God in a burning bush and high on Mt. Sinai. Elijah found God in a still small voice. Isaiah saw God in a vision.

Pursuing God is a frame of mind and an approach to life. Walking into a church, in its purist sense, is an unconscious statement of spiritual desire. Unfortunately, our culture has contaminated this statement and many enter the church without any spiritual motives. Yet going to church together, and worshipping God side by side is bonding. Allowing the architecture, symbols, and stained glass to draw you in; following the ceremony and ritual as it points you heavenward; being lifted by hymns, music, and Scripture; all of this assists you to focus on God and his impact on your marriage.

Many people pray on a regular basis and still more believe prayer is a good idea, especially in time of crisis. Praying with your spouse can be both a frightening and an exhilarating experience if done with depth and sincerity. Exposing your soul to God is humbling, and inviting your partner to join you increases vulnerability. Standing before God—whether it is with praise, thanksgiving, confession, or petition—is an intimate experience. There is something about this process that strips away pretense. Once you break through the fear and pray together, it brings about the deepest of all togetherness.

Another means of seeking God is through reading the Bible and devotional literature. Grappling with words that pull us heavenward and remind us of eternal truths also builds spiritual togetherness. Some couples read through the Bible. Others share devotional writings, discovering more about God and how he interacts with the universe.

One of the difficulties with reading together is finding a quality time that is convenient for both. It is best to find a time that is consistent, free of interruption and when both partners are alert. Study takes concentration and meditation. Sharing together reflections and illuminations bring two people closer. Many denominations publish daily devotional guides. To help you get started, here is a list of five excellent books that promote meditation:

- *The Confessions of St. Augustine*
- *Knowledge of the Holy* by A. W. Tozer

- *Mere Christianity* by C. S. Lewis
- *Orthodoxy* by G. K. Chesterton
- *Knowing God* by J. I. Packer

Reflecting God. If we sincerely pursue God we will, in time, begin to reflect God. As the moon reflects the sun, so true spirituality ultimately reflects God. This is called godliness, morality, and perfection. Here, two encourage each other toward a higher level of conduct than society at large. This struggle for moral excellence is essential to spirituality yet it is impossible to attain. There is no way any of us can be truly godly for we all struggle with a dark side that thinks, feels, and does things we wish we didn't. As a result, this challenge to our spirituality often creates high levels of guilt. However, we can move toward our goal if we accept our humanness and understand that since God is willing to forgive us, we ought to forgive ourselves as well.

Virtue and godliness have many definitions. One widely accepted definition is what the apostle Paul calls the "fruit of the Spirit."[8] His list of godly characteristics is as follows:

- Showing **love** when those around are not lovable.

- Having **joy** when those around are discouraged and discontent.

- Exuding **peace** when those around are anxious.

- Practicing **patience** when those around are hurried and frantic.

- Reaching out in **kindness** when those around are difficult.

- Shining with **goodness** when those around do evil.

- Standing in **faithfulness** when those around have no commitment.

- Flowing with **gentleness** when those around are harsh and cruel.

- Demonstrating **self-control** when those around have none.

The most difficult area of togetherness for many is the spiritual. This might have to do with couples having different religious heritages, different levels of spiritual sensitivity, or different spiritual experiences.

Another factor might have to do with psychological types. Extroverts are more likely to talk about their spirituality for they experience it in community. Introverts see spirituality as a private affair and they tend to have a quiet faith.

Ultimately, spiritual togetherness unites all other forms of togetherness. Intellectually, we think about who God is and how he touches our everyday life. Emotionally, he moves us and softens our heart. Aesthetically, we marvel at the beauty of God's handiwork. Recreationally, we frolic in his playground. In crisis, we lean on him, learning to trust him through difficult times. During household work we ask for strength. Sexually, we thank him for the pleasure and affirmation of physical closeness. Thus, the core of all forms of togetherness is the spiritual.

SPACES IN YOUR TOGETHERNESS

Individuality is critical to good mental health, but so is togetherness. A danger is imminent when we fall into "either/or" thinking. Individuality at its extreme fosters selfishness, insensitivity, isolation, and loneliness. Togetherness, at its extreme, fosters enmeshment, codependency, constriction, and strangulation.

Individuality and togetherness are both important to a healthy marriage. We need breathing space to express our uniqueness, yet we must be careful that this distance does not lead to a permanent separateness. At certain times we separate for individual journeys, only to excitedly reunite, sharing with our partner what we have learned from our separate adventures. As we grow closer, we must not erase or overshadow the two individuals. Kahil Gibran, the famous poet, wrote in *The Prophet*, "Let there be spaces in your togetherness."[9]

We draw together in our coupling, we draw apart in our individuality. Balance is the key. We do need space in our togetherness.

Discussion Questions

1. When do you feel most in touch with your mate's emotions?

2. Are you more likely to ignore, deny, moralize, ridicule, attack, or affirm your partner's emotions?

    How does he/she respond when you do each of the above?

3. When was the last time the two of you read a book together?

    What did you enjoy most about that experience?

4. What specific places or types of natural beauty does your spouse enjoy the most?

5. What are the most memorable scenes of aesthetic togetherness you and your mate have experienced?

6. When was the last time the two of you set aside an entire day just to play?

7. If tomorrow you and your partner had the whole day alone with no distractions or responsibilities, what would you do?

8. What common everyday tasks would you rather do with your spouse than alone?

9. What is the biggest crisis the two of you have experienced together?

10. When was the last time the two of you talked about your sexual needs and how to be better lovers?

    Is this easy or awkward? Why?

11. What is it that you enjoy most about each of the three levels of intimacy?

> a) Touching
> b) Cuddling
> c) Lovemaking

12. What have the two of you done together in the past week to grow closer to God?

13. On a scale from 1 to 10 (1 = excellent, 10 = poor) how well does your marriage rate in the following eight types of togetherness?

> a) Emotional   e) Work
> b) Intellectual   f) Crisis
> c) Aesthetic   g) Sexual
> d) Recreational   h) Spiritual

14. What specific things can you do in the next three months to improve your rating in each of the above types?

Notes

1. Ecclesiastes 4:9-11.

2. These eight catagories are drawn and adapted from Charlotte Clinebell and Howard Clinebell, *The Intimate Marriage* (New York: Harper, 1970). In this book they present the following twelve facets of intimacy: sexual, emotional, intellectual, aesthetic, creative, recreational, work, crisis, conflict, commitment, spiritual, and communication.

3. Gregory Stock, *The Book of Questions* (New York: Workman Publishing, 1987).

4. Psalm 19:1, TLB.

5. 2 Kings 6:16-17, TLB.

6. John 18:38.

7. Viktor E. Frankl, *Man's Search for Meaning* (New York: Pocket Books, 1963).

8. Galatians 5:22-23.

9. Kahil Gibran, *The Prophet* (New York: Knopf, 1976), 15.

9

ROMANCE

"O Romeo, Romeo! Wherefore art thou Romeo?" Everybody knows these words from the romantic balcony scene of Shakespeare's *Romeo and Juliet*. Romeo is a Montague, Juliet is a Capulet. Their two families are locked in a deadly conflict, but love will not be blocked in the world's most famous romance. Romeo risks his life to climb the orchard walls and sneak to Juliet's window.

"With love's light wings did I o'er-perch these walls; For stony limits cannot hold love out."

Juliet looks down on the man she loves and warns him that if her family finds him, they will kill him. Romeo proclaims his "heart's dear love" and begs,
"The exchange of thy love's faithful vow for mine."

Juliet replies,

"I gave thee mine before thou didst request it.... My bounty is as boundless as the sea, My love as deep; the more I give to thee, The more I have, for both are infinite."[1]

Romeo and Juliet are one of many couples illustrating romance. History is full of well-known examples: Anthony and Cleopatra, Dante and Beatrice, Napoleon and Josephine, Heathcliff and Catherine, Rhett Butler and Scarlet O'Hara, Edward VIII and Mrs. Simpson, C. S. Lewis and Joy Davidman.

In today's world we are hungry for romance. Love is the prevailing theme in popular music. Over 60 percent of current movies have a romantic element.[2] This year alone, romance novels account for 40 percent of all fiction published.[3] I believe that every one of us has a romantic side; for some it is obvious, for others it is deeply buried. Romance is most active during courtship. It is unfortunate that it is prone to dwindle as a marriage matures.

Every marriage needs romance. As a psychologist I've noticed five interesting patterns in terms of men, women, and romance.

1. Men tend to be less romantic than women.

2. Men tend to take relationships for granted more than women.

3. Women tend to leave relationships more frequently than men.

4. Men tend to be surprised when the woman leaves.

5. Women report that if men would work on basic issues of romance they would not leave.

We all need to become artists of romance (especially men) and we need to practice this art daily. It's the little things in romance that count, for without them a marriage lacks warmth and richness. A relationship without romance is listless, dry, and dreary. It is a divorce waiting to happen. André Maurois, the French novelist and historian, wrote that "marriage is an edifice that must be rebuilt every day." Life wears down relationships. Romance is an important aspect of renewing and rebuilding them.

So what exactly is romance? My dictionary says it's a *love affair* and as such it takes many shapes: a kiss, a note, a walk hand-in-hand, a glance, a vow, a gift, and an infinite number of other expressions. Romance is caring. It is saying and showing that you love someone. It reaches beyond our own selfishness and egocentricity to focus on our mate. Romance should be the natural result of every marriage. The relationship might not be easy, smooth, or anywhere near perfect, but it can still be romantic.

Romance is the interweaving

Commitment, positive regard, communication, giving, and togetherness all build toward romance; facing the enemy, making peace, and forgiveness protects romance from being undermined.

236

and fruition of the previous eight chapters of this book. Commitment, positive regard, communication, giving, and togetherness all build toward romance; facing the enemy, making peace, and forgiveness protects romance from being undermined. Anyone can be romantic. Just remember what preceded this chapter, then spend the time to develop the following five elements.

THE ELEMENTS OF ROMANCE

God has made each one of us unique. What we think of as romantic is often different from what our mate thinks. One might like formal occasions where you each dress up, the other might enjoy being casual. One might be drawn to the city, but the other loves the rugged countryside. One might think romance belongs to the day, whereas the other thinks it belongs to evening or late night.

Men tend to consider visual images romantic—how she looks and moves. Women are more attracted by verbal expression—what he says and how he says it. Everyone has a different version of what is romantic. Don't force your partner to do what you think should be romantic, then pout when they don't enjoy it as much as you do. The key is to understand what touches their romantic button.

Share with each other the time of day and the places you consider romantic. Talk about the actions that stimulate each of you as well as the activities you desire to share with each other. Don't be frustrated if you both see romance differently. Just remember, you can always find common ground.

Romance has five basic elements and one or more of those are present in every romantic encounter. Build on them in a way that increases the romance for both of you.

JOY

Before you and your spouse were married you had fun together. You walked through the park, built sand castles, flew kites, and laughed until your sides ached. You enjoyed each other's company and were happy beyond belief. As you grow older though, life becomes more complicated and you don't have time for frivolous fun anymore. It's easy to lose track of the joy that brought you together. People get too serious and misplace their spirit of romance.

Romance involves relaxation, playfulness, and laughter. Single people tell me that a sense of humor is one of the most important qualities they look for in a potential relationship. My wife makes me laugh...just who she is makes me joyful and that joy wells into laughter. She frequently looks at me and says, "Stop laughing at me." I try to swallow my grin and say, "I'm not laughing at you, I'm laughing with you." She smiles and says, "But I'm not laughing."

Your marriage should bring joy into your life. If it doesn't, don't blame your mate; instead, ask yourself what happened to your ability to relax and be playful. Happiness is a state of mind and it's contagious. As you laugh and have fun your spouse will soon join you.

I like the humor in *Reader's Digest* and I periodically read it late at night just before going to sleep. I lie in bed next to my wife, who is trying hard to concentrate on the book she's reading, and I start to chuckle. Something has struck me funny and I just can't hold it in, but I try. My whole body shakes as I laugh on the inside and soon the bed is shaking. Tami gives me one of those why-don't-you-be-quiet looks and says, "You might as well read me the joke so I can laugh too." I do and soon we're both lying in bed chuckling. Couples need to laugh and have more fun. It's the beginning of romance.

EXCITEMENT

Excitement means to be stirred up and romance stirs the emotions. It stirs enthusiasm, zest, and at times, passion. It energizes a marriage. The opposite of excitement is dullness. Becoming stuck in a rut or trapped in a routine makes for a dull marriage. Marriage is a growing, changing, interacting organism. If it becomes a rigid institution, with everything predictable and repetitive, the relationship is boring and dull.

We all need excitement and if it isn't present in our marriage, we look for it elsewhere: jobs, sports, hobbies, friendships, romance novels, television, or wherever else we can find it. This can be dangerous because it pulls one away from their partner and allows another activity or person to meet a need that is best met within the marriage. I'm not saying that all your excitement must come from your spouse, but if there is no excitement within a relationship, then it's time to become romantic.

Last summer, I took two of my children to the Rose Festival Parade. They were so excited. Brittany loved the brightly colored floats and Dylan loved the marching bands. I had a great time watching the delight on their faces. As adults we become jaded and lose that child-like excitement.

Three words come to mind as I think about excitement. *Adventure* is the first. A romantic marriage goes on adventures where the couple has new and refreshing experiences. They experiment and explore; trying new restaurants, new vacation spots, new hobbies.

The next word is *discovery.* A romantic marriage is not static. Each partner is constantly finding out new information about the other and the world around them. We never have absolute knowledge or understanding of our partner. It's exciting to learn new things about them, who they are, and what they experience. It's also exciting to discover new things about our world. Share what you learn and let your partner share with you.

The last word is *amazement.* Life is amazing, but we tend to race through each hectic day without even noticing the wonders that surround us. Romance involves letting yourself be amazed by the beauty in your world. Beauty comes in many forms. There is the natural beauty of waterfalls, sunsets, blooming flowers, or snow-topped mountains. Then there is the artistic beauty of well-crafted music, dance, poetry, painting, or prose. Last, but most important, is the inner beauty of faith, love, kindness, courage, and honesty. Allow yourself to be amazed and create wonder in your spouse by enjoying the excitement of this beauty together.

Robert Browning was an exciting, energetic man who loved romance. He was thirty-six when he met Elizabeth Barrett, a pale forty-year-old invalid who is considered one of the outstanding poets of her day.

In childhood, Elizabeth suffered a spinal injury and, even as an adult, she rarely left her father's house. When Robert and Elizabeth met they fell madly in love. Their courtship was filled with adventure, discovery, and amazement. During the next year she grew physically stronger as her love for Robert grew deeper. Soon they were married and moved from England to Italy. Several years later she captured the excitement of her love in a collection of poems that she presented to Robert as a gift. In 1850 they were published as *Sonnets from the Portuguese* and the forty-second sonnet of this book has come to be one of the best-known love poems of all time. Here is a portion of it.

> How do I love thee? Let me count the ways.
> I love thee to the depth and breadth and height
> My soul can reach....
>   —I love thee with the breath,
> Smiles, tears, of all my life! and, if God choose,
> I shall but love thee better after death.[4]

That's romantic excitement!

CREATIVITY

Excitement and creativity are close cousins, for what is creative is usually exciting. Creativity gives us variety. God could have easily created just one type of tree, or flower, or dog, but he gave us an amazing variety that enriches our lives. Variety comes from innovation and imagination. Discover what excites your mate and creatively surprise them.

Romance is creative and comes up with unlimited ways to communicate its love.

Variety and imagination keep us alert and focused. In college I had a professor who taught in a monotone voice. I tried so hard to follow his lectures, but soon I'd be daydreaming or half-asleep. A monotonous marriage will cause couples to daydream or "fall asleep" too. Romance is the color and music of marriage and is never boring.

Creative romance knows how to surprise one's mate. Doug and Gina were hiking through the woods one sunny afternoon when they came across a table with a crisply starched white linen tablecloth. The table was set with fine china, crystal goblets, and gleaming silver. Doug encouraged Gina to sit at the table and rest. She was surprised and asked how all this got so deep in the woods. Doug shrugged his shoulders as he sat down too. A moment later a good friend appeared in a tuxedo and offered them hors d'oeuvres.

Now Gina realized this was all planned. The two were served a wonderful five-course meal and as they relaxed after dessert, violin music floated from nearby bushes. It was the perfect romantic surprise that Gina will never forget.

Surprises are unexpected and, sometimes, impractical acts of creativity. They add pizazz to life and pull our everyday existence out of the ordinary. Romance is creative and comes up with unlimited ways to communicate its love.

COURTESY

In 1178 Andrew the Chaplain laid down thirty-one codes and principles of courtly love. A summary of these rules is simple: Romance has good manners. The apostle Paul said it this way in his first letter to the Corinthians:

> Love is patient, love is kind.
> It does not envy, it does not boast,
> it is not proud. It is not rude, it
> is not self-seeking, it is not easily
> angered, it keeps no record of wrongs.[5]

We live in a time when good manners are thought of as old-fashioned and inconvenient. Good manners are never old-fashioned, but they are frequently inconvenient. It takes time to open the car door for your wife, or patiently listen to your husband's story for the hundredth time without interrupting him. Saying *please, thank you,* or *excuse me* slows down the conversation; as does asking if your partner minds if you do something, rather than just telling them what you're going to do.

Courtesy makes it clear that your spouse is very important to you.

Thoughtfulness and politeness are romantic. It communicates to your partner that they are special. Walking beside them, instead of three feet in front of them shows respect. So does smiling at them and not doing anything that would embarrass them in either public or private. Being sensitive to

241

each other when showing gentleness, tenderness, and concern is also romantic. All these actions melt the heart of your spouse. It is romantic to be able to say, "He was a true gentleman," or "She was a real lady."

Courtesy makes it clear that your spouse is very important to you. Romance sets aside time and gives consideration to make sure they understand without any doubt that they hold a special place in your heart.

Harry Truman was the thirty-third president of the United States. He was also a true romantic. He courted his wife, Bess, for eight years before they married. During this time he wrote her many notes telling her how much he treasured her. His romance didn't end with marriage. He continued to write her, expressing how lucky he was to have such a fine woman. When Mr. Truman died he left over twelve-hundred love letters to his dear wife. Some eight hundred years earlier, on April 27, 1174, Marie of Champagne was asked if romance can really exist between married people. Her answer was an emphatic "No!" but she was wrong. Just ask Bess Truman. When there is a declaration of affection in a marriage, whether through word or deed, there is romance.

INTIMACY

Romance without intimacy is shallow. Joy, excitement, creativity, and courtesy may add to a fantastic evening, but all of these elements will fade. The heart of romance is intimacy, when two people connect. It is a relationship that is both emotional and physical. Women connect romance with meeting emotional needs, such as holding hands along a moonlit beach or personal conversations over a candlelight dinner. Men connect romance with meeting physical needs and find most forms of sexual encounter romantic.

Every couple is unique and has different emotional and sexual needs, but most couples need at least one emotional and one sexual time per week. Less than that can potentially cause resentment, insecurity, and lack of attachment. For women, emotional intimacy opens the door to sexual intimacy; for men, sexual intimacy opens the door to emotional intimacy.

Every couple needs regular emotional times where they can really talk and connect. This is your special time to relax and enjoy each other's company. One couple I know goes out to the movies every

Monday night, and another couple sets aside Saturday mornings for breakfast at a local pastry shop. It's important to get out of the house and do something special together. Go out to a concert, or a sports event, or simply take a walk through the park. Most couples agree that dating is important, but it still doesn't happen on a regular basis. There are three common excuses I hear for why it doesn't.

Our lives are too busy. Dating is an issue of priorities. If your marriage is important to you, you will make the time to be together with your mate. It may be only a short time squeezed into a lunch break. Maybe you need to drop an activity you enjoy to make the extra time. Whatever it takes, if you're motivated and creative, you will find quality time.

We don't have the money. Dating doesn't have to cost much. Go to the mall and watch people, play tennis or Frisbee, visit the library, rent a video, ride bikes, or go for a drive. One couple told me they have "in-house date nights." They put the kids to bed early, turn off the TV, snuggle up on the sofa together, share a pint of frozen yogurt, and visit. Total cost of their date is $2.50.

We both enjoy doing different things. Because a couple has different interests doesn't mean they need to keep from having great emotional times together. Go out and enjoy your mate's company, regardless of the setting or activity. The purpose is to connect and build your relationship. That can be accomplished even as you do activities that are not your preference. Besides you can always take turns choosing what to do on each date. Let your mate decide what to do next time; then you decide the time after that.

In addition to your emotional time, set aside quality sexual time. Be sensitive to each other's sexual needs, anxieties, and comfort zones. Create a romantic atmosphere in the bedroom and beyond. Let all the elements of romance enhance your sexual interactions: joy, excitement, creativity, courtesy, and intimacy. Fill your senses with romance: perfect music, alluring night wear, pleasant perfume or cologne, scented body oils. Prepare for amorous times with whatever will increase your sense of romance, such as bubble baths, brushed teeth, locked doors, fresh sheets (or maybe silk sheets), a glass of sparkling cider, tender words, a special dessert, a love poem. Set the mood and focus on bringing pleasure to your partner.

The lack of either emotional or sexual bonding can block intimacy and set a marriage adrift. Intimacy is a lover's knot that keeps a relationship close. In *Love Life for Every Married Couple* there is a list of some of the strands that strengthen the bond of intimacy between husband and wife:

- Physical touching of an affectionate, non-sexual nature

- Shared feelings

- Closeness without inhibitions

- Absence of psychological defenses

- Open communication and honesty

- Intellectual agreement on major issues

- Spiritual harmony

- Sensitive appreciation of the mate's physical and emotional responses

- Similar values held

- Imparted secrets

- Genuine understanding

- Mutual confidence

- A sense of warmth, safety, and relaxation when together

- Sensuous nearness

- Sexual pleasures lovingly shared

- Signs of love freely given and received

- Mutual responsibility and caring

- Abiding trust[6]

Each of these strands increases the romance in your marriage and deepens your love.

These five elements are more than abstract philosophical concepts; they are attitudes that find fulfillment in action. A romantic is not passive or quiet. They live life to the fullest and love their mate with supernatural love. In doing so they reflect God's romance with us, for God's love is unquenchable.

THE ACTIVITIES OF ROMANCE

It's Saturday night, that special evening set aside for romance. Couples all over the world are going out to dinners, movies, dances, concerts, or some other romantic activity. So what am I doing? I'm sitting at home writing this chapter and my wife is doing the laundry. Both my neighbors have taken their wives out for the evening. One arranged baby-sitting for their children and took his wife to a western barbecue party. The other took his wife to dinner and a movie. I'm feeling guilty sitting here writing about romance and not showing it. I finally put down my pen and go outside to the rose garden. I carefully cut four of the most beautiful roses and present them to Tami with a kiss and an "I love you."

I wish I were more romantic but it doesn't come naturally to me. This afternoon I mentioned to my wife I was writing a chapter on romance and that it would probably be the shortest chapter in the book. She asked if it was the shortest because it was the aspect of marriage that was the hardest for me. She didn't ask in a spirit of meanness or humiliation but out of insight and observation. It was a gentle reminder that I need to spend more time on romance.

We need a reminder that there are both strong and weak areas in any marriage. Happily, it is possible to improve the weak ones. Specific ideas of how to be romantic help me to follow through, so I have collected seventy-five ideas that I want to try during the next year. I share them with you hoping it helps you to also romance your marriage.

1. Kiss hello at the door.

2. Send a plant or a bouquet thanking them for last night.

3. Fill the gas tank after using their car.

4. Set aside money for recreation and fun.

5. Let them decide which movie or concert to go to. Then go and be pleasant for their full enjoyment.

6. Pray for them.

7. Call them at work or home and tell them you are thinking of them.

8. Carry a picture of them in your purse or wallet.

9. Smell good when you meet for dinner.

10. Buy or make a card for no special reason.

11. Ask what they want to watch on TV, then watch it with them.

12. Buy a cassette or CD of their favorite music and hide it under their pillow.

13. Fix their special breakfast and serve it to them in bed.

14. Give a back rub or neck rub.

15. Ask them out to lunch and dress up for them.

16. Wash their car.

17. Bring home their favorite ice cream.

18. Run bath water for them.

19. Set up a romantic getaway.

20. Buy them something sexy.

21. Send a telegram to tell them what a great partner they are.

22. Make a tape-recorded love letter.

23. Buy their favorite magazine for them.

24. Greet them with a hug and kiss before they get out of bed in the morning.

25. Attempt to be cheerful even though you don't feel that way.

26. Try to use the word "ours" instead of "mine" whenever you can.

27. Leave a love letter hidden in a place they are bound to find.

28. Reminisce about your wedding.

29. Rent a classic romantic movie (such as *An Affair to Remember, Casablanca, African Queen, Father Goose, Sound of Music, South Pacific*), then watch it cuddled up together with the lights out.

30. Agree on a place you would like to travel together. Begin to collect brochures and books describing it.

31. Make a special candlelight dinner at home with flowers on the table.

32. Sit close together when watching TV, riding in the car, or reading a book.

33. Hold hands when walking.

34. Ask, "What can I do to make you happier?"

35. Never criticize them or apologize for them in public.

36. Never say, "I told you so."

37. Notice the nice things they do around the house.

38. Live every day with your spouse as if it were your last.

39. Bring them iced tea or lemonade on hot days; hot chocolate or latte on cold days.

40. Turn on the stereo and dance with them by candlelight.

41. Go to bed when they do.

42. Plan an indoor picnic lunch on the floor.

43. Wear perfume or cologne.

44. Put together a scrapbook of pictures and mementos showing the high points of your marriage.

45. Tell them you are glad they are there when you reach out in the middle of the night.

46. Read a romantic book to each other at bedtime.

47. Rent a remote cottage where you can swim together in the nude at midnight.

48. Plan at least ten different details to make a romantic night.

49. Stay a night at your honeymoon hotel.

50. Wash their back in the shower or tub, using a tube of liquid body shampoo.

51. Give each other a complete body massage with scented body oil.

52. Take the phone off the hook some evening for some special together time.

53. If your spouse has a daily calendar, write romantic messages on several of the dates.

54. Try to look your best when your spouse is around.

55. Watch a sunset together.

56. Record a cassette of their favorite songs and surprise them with it.

57. On their pillow pin a note saying how you love them.

58. Listen to them with full attention and without interrupting.

59. Send a romantic pair of boxers or lingerie to them. Mark the envelope "Personal and Confidential."

60. Tell the children in front of your spouse that they are a great parent and a wonderful person.

61. Plan a trip to the beach, the woods, or some other outdoors location where you can build a campfire. Pack up blankets, lawn chairs, marshmallows for toasting, and a thermos of hot chocolate.

62. On a clear night take a walk in the moonlight—especially if it's full.

63. Go to a drive-in.

64. Purchase a dozen Valentines in February and send one to your spouse each month of the year.

65. If you have a telephone answering recorder, leave an "I love you" message on it for your spouse.

66. Buy season tickets to the theater, symphony, opera, ballet, sports events for you and your spouse. This forces you to go out on a date regularly.

67. Find out how to say "I love you" in different languages and say it to your spouse during romantic moments.

68. Reenact your wedding day.

69. Find a lake resort where a rowboat or canoe can be rented and go boating.

70. Hold them close at night before you go to sleep.

71. When you sit together, put your arm around them.

72. Instead of hiring a baby sitter to watch the kids when you're out, have the baby sitter take the kids to a double feature or a park while you stay home for three hours of uninterrupted time for romance.

73. Write a romantic poem.

74. Get a book of matches from a romantic restaurant. Send them to your mate with a note: "I've been missing you all day. Meet me at this restaurant tonight at seven."

75. When you are out with your spouse, wink at them or blow them a kiss.

This list may help you be more romantic, but remember that romance is more than an activity to perform. It's also more than checking another item off a list. Romance is an attitude and a way of life.

THE GREATEST ROMANTIC POEM

The greatest romantic poem ever written is called the *Song of Songs* and in Hebrew it means "greatest of all songs." It was written by King Solomon, the wisest man in the world, between 930 and 970 B.C. This song speaks of true love between a husband and wife. It tells of loving and being loved, bringing together all the basic elements of romance. It is a beautiful poem, just as romance and love are beautiful. Take your partner by the hand and lead them to a quiet place. Sit close beside them, tell them how special they are, and read to them the following words. Let each line speak to your soul, allowing them to shape your actions and soften your heart.

Act I

The Bride

"Kiss me again and again, for your love is sweeter than wine. How fragrant your cologne, and how great your name! No wonder all the young girls love you! Tell me, O one I love, where are you leading your flock today?"

The King

"If you don't know, O most beautiful woman in all the world, follow the trail of my flock to the shepherds' tents, and there feed your sheep and their lambs. What a lovely filly you are, my love! How lovely your cheeks are, with your hair falling down upon them! How stately your neck with that long string of jewels. We shall make you golden earrings and silver beads."

The Bride

"My beloved one is a sachet of myrrh lying between my breasts."

The King

"My beloved is a bouquet of flowers in the gardens of Engedi. How beautiful you are, my love, how beautiful! Your eyes are soft as doves. What a lovely, pleasant thing you are, lying here upon the grass, shaded by the cedar trees and firs."

The Bride

"I am the rose of Sharon, the lily of the valley."

The King

"Yes, a lily among thorns, so is my beloved as compared with any other girls."

The Bride

"My lover is an apple tree, the finest in the orchard as

compared with any of the other youths. I am seated in his much-desired shade and his fruit is lovely to eat. He brings me to the banquet hall and everyone can see how much he loves me. Oh feed me with your love—your raisins and your apples—for I am utterly lovesick. His left hand is under my head and with his right hand he embraces me."

Act II

The Bride

"Ah, I hear him—my beloved! Here he comes, leaping upon the mountains and bounding over the hills. My beloved is like a gazelle or young deer. Look, there he is behind the wall, now looking in at the windows.

"My beloved said to me, 'Rise up, my love, my fair one, and come away. For the winter is past, the rain is over and gone. The flowers are springing up and the time of the singing of birds has come. Yes, spring is here. The leaves are coming out and the grape vines are in blossom. How delicious they smell! Arise, my love, my fair one, and come away.'

"My dove is hiding behind some rocks, behind an outcrop of the cliff. Call to me and let me hear your lovely voice and see your handsome face.

"My beloved is mine and I am his. He is feeding among the lilies! Before the dawn come and the shadows flee away, come to me, my beloved, and be like a gazelle or a young stag on the mountains of spices."

Act III

The King

"How beautiful you are, my love, how beautiful! Your eyes are those of doves. Your hair falls across your face like flocks of goats that frisk across the slopes of Gilead. Your lips are like a thread of scarlet—and how beautiful your mouth. Your cheeks are matched loveliness behind our locks. Your neck is stately as the tower of David. Your breasts are like twin fawns of a gazelle, feeding among the lilies. Until the morning dawns and the shadows flee away, I will go to the mountain of myrrh and to the hill of frankincense. You are so beautiful, my love, in every part of you.

"Come with me from Lebanon, my bride. We will look down from the summit of the mountain, from the top of Mount Hermon, where the lions have their dens, and panthers prowl. You have ravished my heart, my lovely one, my bride; I am overcome by one glance of your eyes, by a single bead of your necklace. How sweet is your love, my darling, my bride. How much better it is than mere wine. The perfume of your love is more fragrant than all the richest spices. Your lips, my dear, are made of honey. Yes, honey and cream are under your tongue, and the scent of your garments is like the scent of the mountains and cedars of Lebanon.

"My darling bride is like a private garden, a spring that no one else can have, a fountain of my own. You are like a lovely orchard bearing precious fruit, with the rarest of perfumes; nard and saffron, calamus and cinnamon, and perfume from every other incense tree, as well as myrrh and aloes, and every other lovely spice. You are a garden fountain, a well of living water, refreshing as the streams from the Lebanon mountains."

The Bride

"Come, north wind, awaken; come, south wind, blow upon my garden and waft its lovely perfume to my beloved. Let him come into his garden and eat its choicest fruits."

The King

"I am here in my garden, my darling, my bride! I gather my myrrh with my spices and eat my honeycomb with my honey."

Act IV

The Bride

"My beloved one is tanned and handsome, better than ten thousand others! His head is purest gold, and he has wavy raven hair. His eyes are like doves beside the water brooks, deep and quiet. His cheeks are like sweetly scented beds of spices. His lips are perfumed lilies, his breath like myrrh. His arms are round bars of gold set with topaz; his body is bright ivory encrusted with jewels. His legs are as pillars of marble set in sockets of finest gold, like cedars of Lebanon; none can rival him. His mouth is altogether sweet, lovable in every way."

The King

"O my beloved, you are as beautiful as the lovely land of Tirzah, yes, beautiful as Jerusalem, and how you capture my heart. Look the other way, for your eyes have overcome me!

"Oh, how delightful you are; how pleasant, O love, for utter delight! You are tall and slim like a palm tree, and your breasts are like its clusters of dates. I said, I will climb up into the palm tree and take hold of its branches. Now may your breasts be like grape clusters, and the scent of your breath like apples, and your kisses as exciting as the best of wine, smooth and sweet, causing the lips of those who are asleep to speak."

The Bride

"I am my beloved's and I am the one he desires. Come, my beloved, let us go out into the fields and stay in the villages. Let us get up early and go out to the vineyards and see whether the vines have budded and whether the blossoms have opened and whether the pomegranates are in flower. And there I will give you my love.

"Seal me in your heart with permanent betrothal, for love is strong as death and jealously is as cruel as Sheol. It flashes fire, the very flame of Jehovah. Many waters cannot quench the flame of love, neither can the flood drown it. Come quickly, my beloved, and be like a gazelle or young deer upon the mountains of spices."[7]

Wow! Solomon was romantic. How is it with you and your lover? Feeling romantic? Enjoy! If you aren't, read this chapter again. Ask God to bless your marriage with some of the romantic verve he gave to Solomon.

Discussion Questions

1. Who is more romantic—you or your partner?

   Would your partner agree?

2. On a scale from 1 to 10 (1 = excellent, 10 = poor) how would you rate your marriage in the following five elements of romance?

   a) Joy
   b) Excitement
   c) Creativity
   d) Courtesy
   e) Intimacy

3. When was the last time you and your spouse laughed together? Describe the situation.

4. What examples of adventure, discovery, and amazement have the two of you experienced in your relationship?

5. What is the most creative thing you have done for your mate?

   How did he/she respond?

6. Give three examples of courtesy in marriage?

   a)
   b)
   c)

7. When was the last time you and your partner went on a date?

   What did you do?

   Was it a positive time?

8. Which of the following excuses keep the two of you from dating more often?

   a) Our lives are too busy.
   b) We don't have the money.
   c) We both enjoy different things.

9. How can you resolve these obstacles?

10. Which of the following bonds of intimacy cause you to feel the closest to your spouse?

Non-sexual touch	Imparted secrets
Shared feelings	Genuine understanding
Open communication	Mutual confidence
Intellectual agreement	Sensuous nearness
Spiritual harmony	Sexual pleasures
Similar values	Abiding trust

11. What five activities of romance are you willing to do during the next month?

   a)   d)
   b)   e)
   c)

12. Are you more romantic now than you were during your first year of marriage? What has changed?

Notes

1. A. L. Rowse, ed., *The Annotated Shakespeare*, Vol. III, "Romeo and Juliet," ii, 1 (New York: Clarkson N. Potter, 1978), 90-91.

2. Personal research using *The Oregonian's* listing of movies shown throughout 1994.

3. Norman Wright, *Holding on to Romance* (Ventura, Calif.: Regal, 1992), 31.

4. Elizabeth Barrett Browning, *Sonnets from the Portuguese*, Sonnet XLII (New York: Grosset, 1974) 89.

5. 1 Corinthians 13:4-5.

6. Ed Wheat and Gloria Perkins, *Love Life for Every Married Couple* (Grand Rapids: Zondervan, 1980), 133-4.

7. The Song of Solomon, TLB (adaptation mine).
   Act I: 1:2-3, 7a, 8-11, 13-16; 2:1-6
   Act II: 2:8-14, 16-17
   Act III: 4:1, 3-4a, 5-16: 5:1a
   Act IV: 5:10-16a; 6:4-5a; 7:6-12; 8:6-7a, 14.

10

MINISTRY

In 1946 a thirty-six-year-old Yugoslavian nun was riding a rickety train through India when she heard a still, small voice. The voice told her to follow God and serve him among the poorest of the poor in the streets of Calcutta. The little nun followed the call and was soon teaching, feeding, and comforting the suffering masses in the most disgusting slums of this large city. With a tough faith and a strong stomach, the simple servant worked in filth, starvation, and sickness from dawn until dusk.

Four years later this gentle nun received special permission from the Pope to form the Missionaries of Charity. She has received hundreds of humanitarian awards in her some fifty-plus years of serving the poor. Yet she did not serve for the awards or the recognition. She served because God asked her to serve. She also served because she saw wounded hearts and had compassion. Today she is known throughout the world for her Christian charity and if anyone is thought of as the epitome of goodness, selflessness, and service it is Mother Teresa.

The ultimate goal of marriage is ministry. Anything less reduces the relationship to mediocrity.

The ultimate goal of marriage is ministry. Anything less reduces the relationship to mediocrity. The word *ministry* is from a Latin word meaning "to assist." It is serving, giving, helping, even putting aside your needs to focus on the needs of others. In its purist form, ministry is love in action. When they asked Jesus what was the greatest commandment he replied, "'Love the Lord your God with all your heart and with all your soul and with all your strength and with all your mind'; and, 'Love your neighbor as yourself.'"[1] Ministry demonstrates love. It is in serving God and others that we accomplish life's highest calling.

Ministry is the most important work of any marriage. Everything else, including the previous nine chapters, is merely preparatory to this. These essentials refine the marriage and perfect the marital relationship toward an appropriate ministry.

Many marriages have lost their way. Comfort, pleasure, compatibility, and fairness have become the desired goals of today's couples. These are not bad goals but they are superficial, selfish, and impossible to achieve in any marriage day in and day out; yet if they aren't attained, partners begin to consider the marriage a failure and contemplate divorce. Such goals and attitudes are analogous to those of children who wish everything to go their own way.

Let me be so bold as to suggest that the primary goal of marriage, and possibly every relationship, should be to serve God and others.

This is the most crucial chapter in this book. All the other chapters hold valuable information, but information without direction leads a marriage down a dead-end road. The aim of the relationship becomes one of maintenance. *Ministry stretches a couple beyond themselves and makes them less self-absorbed.* It broadens their vision and moves them beyond their comfort zones. It provides joy, satisfaction, and purpose. It teaches them about the realities of life and helps them develop new friendships. Most important—it pleases God.

SERVING GOD

Serving God is not always easy, and often we come up with all sorts of excuses as to why we can't do it. Over three thousand years ago, in the desert of the Sinai Peninsula, God called Moses to serve him. And Moses, like many of us, came up with some good excuses, but God met each excuse with a solution.[2]

Moses said: I am afraid.

God said: Don't worry, I will be with you.

Moses said: I don't know what to say.

God said: Just tell the people who I am.

Moses said: But what if they won't believe me?

God said: I will give you special evidence to show them who I am.

Moses said: I don't think I can do it.

God said: I will guide you and give you everything you need.

Moses said: Why don't you send somebody else?

God said: I will send somebody else to help, but I still want you.

In the end Moses saw that his excuses were merely ways to avoid service. If we take our faith seriously, then our belief must impact our behavior. To speak of generosity without ever giving is hypocritical. The New Testament says that "faith without deeds is dead."[3] Faith must be demonstrated. True allegiance always comes down to service. It is easy to say you believe and love, but the proof is in the action.

True allegiance always comes down to service. It is easy to say you believe and love, but the proof is in the action.

Serving God is submission of our will to his; it is the yielding of the finite to the infinite. It is a couple giving themselves to their creator so he can direct them to their greatest potential.

Serving God begins as a frame of mind which permeates our being and prepares us for action. So we look to God and ask, "What do you wish of us?" The desire to please God supersedes the desire to please ourselves. This is so contrary to human nature for we are all innately selfish. To serve God we must take our eyes off ourselves and focus totally on him. Otherwise, our service may appear selfless when in reality it is to meet some internal need for attention, appreciation, status, self-righteousness, power, or achievement. Only as we fully submit to God can our service be genuine and our marriage eternally meaningful.

Marriage is a test of one's faith. It's a refiner's fire that either draws us closer to God or pushes us away from him. At best it is difficult and reveals our true character. The challenge of marriage is to serve God in spite of the struggles. Yet we frequently become distracted from God. He seems distant to the hurts and frustrations of our relationship—*but he isn't*. The following statement is a wise mission statement for any marriage:

> In everything, good or bad,
> we will trust and honor God.

TRUST

After reviewing the previous nine chapters with a colleague, he shrugged and said, "This all feels overwhelming. How can anyone do all these things without help? The only way I can have a successful marriage is by keeping my eyes firmly fixed on God. If I look away, everything falls apart. My goal is to cherish my wife and I can't do that apart from God. He is my guide and strength. With God, all things possible."

Trusting God is like swinging on a trapeze high above the sawdust floor of a circus tent. You swing toward the center where someone will catch you and take you to the other side. There are at least four steps to this daring act.

Knowing. To start the process you must know whether the one who is to catch you is capable and willing. Trusting God involves believing he is both. At times a healthy marriage appears impossible, but if God is who he says he is, then he can make it happen. The Holy Scriptures describe many of God's attributes. Here are seven of them.

Omnipresent
God is everywhere.

Omniscient
God knows everything.

Omnipotent
God is all powerful.

Infinite
God has no limitations.

Sovereign
God has ultimate control over everything.

Good
God is morally perfect and is the ultimate yardstick for every virtue.

Love
God cares intimately about every individual.

God is both capable and willing to help us in all that we do. The more we know him the more we recognize our need for him.

There is only one person worth focusing on as you fly through the air. It is the One who is going to catch you.

Focusing. If we do not focus on the One who catches us, we risk missing his hands and falling. Without God our relationship with each other has lost its focus. So what if we have commitment, positive regard, and togetherness; deep inside we know something is missing. A marriage may look perfect—only the couple knows if it's a charade.

Too many times I have heard about the perfect couple who has experienced unfaithfulness or divorce. What went wrong? It's simple. They took their eyes off God and focused on either their partner or themselves. There is only one person worth focusing on as you fly through the air. It is the One who is going to catch you.

Moving Closer. To make the move from your trapeze to the hands of the One who is catching you, you must get as close as you can. Getting close to God allows him to help you. Marriage is like an equilateral triangle: the apex is God, one angle of the base is the husband, and the other is the wife. The closer the husband and wife move to God, the closer they will come to each other.

Likewise, the further they move from God, the more distant they will be from each other. Closeness is critical to trusting God and catching the trapeze.

Letting Go. As the trapeze swings over the crowd and the moment of relinquishing the bar arrives, you must let go. Now I hate heights and I can imagine my sweaty palms glued to the trapeze bar. My mind says let go but my emotions want to cling to the bar forever. However, if we have done the previous three steps, then letting go becomes easy. We have developed a confidence in God's character —his attributes—that allows us to relax and trust him. We know him, we focus on him, and we are close to him. Letting go now becomes a point of excitement as we anticipate God carrying us to the other side and we hear the burst of applause. Then, above it all, the voice of God echoes, "Well done, good, and faithful servant."

HONOR

"The chief end of man is to glorify God." Those words ring out from an ancient catechism with an indisputable truth. If this is true of individuals, why not of marriages? We glorify God by acknowledging who he is and what we owe him. We owe him everything, for everything we have is from him. Our gratitude is best expressed by obedience and obedience demonstrates our respect and honor. Two significant ways to honor God are to reflect virtues and to avoid vices.

Reflecting Virtues. Honor is shown through imitation. Since God is the ultimate yardstick for every virtue, then imitating him reflects his virtues. We become like the full moon reflecting the light of the sun. By actively modeling virtuous behavior we become beacons of light in a world that views values and morals as relative.

Here are ten basic virtues to incorporate into your marriage.

- Compassion
- Kindness
- Humility
- Patience
- Faithfulness
- Self-discipline
- Truthfulness
- Respect
- Courage
- Goodness

As we practice these within our marriage and toward others, we honor God. We also become models of healthy marriages and set an example for other marriages.

Avoiding Vices. The flip side of reflecting virtues is avoiding vices. Vices destroy relationships and distance us from God. They steal our joy, leaving us lonely and alienated. Unfortunately, vices are usually easier to practice than virtues. Here are ten basic vices to avoid.

- Laziness
- Lust
- Hatred/Bitterness
- Pride
- Envy

- Greed
- Hard-heartedness
- Discord
- Dishonesty
- Addiction

Vices create pain, block growth, and keep us focused on ourselves rather than serving God. It is impossible to serve two masters. If your focus is on self, you cannot serve God.

Serving God often leads to serving others. Looking up gives us the strength and motivation to reach out. The two types of service are actually one, for in serving others we actually serve God. Remember that Jesus said the second commandment is like the first, "Love your neighbor as yourself." Reflecting virtues and avoiding vices reveals your commitment to serve God. It also sets the foundation for your service to others.

SERVING OTHERS

Once there was a great rabbi who traveled from town to town sharing his vast wisdom in each synagogue along the way. When the villagers heard he was coming to their town the response was overwhelming. They cleaned the streets, painted the houses, and the men even put a new roof on the synagogue. On the evening he was to speak, the people packed the small white building and overflowed into the street.

On the other side of town, a young widow sat in a modest house with her three small children. As the time approached that the rabbi was to speak, she settled her children into bed and left them alone while she went to hear the wise rabbi. When she arrived at the synagogue, he wasn't there. The crowd waited. It grew late...an hour passed, then two. Finally the mother walked home, head bent in disappointment. As she neared her house, she heard her children's laughter. Bursting through the door she saw a strange, gray-haired man sitting on the floor. He had a child on each side of him and one on his lap.

"Who are you?" she demanded.

"I am a traveling rabbi," the man explained. "I was passing your house when I heard children crying. I knocked on the door and no one answered, so I came in to comfort them. They were afraid to be alone and they begged me to stay. I told them I'd stay until their mother came. Since you are obviously the mother, I'll go now."

"But you were supposed to be at the synagogue serving God and sharing your wisdom."

The old man smiled. "Sometimes the best way to serve God is by serving others. When I see someone in need, I try to meet that need."[4]

The rabbi knew the importance of serving others. He was sensitive to the cries of the children and took action. He could have ignored their cries and told himself that what he was doing was more important, but he didn't. He saw the need and did what he could to help. Sensitivity and action are two aspects of serving.

SENSITIVITY

As a psychologist, I have learned a number of basic truths about people. One is that *everybody* hurts. No matter how wealthy, talented, attractive, or successful a person is, he carries a certain amount of pain. If you ask people the right questions, their eyes will tear or a lump will form in their throat.

Another basic truth is that *everybody* wants to be loved. We want to know that somebody cares and is willing to go out of their way if we have a need.

We all lead busy lives and do not often have the time to notice the hurts or needs of those outside our small circle of friends. We have developed comfort zones that regulate our behavior. Unless forced to, we rarely leave our cozy little patterns. Jerzy Kosinski wrote a wonderful little book entitled *Being There* which later became a major motion picture starring Peter Sellers. The first few pages describes the world of the main character, Chance Gardiner.

It was safe and secure in the garden, which was separated from the street by a high, red brick wall covered with ivy and not even the passing cars disturbed the peace. Chance ignored the streets. Though he had never stepped outside the house and its garden, he was not curious about life on the other side of the wall.[5]

Trapped by his own private comfort zone, the world outside his garden seemed distant and unreal.

We risk the same insensitivity if we are not careful. Needy people surround us; we must increase our awareness and open our eyes. If we look for needs, we will find them. Once people see us as a sensitive and caring couple, they will come to us and share their needs. Until then, *we* must notice, and maybe even study, each person who crosses our comfort zone. Pray that God will show you their needs and he will.

He gave me a Dad-that-is-a-dumb-question look and said, "She looked like she needed a friend."

Let's look at four categories of needs.

1. Physical Needs
Food, shelter, money, medical help, child care, employment.

2. Emotional Needs
Love, belonging, security, hope, trust, laughter, gentleness.

3. Spiritual Needs
Salvation, guidance, prayer, faith, forgiveness, wisdom.

4. Social Needs
Support, company, friendship, communication, encouragement, touch.

These four areas of need are present at every level of humanity. It's easiest to see these needs at the family level as we deal with children, parents, grandparents, siblings, and other relatives. We usually feel closest to our family and are most sensitive to their needs.

The second level of interaction is community. This involves the people we deal with and meet during our daily routines; neighbors, co-workers, church acquaintances, friends, business people—anybody whose life touches ours. Some people are easier to be sensitive toward than others; then there are those we prefer to ignore.

Dylan, my four-year-old son, told me today that he was friends with everybody. Several hours later, while we were at the grocery store, he started talking to a stranger. When their conversation was over, I asked Dylan why he had spoken to this particular individual. He gave me a Dad-that-is-a-dumb-question look and said, "She looked like she needed a friend." I wish I could be more like Dylan, but most of us ignore strangers instead of thinking of them as someone with a need.

The last level of interaction is the world. This is the national and international arena of life that seems beyond our reach. We read about struggles and catastrophes in the newspaper or see them on television, but the places seem distant and the people unreal. We recognize there is suffering in the world, but it's so immense or far away. Yet if we do live in a global village, then these people are our neighbors. Distance is no excuse for insensitivity.

Sensitivity is the opposite of selfishness. Society today encourages us to take care of ourselves even if it hurts others. We have become materialistic and self-absorbed.

Several years ago a popular young girl from a good family committed suicide. The note she left told of great emotional pain and her inability to cope with it any longer. The last line of her note still haunts me. She wrote, "What bothers me most is that with all my pain and confusion, nobody even noticed."

Do we notice the physical, emotional, spiritual, and social needs all around us? Do we see them in our family, our community, our world? Have we become so callused and narcissistic that we are blind? Ministry and service is impossible unless we first have a sensitive, compassionate heart to move our feet and hands to action. Someone once said that sensitivity without action is worthless.

ACTION

To love your neighbor as yourself involves actively serving anybody you possibly can. Yes, anybody! It's easy to serve those we like or agree with, but what about those who are difficult, obnoxious, disgusting, confusing, or frightening? How about those who hurt, cheat, or slander us? Certainly God does not expect us to love and serve them? Yes, he does.

The parable of the Good Samaritan is a model of how we should serve. Though it is a familiar parable, please read it carefully. Place yourself in the sandals of the wounded and robbed traveler.

A Jewish person was traveling from Jerusalem to Jericho. As he moved through the desert hills, some thieves attacked and beat him. Bruised, bleeding, and left to die, he lay by the side of the road in the hot Middle East sun.

Soon a priest came down the road, saw the injured man, and passed by without even stopping. A little later a Levite, a priest of higher rank, came down the road, saw the injured man, and also passed by without stopping. Maybe they were busy or simply didn't want to become involved. Whatever their excuse, they hurried on to their destinations.

To be passive and avoid action is to die.

Some time later, a Samaritan man, whose country hated the Jews, saw the wounded man and, moved with compassion, went to his side, bandaged his wounds, and carried him to a comfortable place. But the Samaritan didn't stop with that. He also arranged and paid for housing, medical care, and whatever else the wounded man needed.[6]

Satan does not want us to take action. We can think all the good thoughts in the world, but he does not want us to act on any of them. Too many of us are more like the priest and Levite than the Samaritan. We have all sorts of excuses for not serving: we are too busy, we don't know what to do, somebody else will take care of it, we are afraid, we don't want to be codependent. There are a hundred more good excuses, but they are just excuses. Taking action is frequently inconvenient and might even cost us something, but that is how we grow.

To be passive and avoid action is to die. Action is focused energy. We see a need and provide something to meet that need. We evaluate the situation and ask, "What has God given me that I can give to best take care of this situation?" It might be time, talent, money, things, prayer, or encouragement.

Ultimately, service is to be a cheerful and wholehearted giving of ourselves to someone else; not begrudging or tightfisted. King Solomon wrote, "If one falls down, his friend can help him up. But pity the man who falls and has no one to help him up."[7] Sometimes I wonder what would have happened to the wounded man if the Samaritan had walked on by without stopping. Can you recall a time when you experienced the ministry of a Good Samaritan? I can.

It was a cold winter morning and sleet pounded my windshield as I drove the freeway to work. Suddenly, my car sputtered and choked. I eased it to the side of the road as I chastised myself for not stopping at a gas station before entering the freeway. The fuel gauge read empty. I climbed out of the car and started walking toward the next exit. Within a minute a car pulled in front of me and a man in a business suit asked if I needed a ride. He was late for a meeting, but he drove me to a gas station and back to my car. When I asked him why he helped me, he smiled and said, "Because I'm a Christian." Then he drove off. I guess there wasn't anything else to say. Next time I see a needy motorist I want to be a Good Samaritan.

Serving can be directed three ways: toward your family, your community, and the world.

Serving Your Family. My parents are great at serving. My mother takes care of my eighty-eight-year-old grandmother. She buys her clothes, bathes her, and reads to her.

My father does projects with each of his six kids. He builds shelves in our garages, helps with moves, and mows our lawns.

Together, my parents make loans, celebrate birthdays, baby-sit grandchildren, and provide encouragement.

Serving your family can be both the easiest and the most difficult of tasks. It is easy in that they are frequently present and there is a sense of obligation. It is sometimes difficult because we take them for granted.

When people are too close we can lose our sensitivity toward them. There is also more opportunity for hurts and misunderstandings to occur. As a result, we do not feel like serving, nor do we feel they deserve being served, so we hold back.

Serving strangers seems more attractive and even romantic. It is sad to see couples selflessly serving their community and the world, and at the same time ignoring their own family.

Serving Your Community. The only limitation to serving is your imagination. Robert F. Kennedy once said, "Some men see things as they are and say, 'Why?' I dream of things that never were and say, 'Why not?'"

Serving your community can be exciting. I know a couple who spends every Thanksgiving serving the homeless a turkey dinner at the Portland Rescue Mission. Another couple adopts a needy family each Christmas and showers them with food and gifts.

Look for opportunities to serve, and then take action. Here are twenty local ways to serve.

1. Assist youth organizations such as the Boy Scouts, Girl Scouts, Awana, or Young Life.

2. Find some area of service at your church. Help the youth, teach Sunday school, sweep floors, maintain the church grounds, or help prepare newsletters for mailing.

3. Volunteer to help at your local school.

4. Visit a convalescent care facility to cheer up the residents.

5. Prepare a meal for a shut-in.

6. Fix a vehicle for someone in need.

7. Provide time, money, blankets, or food for the homeless.

8. Fix a food basket for someone in need.

9. Volunteer to baby-sit for a single parent.

10. Adopt a grandparent at a nursing home facility.

11. Be a camp counselor.

12. Get involved in local politics.

13. Open your house to people who need a short-term place to stay.

14. Donate unused items to worthy causes.

15. Volunteer to read for the visually impaired.

16. Adopt a child for a day and take them someplace special.

17. Spend an hour or two and pick up litter in your community.

18. Help a neighbor with a house or yard project.

19. Look for opportunities to help and encourage other couples who might be struggling in their relationship.

20. Contact Love, Inc. to connect your abilities with specific, legitimate needs in your community.

Serving the World. It is easy to live by the philosophy, "If I don't see a need, it doesn't exist." This is a great strategy for ignoring the poverty, starvation, and sickness throughout the world.

Not all couples are as sheltered as most of us. Recently, I spoke to a couple who spent a month helping build a church in Mexico. Another couple, a physician and nurse, spent a week in Jamaica meeting needs. One couple even became full-time missionaries directing a camp in Ireland.

Needs exist, whether or not we see them. Here are twenty national and international ways to serve.

1. Support a needy child through Compassion International.

2. Build low-cost housing for the underprivileged through organizations such as President Carter's Habitat for Humanity.

3. Provide food, clothing, and blankets for the International Red Cross.

4. Be a short-term missionary (e.g., Youth with a Mission or Harvest Ministry).

5. Support international evangelistic crusades (e.g., Billy Graham or Luis Palau).

6. Research and pray about a specific culture or country.

7. Get involved with national politics.

8. Help get Bibles placed nationally and internationally through the Gideons.

9. Help get Bibles translated through Wycliffe Bible Translators.

10. Encourage teenagers and college students to get international experience.

11. Write letters and send care packages to missionaries.

12. Visit a mission field on your vacation.

13. House an exchange student for a year.

14. Ask an international student to dinner.

15. Host a missionary and hear about life in foreign cultures.

16. Help build or repair churches.

17. Get involved with national fund raisers for medical problems (e.g., March of Dimes, Muscular Dystrophy, or AIDS research).

18. Assist a family whose major breadwinner is in prison.

19. Skip one meal per week and send the money to an international orphanage.

20. Discover what you can do to help a hospital ship provide medical assistance, (e.g., the mercy ships operated by Youth with a Mission).

Ministry and service are not popular words in a culture that is so self-centered. In our topsy-turvy world, God and others become our servants. We become angry and disappointed when life is too difficult. We might even shake our fist at the sky and yell, "This is not fair!" Yet in spite of our narcissistic tendencies, serving God and serving others is our greatest calling. It raises our marriage above the selfish mundane.

This is more than just an interesting philosophical ideal. It can be a practical reality. It involves seeing life as more than a means to gain personal comfort and pleasure. It occurs when a husband and wife take each other's hand and walk with God. This is an act of faith, for we are not always sure where he will lead. What we can be sure of is that he will lead us to a place of greater fulfillment. The journey may be difficult, but at the end we will feel it was worthwhile.

Marriage is like a basketball game. A lot of skill building, working out, practice, and play making happens before the team ever steps onto the court. Facing the enemy, commitment, positive regard, communication, making peace, giving and receiving, forgiving, togetherness, and romance is the preparation for the game. Each of these aspects is important, for without them the game might not happen, or if it does, it will falter throughout the play.

The game itself is ministry. Ministry is the purpose for all the preparation: it is the goal, the endpoint, the grand finale, the keystone, the coup de grace. To prepare for the game without ever playing it does not make sense. The game is the reason for the practice, even as service is the reason for our marriage.

It is easy to become so focused on different aspects of preparation that we come to believe they are the reason for the relationship. Thus, communication, togetherness, romance, or some other piece becomes our goal. Dribbling, passing, and free-throw shooting is critical to a basketball game, but used apart from a game plan, the team will lose. For a team to be successful, they must follow their coach and work together as a team. All this is for the purpose of the game.

Ministry is the big game. In marriage we must follow our God, work together as a team, and be ready to serve.

THE SPOILED RICH KID

In 1207 outside a small town in Italy, a twenty-five-year-old man was riding horseback when a beggar approached him. The young man had a reputation for being a spoiled rich kid and a playboy, but on this particular day he was searching for a purpose in life. As the beggar moved closer, the man felt a deep repugnance. This was no regular beggar—he was a leper. Of all diseases, leprosy was what this rich kid feared most. It was an ugly disease with its rotting flesh, crusty sores, and slow, hideous death. Worst of all, everybody said that a single touch could spread the disease.

On a typical day the playboy would nonchalantly toss a silver coin at a beggar and gallop away, but not today. Something about the leper moved him. Maybe it was the pain in his eyes or the hopelessness of his shuffle. Whatever it was, it prompted the rich kid to dismount and walk toward the leper. He placed his silver piece in the twisted palm of the beggar, then kissed the leper's hand.

Francis of Assisi's life was never the same after that act of compassion. At that moment he decided to become a servant to the poor and downtrodden of the world. Two years later, Pope Innocent III established the Franciscan Order. Serving God and serving others became a way of life for St. Francis of Assisi.

Let us not be like the spoiled rich kid, searching for personal comfort and happiness. Let us be like Francis of Assisi, looking beyond ourselves to serve others and, in so doing, reflect to the world the love of God. With slight alteration, let us make *The Prayer of Saint Francis* the prayer of our marriage.

Lord,
make us an instrument
of Thy peace.
Where there is hatred,
let us sow love;
where there is despair,
hope;
where there is sadness,
joy;
where there is darkness,
light.

O Divine Master,
grant that we may not so much
seek to be consoled,
as to console;
not so much to be loved,
as to love.
For it is in giving that we
receive,
it is in pardoning that we are
pardoned,
it is in dying that we are born again
to eternal life.[8]

Discussion Questions

1. Why is service important to a marriage?

2. When is it easiest for you, as a couple, to serve God?

3. What excuses have you used in the past to not serve God?

4. What have you done in the past month to serve him?

5. Which virtue does your marriage reflect most?

Compassion	Patience	Respect
Kindness	Faithfulness	Truthfulness
Goodness	Humility	Courage
Self-discipline		

6. Which virtue would you and your partner like to work on during the next month?

7. Which vice do you struggle with the most, both individually and as a couple?

Laziness	Lust	Hatred/Bitterness
Pride	Envy	Hard-heartedness
Greed	Discord	Dishonesty
Addiction		

8. How can you deal more effectively with this tough area? Be specific in your answer.

9. Of the four needs listed below, circle those you as a couple are best at helping others with:

   a) Physical   c) Spiritual
   b) Emotional   d) Social

   Explain what you do.

10. On a scale from 1 to 10 (1 = excellent, 10 = not at all) how would you rate yourselves as a couple in meeting needs in the following areas:

    a) Family level
    b) Community level
    c) National level
    d) International level

11. In serving your community:

    a) Which of the twenty suggestions have you done in the past?
    b) Which would you like to begin doing?

12. In serving the world:

    a) Which of the twenty suggestions have you done in the past?
    b) Which would you like to begin doing?

Notes

1. Luke 10:27.
2. Exodus 3:1-4:17 (author's paraphrase).
3. James 2:26.
4. An old traditional rabbinical folktale.
5. Jerzy Kosinski, *Being There* (New York: Harcourt Brace Jovanovich, 1970), 4.
6. Luke 10:30-37.
7. Ecclesiastes 4:10.
8. This prayer, though attributed to St. Francis, was not actually written by him. It is believed to have been composed at a Catholic Congress in Chicago in 1925.

CONCLUSION

Groucho Marx once quipped, "Marriage is a wonderful institution, but who wants to live in an institution?" Marriage today is attacked, demeaned, ridiculed, minimized, and ignored. Some twenty years ago I sat in a Courtship and Marriage class where the sociology professor announced that marriage is hopelessly old-fashioned and practically dead. Recently, the cover of *Time* magazine suggested that infidelity may be genetic. The implication is that people who are faithful are expecting too much of marriage. Yet marriage is a wonderful institution and it is neither dying nor dead.

Marriage is a sacred state—a partnership of grace where friendship, love, and godliness can take root and bloom. Unfortunately, without proper care, the opposite can also take root and bloom. Some marriages are good and some are hard—even difficult. Nevertheless, the marriage relationship was instituted and blessed by God. Marriage is a wonderful thing—even if we are human and our flawed state mars its wonder.

Last weekend Tami and I went to a wedding. It was a beautiful summer day and I'd rather have been outside relaxing in the sunshine. Nevertheless, going to weddings is important for both us and the couple getting married. So Tami and I dressed up and went to a warm church in the middle of a lovely Saturday afternoon. The sanctuary, elegantly decorated with long, white gladiolas and baby's breath, was transformed into the perfect mood by the glow of candlelight and romantic melodies from the baby grand. I sat down, slipped my arm around Tami, and let my mind drift back to our wedding day.

We go to weddings to remind us of the sacredness of marriage; to make sure we don't forget those holy commitments we made to each other and to God. As we listen to the bride and groom saying their vows, in our hearts we renew those vows we made at our wedding. Looking into their glowing young faces with eyes full of dreams, we see ourselves, however many years ago, when life seemed so simple. However, marriage is no easy adventure. It is a test of everything we are. There are days we pass and there are others we fail. To borrow from Charles Dickens, "It was the best of times, it was the worst of times." Yet through it all, we learn the meaning of love.

We start so hopeful and naive. Then reality hits and many fall to the wayside, dazed and confused. Others run away, either angry and bitter, or optimistic that next time they will have better luck. Some still stand by their commitment—struggling, growing, learning, and loving. We all have many areas in which to improve. The danger of books on marriage is that they leave us feeling inadequate, guilty, and frustrated. They point out the obvious—we fail and our marriage isn't perfect. So what's new?

Marriage is a process. None of us can accomplish everything on the previous pages, but, step by step, we can apply certain concepts and do better today than we did yesterday. Don't be overwhelmed by where you are versus where you want to be. Instead, choose one concept, pray like crazy, and implement that one concept to the best of your ability. When you have that one down, choose another. It takes time and it's hard work, but it's worth the effort. With God's help and a stubborn determination to love your partner, your marriage can be great.

I didn't write this book because I have the perfect marriage (just ask Tami). I struggle and fail the same as everyone else. Perfection is out of my reach but a great marriage isn't. Anybody can have a wonderful relationship if they're both willing to work together and make it a priority.

I've counseled thousands of couples, and I've learned a lot from their mistakes and their successes. God doesn't need perfect couples. He needs committed couples with positive regard who are willing to try their best to communicate, make peace, forgive, give generously, stand together, romance each other, and minister beyond themselves. The previous ten chapters provide the building blocks to do this. If you ignore any one of them, you risk failure. If together you cling to these principles and practice them daily, you will grow and so will your marriage.

If death does not separate you beforehand, there will come a day when the two of you will sit side by side, gray and wrinkled, reminiscing over a long marriage. You will laugh and cry as you recall all you have experienced together—the ups and downs, the joys and sorrows, the foolishness and the frustrations. Then your shaky hands will touch, and a gentle squeeze will remind you both of the young bride and groom who started this sometimes rocky, sometimes smooth journey so many years ago. A smile will part the dry lips that kissed so passionately on that long-ago wedding day. The day when two friends turned lovers and committed their lives "till death do we part." Your cloudy eyes will meet and there will be silence, for you both know that words can't express what you feel.

Marriage is a wonderful institution. Yours can be the absolute best.

Recommended Reading

Chapin, Alice, *400 Creative Ways to Say I Love You*, Tyndale House, 1986.

Chesser, Barbara Russell, *21 Myths That Can Wreck Your Marriage: How a Couple Can Avoid Head-on Collisions*, Word, 1990.

Dobson, James C., *What Wives Wish Their Husbands Knew About Women*, Tyndale House, 1975.

Harley, Willard F., Jr., *His Needs, Her Needs: Building an Affair-proof Marriage*, Revel, 1986.

Lewis, C. S., *The Four Loves*, Harcourt Brace, 1960.

Mason, Mike, *The Mystery of Marriage: As Iron Sharpens Iron*, Multnomah Press, 1985.

McGinnis, Alan Loy, *The Romance Factor*, Harper, 1982.

— *The Friendship Factor*, Augsburg Fortress, 1979.

Powell, John and Loretta Brady, *Will the Real Me Please Stand Up? (So We Can All Get to Know You!) 25 Guidelines for Good Communication*, Tabor Publishing, 1985.

Sell, Charles M., *Achieving the Impossible: Intimate Marriage*, Multnomah Press, 1982.

Sande, Ken, *The Peacemaker: A Biblical Guide to Resolving Personal Conflict*, Baker Book House, 1991.

Smedes, Lewis B., *Forgive and Forget: Healing the Hurts We Don't Deserve*, Pocket Books, 1984.

Smalley, Gary and John Trent, *Love Is a Decision: Ten Proven Principles to Energize Your Marriage and Family,*Word, 1989.

Swindoll, Charles R., *Strike the Original Match: Rekindling and Preserving Your Marriage Fire,* Multnomah Press, 1980.

Tournier, Paul, *To Understand Each Other,* John Knox, 1976.

Vanauken, Sheldon, *A Severe Mercy,* Harper, 1977.

Wangerin, Walter, Jr., *As for Me and My House: Crafting Your Marriage to Last,* Thomas Nelson Publishers, 1987.

Wheat, Ed and Gloria Perkins, *Love Life for Every Married Couple,* Zondervan Publishing House, 1980.

Wright, Norman H., *Communication: Key to Your Marriage,* G/L Publications, 1974.

— *The Pillars of Marriage,* G/L Publications, 1980.

These twenty books are sitting on my bookshelf and have been read more than once because of the wealth of information they hold. I quickly recommend them to anyone who asks. Each author was cited at least once in this book. Yet the spirit of these books flows through every page of this work. I could have cited each book many more times but I attempted to keep citations and endnotes to a minimum for the ease of reading.

About the Author

Dr. Steve Stephens holds a Master's degree in Pastoral Psychology and a Ph.D. in Counseling/Clinical Psychology. He has worked for Youth for Christ and has served as a youth pastor and an associate pastor. He is currently a licensed psychologist who has counseled couples for seventeen years. He is a clinical member of the American Psychological Association and the American Association of Marriage and Family Therapists. Dr. Stephens is married to Tami and has three children, Brittany, Dylan, and Dustin. He is an author and successful seminar speaker.